A HISTORY
OF
SWEDISH
LITERATURE

A HISTORY
— OF —
SWEDISH
LITERATURE

BY

INGEMAR ALGULIN

THE SWEDISH INSTITUTE

Published by the Swedish Institute
© 1989 Ingemar Algulin and the Swedish Institute
Translated by John Weinstock, revised by Judith Black
Design by Paul Eklund

Printed in Sweden by Bohusläningens Boktryckeri AB, Uddevalla 1989
ISBN 91-520-0239-X

CONTENTS

PREFACE

This History of Swedish Literature was written, mainly in 1984 and 1985, in response to the request from the Swedish Institute's reference group for literature for a short survey of Swedish literature designed for foreign readers. It leads up to recent days, although in less detail for the latest, as yet "unhistorical" years. While writing, I have tried to elucidate the connections with well-known international trends and movements as well as what could be called the Nordic "exoticism" of Swedish literature. However, the task of presenting the literature of one's own country meaningfully to an international readership is a difficult and subjective one. My survey is, ultimately, what I myself wish to introduce to people in other countries who are interested in Swedish literature.

I am grateful to all the people—translators, commentators, staff of the Swedish Institute—who have been involved in the making of this volume and contributed to its final shaping. My particular thanks are due to Professor Jean-François Battail, Université de Paris-Sorbonne, for his committed and constructive scrutiny and comments.

Stockholm 1989

INGEMAR ALGULIN

EDITOR'S NOTE: If the English name of a work is italicized or given within quotation marks, it has been published in English under this title. If not, the work has not appeared in English and the title provided is merely a direct translation of the original Swedish.

FROM THE VIKING AGE TO
THE GREAT POWER ERA

Literary history always begins with silence, with an absence of literary documents that can be dark and enigmatic and give rise to speculations that spur the imagination. Was there perhaps a literature, maybe even a richly abundant one, before the first writings we know about? The fact that there are no written literary sources need not imply that nothing was being written. There was certainly an extensive oral literature; why not also a written one, which simply disappeared with time?

Such questions are particularly relevant in Sweden's case. Before ca. 1300 there is in fact no literature preserved in manuscript form in Swedish. The culturally flourishing Viking Age, for instance, with its lively international relations with the rest of Europe and the Orient, left no literary legacy. There are, however, many signs that a literature existed, one which probably had many similarities with Old Icelandic. It almost certainly consisted of poetry of various kinds, perhaps also stories and sagas. What distinguishes Sweden from medieval Iceland is the attitude toward the pagan literary treasures which prevailed at the time of the introduction of Christianity and the manuscript tradition. In Iceland a great literary culture flourished, nurtured its literary legacy and developed it further. In Sweden, on the other hand, the Christian Church concentrated on breaking with the pagan period and therefore attempted to erase as many of its cultural manifestations as possible. As a result, no literature from the pagan era is preserved in manuscript form.

However, fragments of a Swedish literature from the Viking Age have, paradoxically enough, been better preserved than is usually the case with manuscripts, namely in the form of rune stones. In Swedish literature the preliterary silence is broken by the writing that we find on thousands of stones that were erected over large parts of the country during the Viking era.

The Viking Age—Runic Inscriptions

The runic inscriptions were, unlike the later medieval manuscripts, not exclusive, literary documents to which only a small number of literate persons had access. They were cut on blocks of stone near farms and roads where all the passers-by could see and contemplate them. They formed a literary common ground, on which there was an intimate interplay between writing and rural settlement and between writing and nature. This is a link which to a certain degree characterizes the Swedish landscape even today, where you can come across some 2,500 rune stones—a number that is steadily increasing due to new discoveries. In order to get a feeling for the very oldest Swedish literature you should ideally go out into the countryside, preferably in the province of Uppland where around a thousand of these stones are preserved. You will find them in meadows, valleys and mountains, near roads and watercourses, and it is easy to see that they are also artistic documents of great value. The persons who cut the runes put considerable effort into adornment, mainly ornamental but also figurative. The runic symbols were set within a decorated snake or dragon coil that was sometimes filled in with other ornamental designs. Originally the stones were also painted and must have made a magnificent sight, viewed against summer green or a snowy winter landscape. However, it was not only on stones that runes were cut. The older inscriptions in particular are found on weapons, jewelry and horns. Perhaps the most common material on which runes were cut was wood, but since wood disintegrates such runic inscriptions have as a rule not been preserved.

Very little is known with certainty about the origin of the runes. They probably arose during the second century A.D. and were influenced by old Italic alphabets. We usually distinguish between the *older* and *younger runic alphabets*. The older consists of 24 letters and is used on runic inscriptions from the third to the ninth century A.D. The language of the older runic alphabet is proto-Nordic, and the texts, which are difficult to interpret, are of more linguistic than literary interest. The overwhelming majority of runic inscriptions, however, are in the younger runic alphabet.

This consists of just 16 letters and is thus a simplification of the older runic system, whereby several pairs of sounds are symbolized by the same rune. The younger runic alphabet occurs on inscriptions from the ninth century on; however, most of them are from the eleventh and twelfth centuries, which were really the golden age of runic writing and which coincided with a culmination in trade relations with the east.

To a great extent the texts on these runic memorials are based on a set formula: "Someone erected this stone in memory of someone. Someone cut it." To this typical formulation, however, the rune cutter most often added some additional information of interest. Herein we find a social, political, economic, cultural and to a certain degree literary picture of the Viking Age that is both comprehensive and alive. We meet a great number of people both at home and on long journeys to the east and west. Their social position and achievements emerge from the texts, which vigorously and tersely describe battles, the defense of the homeland, trade and the legal system. The greatest interest, for obvious reasons, is in the stones that attest to the Vikings' extensive journeys. Many men died far from Sweden, and stones were erected in memory of them at home. Here it is easy to trace the Vikings' trade routes east to Finland, Russia and Greece, down to Byzantium, Bagdad and Jerusalem, and west to England, where several Swedes participated in establishing the so-called Danegeld, the tax whereby the English were forced to ransom their land from the Danish Vikings. A broad, international perspective sings out from the rune stones in the idyllic Uppland countryside.

Also of great interest are the rune stones on which the memorial takes the form of a poetic strophe in verse types we know from Old Icelandic poetry: *fornyrdislag* and *drott-kvætt*. These attest to the fact that Scandinavia was a united empire with regard to literature. Seldom is it great and significant poetry, but the fact that it was written is a sure sign that there was an indigenous poetry corresponding to Old Icelandic. Contrary to what one might think, the runic inscriptions are not anonymous literary monuments. With great pride many of the rune cutters put their names on the stones, referring to themselves as "skalds" (poets), for example Thorbjörn the Skald or Grim the Skald.

A text in *fornyrdislag* is found on the most remarkable of all rune stones, the Rök stone in Östergötland, which was cut and erected in the ninth century, at the beginning of the period of the younger runic alphabet. One of the peculiarities of this huge stone is that it is fully covered with runes without any ornamentation whatsoever and is thus the world's longest runic text. But the text in itself is also remarkable and obscure, with an ancient, magical darkness conveyed in evocative, mysterious formulations. The stone was cut by a man named Varin in memory of a dead son, and he alludes to events and stories from the past. So, for example, in the strophe about Theodoric the Great, the famous king of the Ostrogoths who lived around 500 A.D., he wrote: "Theodoric the bold,/ king of sea-warriors,/ rules

The Rök Stone.

over/ Reid-sea shores./ Now he sits armed/ on his Gothic horse,/ shield strapped,/ protector of Maerings." This verse is an excellent example of Old Norse poetry, resembling not only Old Icelandic writing but also Old English. From the darkness and silence of prehistory the Rök stone rises as a powerful literary monument. With it, Swedish literature can be said to begin.

The Middle Ages—Provincial Laws, Ballads, Historical Chronicles

In the history of Sweden, the Middle Ages is the period that began at the end of the Viking era, although there are obviously no clear-cut boundaries. Rather, the period of transition between the pagan Viking era and the Christian Middle Ages during the eleventh and twelfth centuries is a long, drawn-out period that continues to rest in a certain historical chiaroscuro. It is characterized by a strengthening of national unity and royal power centered around the old cult district of the Swedes at Uppsala. Gradually, Christianity became more widely established in the country. The period's most remarkable cultural manifestation is without a doubt the building of hundreds of cathedrals, churches and monasteries, an achievement which was accomplished in a surprisingly short time and with great emphasis on rich ornamentation. With the Christian culture there came a spreading of literacy, book learning and a certain measure of literary culture. All education emanated from the Church and the monasteries. Swedish students soon began to seek out foreign universities, first Bologna, then in the thirteenth century mainly Paris, where colleges were set up for Swedish students from the central dioceses. In such a way, a foundation was laid for an intellectual elite, for whom there was a professional market in two main areas: the Church and the law. At this time, the literate were either clerics or law men.

Pagan culture survived longest on the periphery of Europe. The new continental Christian culture did not gain a foothold in Sweden until very late. During the long period when Christianity was securing its position the kingdom found itself in an obvious cultural backwater, not only in

relation to the countries on the Continent but also in relation to the Scandinavian neighbors Denmark, Norway and
Iceland. The total absence of secular literature during the
twelfth and early thirteenth centuries is especially striking
and puzzling. The medieval renaissance, whose culmination
is usually considered to have occurred in the twelfth century, evidently passed Sweden by without a trace. Only
towards the end of the thirteenth century did this situation
begin to change. The late thirteenth and early fourteenth
centuries constitute the first period in which a Swedish
literary culture developed. This was during the time when
the powerful Folkung dynasty held power and an aristocracy of privilege was established. This aristocracy was finan-
cially prosperous and viewed with interest both the cultural
and material lifestyle of the continental aristocracy.

One of the most important cultural achievements during
the Folkung period was the writing down of the *provincial
laws*. The medieval Swedish provincial laws have their roots
in the society of the Viking era and reflect in an often
illuminating way the period of transition between paganism
and Christianity. Originally, they were preserved in the
minds of people who were entrusted with responsibility for
legal knowledge. These laws were recited orally at the *Ting*
(assembly of freemen) and passed on to the next generation
of law men. This legal knowledge often went from father to
son, and important dynasties established themselves in positions of power during the twelfth and thirteenth centuries,
assuming responsibility for legal matters and jurisdiction in
their particular areas. When the Roman alphabet became
more common there arose a need to record these laws. This
process is thought to have begun in the early thirteenth
century, when an older version of the *Västgötalagen* (Västergötland Laws) seems to have been extant. From the second
half of the thirteenth century comes a later, "modernized"
version, the so-called *Yngre Västgötalagen* (Younger Västergötland Laws), as well as the *Östgötalagen* (Östergötland
Laws) and the *Upplandslagen* (Uppland Laws). The latter
can be dated to 1296 and came into existence through a
royally constituted committee. By the beginning of the fourteenth century, the other provinces had also written down
their laws. However, by the middle of the fourteenth cen-

tury these provincial laws were already out of date, and they were replaced in 1347 by a common law for the entire kingdom, usually called *Magnus Erikssons landslag* (Magnus Eriksson's Law Code) after the monarch in power at that time.

The provincial laws provide us with invaluable information about Swedish society during the early Christian period, both with regard to the overall social structure and simple everyday life. They reflect a conception of the law that goes back to pagan times but that was also obviously modified under the influence of Christian culture. They also give a picture of medieval Sweden that is remarkably alive, and therein lies their literary worth. This ancient legal language with its conventions from a primitive society shunned both the abstract and the generalized. People expressed themselves concretely and by example. Instead of applying general legal principles juridically from case to case, some simple cases would be taken and judgments based on them. These legal examples were often brief, lively tales which give unusually concrete glimpses of everyday medieval life and which can contain quick and matter-of-fact exchanges of great authenticity. The linguistic form of the laws was colored by the oral tradition they once functioned in and are characterized by mnemonic aids such as rhythm, alliteration, repetition and parallelism. They are thus often highly poetic in character, something which contrasts with the brutal legal concepts they frequently express. Often cited is a paragraph from the older Västergötland Laws that shows how "minstrels," the traveling musicians and jesters of the Middle Ages, were without legal rights: "If a minstrel is beaten up, there will be no fine."

From the end of the thirteenth century, the new feudal life at the Folkung rulers' court and the newly established aristocracy stimulated the rise of a secular literature. Courtly writing from the Continent was imported and in certain cases translated for Swedish use. The writing of *ballads and songs*, a fashion which had spread throughout Europe, also figured in this cultural influx. When it reached Sweden and the other Scandinavian countries, it developed a surprisingly independent artistic life. However, we know little about its earliest existence on Swedish soil. Only fragments of ballads are preserved from the Middle Ages. Not until the sixteenth and seventeenth centuries can you find song books with complete ballads. Once part of an aristocratic culture, the ballads came increasingly over the centuries to live on in a popular culture. During the nineteenth century, after the arrival of Romanticism, a more systematic effort to collect ballads and songs was begun, an effort which continues into our own days. It was largely female singers from among the ordinary people who were the bearers of this song tradition and who saved it from oblivion.

These ballads are without exception anonymous and had a concrete social function as cultivated entertainment. The word ballad itself means dance song, and it was as song and dance that they were presented. A lead singer recited the verses of the text, while the dancers, who performed in a circle, sang in chorus the characteristic refrains that are usually repeated after every verse. It is generally thought that modern Christmas dance games of various types are survivals of medieval dance song. Only in one place in Scandinavia has the ballad been preserved as a dance song in a more original form with clear roots in the Middle Ages, namely in the Faeroe Islands, where it lives on as a native tradition.

Beside the lyrical, mood-inducing refrains that create a sort of poetic background illumination to the events of the poem, the ballads are characterized by standardized formulas and by a strongly condensed epic-lyric character. With a limited range of expressions they produce an exciting, dynamic story presented in song from the perspective of the narrator. The ballad stories are episodic and are built on, among other things, lively exchanges, often without elucidative commentary. The concentrated effect which results is reminiscent of the spare and evocative technique of the Old Icelandic saga. This is especially evident in the foremost of the *chivalric songs*, the ballad of Ebbe Skammelsson, which depicts a dark and violent family tragedy with impassive brevity. Another type of ballad is the *nature-mythical song*, which describes a magical relationship between man and nature, as, for example, in "Herr Olov och älvorna" (Mr. Olov and the Elves), which can be interpreted as a late Scandinavian variation of the ancient Greek myth of

Orpheus and Eurydice, only with a happy ending. More popularly burlesque in character are the *heroes' songs*, such as "Holger Dansk och Burman" (Holger the Dane and Burman). This depiction of how the knight rescues the beautiful princess from the terrible troll has themes typical of the medieval saga and the poems of courtly love. The *historical songs*, on the other hand, are based on real events from medieval history. One example of this is the song about the battle between the Swedes and the Danes at Lena at the beginning of the thirteenth century. The final verse turns from the battle arena to the women at home, and its darkly condensed conclusion is one of the highpoints of the entire ballad genre:

> *Fruarna stå i höga loft.*
> *De vänta sina herrar hem komma.*
> *Hästarna komma blodiga hem,*
> *och sadlarna äro tomma.*

> The wives stand high in the loft.
> They wait for their men to come home.
> The horses come home bloody,
> And the saddles are empty.

The writing of history also developed during the cultural life of the Folkung era, from simple annals to the poetry of the anonymous *Erikskrönikan* (The Chronicle of Erik), which probably came into being around 1330. This depicts the destiny of the Folkung dynasty from Birger Jarl's crusade to Finland and the founding of the city of Stockholm in the mid-thirteenth century, through the new feudal court life at the end of that century, to the fateful fraternal quarrels between the king's sons at the beginning of the fourteenth century. The Erik who is the verse chronicle's main character, and who is portrayed as a true medieval knight, is Duke Erik Magnusson, one of these royal sons, whose attempt to form a united Nordic kingdom was brutally scotched when he was murdered by his brother, Birger. The chronicle was undoubtedly intended for Erik's son, Magnus Eriksson, who took over the regency after the bloody struggle between the brothers. This is the same son who, at the end, is hailed with newly awakened national pride as one of the most powerful Christian monarchs in the world, since he had become king of Norway too through his mother. The unknown author of the verse chronicle, who has stubbornly defied all research attempts at identification, was an eminent narrative talent who often recounts the diverse course of events with lively clarity and a pregnant sense of detail. This anonymous writer must have had some literary education, since he alludes to Gawain and Parsifal, the heroes of the Arthurian legends, and, furthermore, to the mad Danish Prince Hamlet, known from Saxo Grammaticus' Danish chronicle. The writing of historical chronicles, but in the form of a coarser, political propaganda, was also cultivated during the fifteenth century.

Of a higher literary class than most, though, is the "Frihetsvisa" (Freedom Song), written in 1439 by Bishop Tomas Simonsson, and whose message of freedom survived the politics of the era and made it a jewel among Swedish songs: "Freedom is the best thing,/ that can be sought in all the world around,/ for him who can carry freedom well."

Saint Birgitta

It is in the field of Christian writing, most of which was written in Latin, that the first more significant authors in Swedish medieval literature came to the fore. Here we find the Dominican monk Petrus da Dacia, a farmer's son from Gotland, who wrote a famous biography of the stigmatized mystic, Kristina from Stommeln. Together with their pre-served correspondence it gives both an analytical and a typi-cally devout picture of medieval mysticism and piety, which has significant value for the history of religion. However, foremost of all was Saint Birgitta, a lawman's daughter from Uppland, whose emergence from the rather spartan Swedish cultural milieu as one of the medieval period's most remark-able and interesting personalities can be seen as a veritable medieval miracle.

Birgitta (1303–73) also figured to a certain degree in the Folkung period's active cultural life. Kinship as well as envi-ronment guaranteed her social status and a relatively thorough education. She was related to several of the kingdom's most powerful families, distantly also to the Folkung dynasty. As a lawman, her father, one of the editors of the Uppland Laws, belonged to the country's small intellectual elite. Thus, her unexpected rise to fame took place against the background of the most privileged possible home circumstances in the Sweden of that time. However, any higher study was naturally out of the question. Instead she was married at a very young age to a man who, in his capacity as knight, lawman and counsellor of the realm, belonged to the most influential in the kingdom. Periodically she was a guest at the court of King Magnus Eriksson, whom she would later criticize in very strong words in her revelations. She did not neglect book learning and a life of piety, and together with her husband she undertook a pilgrimage at the beginning of the 1340s to Santiago de Compostela in Spain. This journey was important for her international perspective in that she saw at close hand the dark consequences of the Popes' Babylonian Captivity and the immense destruction caused by the war between England and France.

The death of her husband shortly after their return home was a turning point, after which her life of piety intensified greatly. She began to get revelations and visions which she allowed her confessors to write down, and she was seized by the idea of founding a new convent in Vadstena in Östergötland. Difficulties in realizing this plan arose, and, after a conflict with King Magnus Eriksson, she left the country and travelled to Rome, where she resided until her death. Her inclination towards playing a significant political role was expressed in her effort to induce the Pope to return to Rome after the long Babylonian Captivity in Avignon. Eventually she succeeded in obtaining a papal sanction for a new convent in Vadstena. A short time before her death she undertook a pilgrimage to Jerusalem. After she died, her remains were taken to Vadstena, which became the center of a rapidly flourishing Birgitta cult and one of Sweden's late medieval cultural centers, with an extensive convent library. Birgitta was canonized in 1391.

It is mainly for her revelations, the so-called *Revelationes celeste*, that Birgitta can lay claim to a place in literary history. As mentioned earlier, they were written down by her confessors, one of whom was Master Mattias, one of the most learned humanists in Sweden at this time, and who also enjoyed a certain international celebrity. Only a small number of manuscripts in Birgitta's own hand have been preserved, but experts usually judge the confessors' writings to be genuine, and we know that at least during her later years Birgitta endeavored to check their wording. Her revelations arose from a life of piety and mysticism, but her visionary disposition and her temperamental, "uncensored" realism imbued them with a highly individual form. The revelations are often put into the mouth of Christ or the Virgin Mary or some apostle or saint. They frequently consist of advice and exhortations, solace and penitential sermons, but just as often they allude to something real in contemporary social, political or religious life, sometimes in allegorical form. When she turns to the king or Pope with criticism in such polemical writings, she speaks with the force and authority of someone with an unusual self-confidence, stemming from religious inspiration.

There are sometimes contemporary theological discussions in Birgitta's revelations. Her critical attitude and will to improve must be viewed primarily against the background of the deep crisis that the Catholic Church went through during the Middle Ages, when it was shaken by the Popes' Babylonian Captivity and many other decadent phenomena and began to lose its authority over the people. Birgitta makes accusations and wants to set things right. In some visions, which take the form of great legal proceedings, Birgitta reveals herself as the lawman's daughter. Her literary fantasy often blossoms in visions of a hallucinatory nature, even if the apocalyptic strain is not so usual with her as with many other mystics of this time. Allegorical imagery figures largely in her style, but she can be said to have revitalized medieval allegory with her realistic observations of life. Her language is often marked by woman's life and occupations, by the everyday tasks and motherly concerns which were not foreign to her after a marriage and many children. Vivid pictures are drawn of farming life and handicrafts. Together they give a concrete and lively presentation of medieval life and occupational activities. This unembellished realism with its unexpectedly effective personal quality contrasts with the more conventional rose and precious stone symbolism that also plays an important role in her allegorical visions.

In many respects Birgitta is still an enigmatic figure. The sources on her life are often contradictory and in several cases were written so late that they could already have been distorted by the legend-making process. Yet her achievement stands out clearly. She gave Swedish medieval literature a comprehensive and original work of international scope. She was without doubt the most luminous personality during the Swedish Middle Ages. With her work, the mystic dimensions of which can be compared favorably with those of other great mystics of the time, Swedish culture took its place in a European cultural community. In spite of the fact that Birgitta hardly became a widely-read author, the surprisingly intensive force with which she testifies to her own spiritual experiences and those of her era can still fascinate us today.

Book Printing and the Reformation—Bible Translations and Renaissance Humanism

The cultural flourishing of the Folkung era during the period 1275–1350 was the late awakening of a secular culture in Sweden. It was to become a parenthesis in medieval history, pinned in between underdevelopment at home and the phenomena of international decadence that made the fourteenth century a period of decay throughout Europe. After 1350, Swedish culture sank back into a gray lethargy and went into a nearly three-hundred-year cultural freeze that was only occasionally broken by some important high point. Gutenberg's invention of book printing, for example, reached Sweden at the end of the fifteenth century and profoundly changed the conditions for the production of literature. The first book printer in the country was a German, Johann Snell, who in 1483 printed the first Swedish book: a little collection of entertaining and moralizing animal fables in Latin. In 1495 came the first printed book in Swedish, with a title typical of the time, *Av djävulsens frestelse* (From the Devil's Temptation). However, as far as secular literature is concerned the new printing presses did not signify any breaking of the ice, let alone a flourishing.

The sixteenth century was, if anything, even poorer in high quality belles-lettres than the previous century. Only some dozen works that in a modern sense could be designated imaginative literature saw the light of day, and the literary works of the Middle Ages were only printed in exceptional cases.

For the Protestant Reformation, however, the new art of book printing came to take on a profound significance. In Sweden, the Reformation coincided with the final consolidation of the national state. During most of the Middle Ages an intensive struggle for political hegemony over Swedish territory was conducted against above all German and Danish interests. Not until the beginning of the 1520s could the Danish invaders be put to flight under the powerful leadership of Gustav Vasa who, in 1523, was made king of Sweden. As an absolute and despotic ruler he strengthened the power of the crown and the unity of the national state and in 1527 carried out a Lutheran Church reformation, an important cornerstone in his national policy. For his Church policy he made use of trusted men such as Laurentius Andreae, who as head of the new royal chancellery dealt especially with Church matters, and Olaus Petri, who preached the new doctrine in Stockholm and became the spiritual central figure of the Reformation, together with his brother, Laurentius Petri, who became the country's first Protestant archbishop. From the royal printing press, which was founded at this time, flowed a stream of theological writings, and by royal order a Swedish translation of the New Testament was accomplished with impressive speed and published in 1526. There is no indication of how the translation was carried out or who the translators were, but it is likely that both Luther's translation and the Danish one were used as models.

In 1541, the whole Bible was translated and printed, bearing the long title *Biblia, det är all den helga skrift på svensko* (Bible, all the holy scriptures in Swedish). It came to be known as Gustav Vasa's Bible and was the official Church Bible for some four hundred years up to 1917. The new editions that came in 1618 under Gustav II Adolf and in 1703 under Karl XII were only lesser revisions. Gustav Vasa's Bible was without doubt the most important literary work to appear in Sweden in the sixteenth century. As a linguistic achievement the translation is impressive. A classically pure Swedish emerged here with the ability to be both realistically forceful and lyrically sublime, to unite expressiveness with solemnity. To its religious importance must be added its linguistic and literary significance. It was through the Bible's pithy turns of phrase that people came in contact with a language that was beyond everyday usage. Even if it became heavy and archaic with time, this translation was responsible for that consciousness of religious, linguistic and literary tradition that links the sixteenth century with the early twentieth century and that was not lost until our own time. Herein lies one of the paradoxes of the Swedish sixteenth century: although impoverished in terms of literary production, this century produced perhaps the most important literary work of all time. For Gustav Vasa's Bible is the classic of the Swedish language. Even in the modern era, poets and other writers have cited its language as perhaps the best, most expressive and most sonorous Swedish that was ever written, and many of its solemnly archaic expressions and turns of phrase are still alive today.

With the Reformation came a very rough-handed settlement of accounts with medieval Catholic culture. All resistance was broken down by brutal means. The property of the churches and monasteries was confiscated, which in practice meant a veritable pillaging of their treasures by Gustav Vasa's bailiffs and soldiers. Not least, the priceless book collections of the monasteries were subjected to this plundering, as was the case with the Vadstena convent. In Swedish cultural history, Gustav Vasa's reign stands out to a considerable degree as a dictatorship hostile to culture. Scholarship and education declined catastrophically. At Uppsala University, founded in 1477, teaching lay fallow and was not revived until the end of the sixteenth century. The number of Swedish students at foreign universities also decreased drastically. However, continental Humanism offered a counterbalance to this cultural decline. Its newly awakened inspiration, derived from classical antiquity, began to reach Sweden around 1500, brought by Swedish students returning from Italy. In their writings they recommended the study of antiquity, and some of them founded private book collections of significant size in which the classical authors as well as those of the Italian Renaissance were represented. Gradually it became clear that Humanism could coexist very well with Lutheranism in a Protestant state. Later in his reign, Gustav Vasa liked to present himself as a typical Renaissance sovereign and a worthy equal to the classical champions of freedom. He surrounded himself with classical insignia and classical rhetoric on solemn occasions and called in a court poet from the Continent, who wrote in Latin. Furthermore, he gave his sons, the aesthetically gifted Erik XIV and Johan III, an education that befitted young princes of the time.

It is also with these Vasa sons that one can talk about a humanistic breakthrough in the history of Swedish education. As humanistically schooled Renaissance princes they defended literary culture, and it has been claimed that few monarchs of the time, i.e. around the 1560s, had such a thorough humanistic education as Erik XIV. The royal court and the aristocracy were permeated by Roman rhetoric; an indigenous Latin writing made its breakthrough, and in Johan III's school regulations from 1571 it was even made a compulsory subject. However, Latin writing, being unoriginal and artifical, was never of any real significance. Of greater interest is the drama of the humanistic school that developed at the beginning of the seventeenth century, with above all Terence as the prototype. It is characterized by a didactic tendency and was produced by students, often for public performance. In comparison with the level attained by Italian, English and Spanish dramatic art at this time these plays appear modest, but with their coarse realism, erotic openness and their burlesque popular element they are clearly related to the English traveling theater. The little comedy *Tisbe* from 1610 is one such example. At the beginning of the seventeenth century, instruction at Swedish universities and schools was also intensified to a more international level and independent research began to emerge. This upturn in educational life was one of the prerequisites for the growth of the Swedish Great Power state during the seventeenth century.

The Writing of "Gothic" History

During its period of consolidation in the sixteenth century and its emergence as a European Great Power during the seventeenth century, the new Swedish national state was permeated more and more by a national myth, the aim of which was to assert the country's position among contemporary nations by giving it a glorious past. This was achieved with the myth about Sweden's Gothic origins. It is a myth that played a great role in the history of ideas in Sweden, and is usually called *Gothicism*. Its roots can be found in the Gothic chronicle of the sixth-century historian Jordanes, where it was stated that the Ostrogothic and Visigothic people emigrated from the island Scandza, an island that was identified with Scandinavia. This myth was exploited by the chauvinistic propaganda machinery as early as the late Middle Ages. At the synod of Basel in 1434, the Swedish delegate demanded that he should have the most prominent seating, given that Sweden was "older, stronger and more noble" than all other kingdoms. He did not obtain his wish, but the myth is confirmed in Ericus Olais *Chronica regni Gothorum* from around 1470. Here, the nationalistic fantasy was twisted further, depicting Uppsala as the center of the old Gothic kingdom in Scandinavia, a place chosen by God, equal in rank to Jerusalem and Rome, from where the Goths emigrated and conquered the world.

This entire megalomaniacal complex of ideas was exploited in the aggressive nationalism of the sixteenth century. To be sure, it was questioned by Olaus Petri in his Swedish chronicle, remarkable at the time for its unusual criticalness and impartiality, as well as its strongly critical treatment of Gustav Vasa. Other chroniclers, though, gradually lent an international notoriety to the king's adventurous life and successful struggle for freedom in the shape of propaganda and legend. But the real codification of the Gothic myth was to be made by the brothers Johannes and Olaus Magnus. As learned Catholic Renaissance humanists they lived in self-chosen exile on the Continent. Although poor, they enjoyed an increasing European reputation. They ended up in Italy where Johannes, shortly before his death in 1544, finished his great national history in Latin, *Historia de omnibus gothorum sveonumque regibus.* Published in Rome in 1554, it aroused great international attention. Through painstaking research he tried to document Sweden's glorious Gothic past. Johannes Magnus was something of a dreamer and visionary, and his myth-creating fantasy presented Swedish prehistory as a free, illustrious golden age, a myth which would later inspire and be exploited by the seventeenth century's patriotic history writers. Johannes's brother, Olaus, was director of the Birgitta House in Rome, where he had a printing press installed to print his own writings as well as those of his brother and Saint Birgitta. He also published a work that could be called a Gothic cultural history: *Historia de gentibus septentrionalibus,* 1555. His aim was to depict the wild Nordic nature and the hardy people who lived there, to give a picture of his homeland that would inspire respect. As a realistic description of travel and the life of the people, this work has a significant cultural-historical value and is still worth reading. It was translated into many languages and, alongside the Bible translation, it is the only sixteenth-century classic in Swedish literature.

In the growing Swedish Great Power state of the seventeenth century the Gothic myth was seized and made into an effective ideology. At the universities it stimulated various kinds of historical research. This could—as in the case of the historian and dramatist Johannes Messenius—be directed toward the collecting of information and manuscripts for archives. Interest in Old Icelandic literary manuscripts grew around the middle of the century, and these were pragmatically incorporated into the Swedish Gothic legacy and systematically sought for collecting. Rune stones also began to arouse the interest of researchers at this time. With Johannes Bureus and his pupil, the poet Georg Stiernhielm, runic research was combined with mystic and Gothic speculation, leading to a linguistic revival of the Gothic myth that Swedish was the first language known to man! The naturalist Olof Rudbeck was responsible for the culmination of this whole stream of Gothic ideas in his work *Atland eller Manhem* (Atlantis, or Manheim), usually called *The Atlantica* and published in four parts 1679–1702. As a physician, Rudbeck had made the meritorious discovery of the lymph nodes and their function, and he was an ingenious and empirically oriented enthusiast amid the vigorous activity at Uppsala University at this time. However, when he tackled historical research the results became fantastical. He tried to show the supremacy of the Swedish language over the classical languages by attempting, for example, to derive proper nouns of Greek etymology from Swedish, in order thereby to prove that Sweden really was the legendary island Atlantis that Plato mentions in some of his dialogues! Rudbeck's work was a great international sensation but was also severely attacked. The famous philosopher Leibnitz, for example, wrote a sharp rejoinder. In fact, *The Atlantica* was just a late shoot on the tree of Gothic myths. When the winds of the Enlightenment began to blow in the eighteenth century, its fantastical constructions crumbled, just as the short-lived Swedish Great Power state was also leaning towards its fall.

The Great Power Era—Queen Kristina's Cultural Policy

Sweden made its entrance into the European power game with Gustav II Adolf's (Gustavus Adolphus) Protestant campaign during the Thirty Years' War. The Peace of Westphalia of 1648 affirmed Sweden's position as a Great Power. From the middle of the century on Sweden was a factor to be reckoned with in Europe, and this quickly brought positive consequences in the cultural arena. The military and political successes were followed by a cultural prosperity that was characterized by a newly won national self-assurance and a need for demonstrations of patriotism. For some two decades, long campaigns on the continent had brought aristocratic as well as common Swedish soldiers into closer contact with European culture than ever before. They returned home with new impressions and new customs and their pompous, nouveau-riche lifestyle exhibited a vulgarity previously unknown. Not least, they brought home immeasurable art and literary treasures, the harvest of widespread despoliation during the war years. In particular, the plundering of Prague in 1648 provided a rich trove of stolen cultural goods, from which, for example, Queen Kristina's royal library received significant additions. The cultural prosperity during the Swedish Great Power Era was based solidly on a barbaric plundering not far behind the pillaging of the Viking Age.

However, these brutally acquired cultural trappings left a taste for more and led to an increasingly ambitious cultural orientation. The teaching system developed rapidly and education advanced in enormous strides. Students thirsty for education sought the foremost universities of the age in numbers far above those studying abroad in earlier periods. The goal was now Germany, just as it had been from the late medieval era on, but Dutch universities were also popular—especially Leyden, which was the leading university city in mid-seventeenth-century Europe. French educational trends were also very much in evidence during the epoch, just as there were certain contacts with the newly founded Royal Society in London. At the same time, an apparent refurbishing of the Swedish university system was taking place. After the revitalization that Uppsala University experienced at the beginning of the century the need arose for new universities in other regions of the expanding realm. In 1632, Dorpat in the newly conquered Baltic provinces got a university; in 1640, Åbo in Finland. In southern Sweden, in the area that was conquered from the Danes, a university was founded in 1668 in Lund. In the North German provinces that were incorporated into the Swedish Great Power state, the flourishing university in Greifswald was taken over. The poet Tomas Thorild was to be a professor there for some years. The standards at these seats of learning were relatively high, even in international terms, and as before, the emphasis in education lay on theology and Humanism.

The cultural upswing during the Great Power Era was, however, generally attributable to one distinct central figure who promoted artistic development: Queen Kristina. In spite of his high educational and cultural ambitions, Gustav II Adolf had been too involved in war to make much of an effort in the field of culture. Only with his daughter Kristina did what we can call a cultural life develop in the capital, where the literary talents of the time mixed with famous learned figures from abroad. Kristina was given an excellent education and showed early on an inclination for serious studies and an interest in philosophy and theology. She retained these scholarly ambitions as an adult, and she tried to fill most of the hours of the day with intellectual pursuits of various kinds. To a high degree, her cultural policy was determined by these ambitions. Understimulated by the Swedish educational environment, she tried to attract famous humanists to the court in Stockholm. A number of international luminaries now gathered in the capital, which suddenly found itself a European intellectual center. Illustrious names such as Vossius, Heinsius and Salmasius from Leyden, Frenchmen such as Samuel Bochart, Pierre-Daniel Huet and Gabriel Naudé came, as well as the jewel in the crown, the philosopher Descartes. However, their sojourns at the court were not always especially long-lived, and in Descartes' case it ended unfortunately when he died after a time as a result of the strains of the raw northern climate.

The task of these famous guests seems otherwise to have been to act as librarians and book buyers. The royal library, originally founded on literary war booty, was completed by means of an ambitious, not to say extravagant, purchase policy with regard to manuscripts and books. Over time, the collections grew to an impressive library of classical manuscripts and first editions which followed Kristina to Rome when she abdicated and converted to Catholicism. Remnants of this collection can be found today in the Vatican Library. Descartes' attempt to form a learned court academy of these guest researchers around the queen, along the lines of the French Academy, was more short-lived, even if this embryo of a Swedish academy does seem to have met for a short period.

There was also a more public facet to Kristina's cultural interests, one which favored theatrical plays, parades and all kinds of pageants. At court, a magnificence and a splendor developed that sought to surpass those of the Continent. Fortune-hunting poets were attracted to this sensational court and wrote poems of praise to the queen. German, Dutch and Italian theater companies visited Stockholm on their tours, and a court theater was founded at the castle. Of greatest interest are the ballets that were produced by the court theater and for which several of the period's foremost writers wrote separately printed texts. Thus, for example,

Stiernhielm wrote the scenario to the ballet *Den fångne Cupido* (Cupid Imprisoned) from 1649, poems in classical meter such as the hexameter and the Sapphic strophe, expressing a worship of antiquity typical of the time. In *Fredsafl* (Peace Notice), also from 1649, Stiernhielm worked with Descartes, who wrote the parallel French text, while *Parnassus triumphans* from 1651 paid homage to Kristina as the patroness of the arts and sciences and proudly proclaimed that the muses had left Greece and settled with the Swedish queen and her people.

This culturally prosperous court life did not last long, becoming increasingly superficial and frivolous. However, beneath the worldly and libertine exterior there was in the queen a streak of serious religious searching which led to her renouncing the throne, adopting the Catholic faith and—just like Saint Birgitta and the brothers Magnus before her—moving to Rome, where she settled for the rest of her life. There too she became a center for intellectual and artistic life, a well-known personality in the Europe of the day. We meet reflections in her scant writings of her agitated and contradictory psyche, which vacillated between passion and intellectualism, between outward joy of life and inner isolation, between religious earnestness and scepticism. Her writings consist partly of autobiographical fragments, partly of *L'Ouvrage de Loisir* and *Sentiments*, collections of aphorisms from her period in Rome, written in French in imitation of La Rochefoucauld. The pithy maxims do not display any deep originality, but they are nevertheless genuine expressions of a firm faith in God and a conception of the world devoid of illusion. Furthermore, they shed interesting light on her remarkable personality and life.

Stiernhielm, the Father of Swedish Poetry, and Baroque Poetry

During Kristina's era there also arose something that might be called a literary Parnassus in Swedish cultural life. At the center of this stood Georg Stiernhielm (1598–1672), whom we have already met as the Gothically inspired language researcher and author of ballet scenarios. His contemporaries recognized the pioneering nature of his poetic work, and the honorary title "the father of Swedish poetry" has been attached to his name. The question is whether it was not in fact he himself who laid the foundation for such a view with the title of his poetry collection from 1668 *Musae suethizantes*. The Swedish subtitle of this work was "it is the muses now first learning to write poetry and to play in Swedish," indicating an awareness of the retarded state of Swedish literature. This proud, lyrical self-declaration was probably not entirely correct, for attempts had already been made to transfer classical meters to Swedish. However, Stiernhielm was undeniably the one who consolidated the classical poetic forms in Swedish poetry and who attained more artistically satisfactory results than earlier attempts had done.

Stiernhielm came from a mine-owning family in Dalecarlia and studied abroad in a manner typical for the time. After returning to Sweden he held a whole series of high state posts, and in the 1640s and 1650s he became the leading professional writer at Kristina's court. In his versatile, light-hearted and robust Renaissance nature there was a serious philosopher and scientist and a speculative mystic. His scientific ambitions stretched from mathematics and mechanics to comparative linguistics. His Gothic language research led him to a linguistic purity that aimed at eradicating all foreign words from the Swedish language, particularly the German-influenced ones, and promoting a return to original, Swedish words and expressions. As a thinker, he belonged to the neoplatonic tradition with its natural-philosophical mysticism. He saw cosmic matter as permeated by the principles of common sense and laughter which together accounted for divine wisdom and harmony.

A strong gust from his world of ideas also passed through his literary work. His literary fame rests largely on his hexameter poem *Hercules*, the full version of which was printed in 1658. The classical motif in this heroic poem about Hercules at the crossroads originally came from Xenophon and was often used in the humanistic poetry of the time as a morality tale. This was also Stiernhielm's purpose. He was clearly addressing himself first and foremost to the young men of the nobility who, as a result of the aristocracy's newly acquired economic power, were easily tempted into a dissolute lifestyle. The allegory depicts Hercules at a crossroads, unsure of which path to take. He is then met by a band consisting of Mistress Lust and her daughters Idleness, Lewdness and Vanity and her son Intoxication. Mistress Lust urges him to appreciate the good things in life, since life is short and death dark and irrevocable. However, as Hercules stands ready to follow her, Mistress Virtue appears and urges him instead to devote his energy to work and scholarly labors, which will gain him everlasting fame. With rhetorical skill Stiernhielm leaves the ending open. We do not learn which path Hercules chooses, but Mistress Virtue has, naturally, the final word.

The poem, because of its hexameter form, mimics the classical; however, in its scholarly, allegorical construction we encounter continental Baroque poetry in all its embellished and affected splendor. Emblematic art, where a maxim tells the reader how to interpret a symbolic image, played a role in Stiernhielm's way of describing the characters. The language is characterized by the Baroque rhetorical ideal of art, with a large arsenal of effective images, antitheses, enumerations, alliteration, inner-rhyme, etc. But the poem also has a Swedish characteristic in the Old Swedish words that the poet uses to elevate its Swedish linguistic purity and in the vigorous and genuine colloquial language, which, in spite of the scholarly form, renders the poem surprisingly alive. In the diversified and lively realism which culminates in Mistress Lust's depiction of drinking bouts, gaming and gambling and erotic adventures, there are many contemporary images. The dark picture of age and death so typical of the time contrasts with the life-affirming hedonism but also with heroic stoicism and faith in an ethical struggle as man's true goal: "Therefore live so that others may count themselves fortunate from the fruit of your mercy: be useful to everyone in the world."

In his other poetry, for example in the ballet texts, Stiernhielm excelled in a variety of lyrical forms which had earlier been inconceivable in Swedish and which effectively broke the monopoly of the Latin-imitating poetry. Still other poets of the era tried new forms in Swedish, such as the classical ode and the sonnet. The ballad experienced a renaissance through poets such as the somewhat older Lars Wivallius and Lars Lucidor Johansson, both adventurous characters and experienced foreign travellers. These both cultivated a more personal ballad form in praise of freedom and nature. There were also court poets who wrote richly ornate poems in the international Baroque style for great occasions. A growing upper middle-class also encouraged an occasional poetry for the solemn events of family life such as weddings and funerals and made it one of poetry's most important forms at this time. While narrative prose was still extremely undeveloped during the entire seventeenth century, some indigenous dramatic activity lived on after Kristina's era. In Uppsala, there was an active student theater troop, and in Stockholm, drama was performed in a venue called *Lejonkulan* (The Lion's Den), Sweden's first permanent theatrical stage, which hosted an artistically modest, native repertory.

The first official Swedish hymn-book was also a creation of this era. It was sanctioned in 1695 and gave expression to the seventeenth century's orthodox Church movement. The main responsibility for the work fell to the court chaplain, Jesper Svedberg, the father of Emanuel Swedenborg. At his side he had the learned, English-oriented bishop, Haqvin Spegel, who celebrated God in inspired psalter paraphrases and who in addition wrote several biblical epics of impressive stature, in which traces of Milton can be detected. As an expression of simple, naive and trusting Christian faith the hymn-book of 1695 had a great influence on the church congregations all over the country, where it was in use during the entire eighteenth century. This was, however, virtually the only literary legacy from the Great Power Era to the new century, a century which was to settle accounts with past ideas and values.

THE ENLIGHTENMENT AND THE GUSTAVIAN GOLDEN AGE

During the early eighteenth century, when Karl XII's (Charles XII) expansionist war policy put a heavy strain on the country, a new trough in Swedish cultural life was reached, not least in the field of literature. To be sure, some new poets emerged and led Swedish poetry towards greater realism and a more sincere, pietistic expression of religious faith. There even arose a small, lively literary salon in the capital, on the French model, and French classical drama was introduced sporadically from the end of the seventeenth century. In most respects, though, a noticeable weakening of cultural life began that lasted a good way into the eighteenth century. With Karl XII's death in 1718 and the hard terms of peace that followed, the Swedish Great Power state dissolved, and the nation went into a calmer phase with a constitutional form of government and a gradually prospering economy. From the 1730s on it is clear that culture was also rallying again, and bit by bit a new literary life began to flourish. However, the culmination of this trend did not occur until late in the century during Gustav III's reign, when Swedish literature experienced a genuine golden age.

It was the ideas of the Enlightenment which accounted for this cultural renaissance, and these swiftly penetrated the new Sweden that emerged after the collapse of the Great Power Era. The so-called Era of Freedom—the period that stretches from 1718 to Gustav III's *coup d'état* in 1772—benefitted from the new concepts of freedom and reason, prosperity and justice. The Enlightenment was introduced from France, and Voltaire, Montesquieu and Rousseau rapidly became well-known names in Swedish cultural life. All who sought education made the pilgrimage primarily to Paris. The French language began to affect Swedish—just as German had earlier—to such a great extent that a hybrid language arose. In aristocratic and other cultivated circles, people often spoke and wrote French. The style and tastes of French Classicism manifested themselves all the more strongly as the leading aesthetic doctrine. Almost equally strong, however, was the influence from England. It was to England that one turned for forms of government and party systems. It was on English models that a Swedish press with newspapers and journals began to emerge. English literature, partly through translations, also started to gain a footing. English writers were introduced on a broad front, and Swift, Addison and Steele, Pope and others became models for Swedish writers. The English influence is noticeable not least in the field of prose, where the literature of the Era of Freedom attained its most outstanding results.

The Breakthrough of Prose and the Press Olof Dalin

At the center of the new ideas of the Enlightenment and the breakthrough of prose and the press in the eighteenth century stood Olof Dalin (1708–63). He ushered in a new phase of the history of Swedish language and literature and was the leading literary figure of the Era of Freedom. For the aristocratic and upper middle-class salons which he frequented, he wrote an extensive occasional poetry of the sort that in French is called "poésie fugitive" and that is based more on the inspiration of the moment than on aspirations to everlasting fame. He also became an admired epic poet and dramatist, with, among other works, a comedy in the style of Molière. But it was in the area of prose that he was to make a lasting impression. In 1732 he began anonymously to publish his one man periodical *Den svenska Argus* (The Swedish Argus), which continued until 1734. This represented something thoroughly new in Swedish literature. As a model Dalin took Addison and Steele's moralistic weekly journals *The Tatler* and *The Spectator*. In accordance with the custom of the time, he drew freely on ideas from these and from many other sources. His articles are not marked by any originality, and their significance lies in Dalin's ability to transfer the ideas to Swedish conditions and to fit the Swedish language to the demands of the genre:

a realistic depiction of society, a nimble and satirical analysis of customs and societal conditions, an enlightening, effective discussion of ideas. *Den svenska Argus* marks the beginning of a new period in the development of the Swedish language through its realism, its clear form and its effective means of expression.

An example of the role the English models played for *Den svenska Argus* is the fictitious frame story that Dalin introduced in the second issue of the journal. As counterparts to the British gentleman's club members in *The Spectator* he presents some Swedish gentlemen (a courtier, an officer, a scholar, a lawyer and a merchant), who get together every week to discuss the questions of the day. In many articles they function as mouthpieces for the ideas of the Enlightenment. But Dalin is at his best when he is able to infuse Swedish life into the foreign models and lash out with indignation and satirical acerbity at the vices and moral defects of his era: the lust for power, the craze for learning, snobbery, and the "madness and decay of the parties."

The most famous article deals with the Swedish language. Dalin depicts allegorically how "Mistress Sweden" sullies her mother tongue "with rouge and French flies" and all sorts of "foreign ingredients, blemishes and constraints," so that hardly anything remains of the original Swedish. Just as Stiernhielm and others had done in the seventeenth century, he storms with purist zeal against the foreign influence on the Swedish language. Dalin gives a long series of brilliantly rendered insights into milieus and people's way of thinking in the eighteenth century. There is an inquisitive joy of discovery and realistic freshness in his contemporary interiors. Among the new linguistic gains are, for example, the rendering of an accurately recorded spoken language in conversations and dialogues from both intellectual and simple environments.

Dalin's prose narrative *Sagan om hästen* (The Story of the Horse), 1740, also became famous. It was written at a time when Parliament (the *Riksdag*) was convened to grant an appropriation to a war of revenge against Russia, and it calls for temperance in war policy. The narrative deals in an allegorical form with Sweden's fate under various rulers. The country is represented as a horse with the kings as its various owners and riders. Its entertaining and engaging effect is based on the contrast between the popularly realistic and burlesque narrative tone and the serious nature of the historical material. Even today it is considered literary entertainment of high class. In *Den svenska Argus* Dalin had often shown a striking mastery of the ironically malicious prose-satire form, for which one of his teachers was no one less than Swift himself. An especially cherished target for the other satires which flowed from his pen on various occasions was the historical research and legacy of seventeenth-century Gothicism and Rudbeckianism. As a man of the Enlightenment he sympathized with natural sciences and with economic research, but had little left over for "useless" sciences such as historical research, least of all in the speculative and outdated form in which it had been pursued in Sweden hitherto. With mercilessly malicious joy he illustrated Rudbeck's methodology in a little mock treatise on the question of which language was spoken in Paradise, concluding with feigned triumph that it must have been Swedish. He had the chance to demonstrate a constructive side of this anti-Rudbeck criticism when he was commissioned by Parliament to write *Svea rikes historia* (History of the Kingdom of Sweden). This came out in four volumes 1747–62 and is characterized by a critical attitude to the Gothic fantasies of the past. It stands out as a significant product of the Enlightenment, a sorely needed sobering up after the megalomaniacal visions of the Great Power Era. Furthermore, it inspired better scholarship in the area of historical research during the latter half of the eighteenth century.

Dalin's *Argus* was the opening shot in a rapid expansion of the Swedish press. The new press became above all a forum for the new commercially oriented bourgeoisie, for whom the debate of ideas and literary news were desirable commodities. In the 1760s, there arose a number of more regular newspapers, and during the Gustavian epoch, the *Stockholms Posten*, which was founded in 1778, provided the forum for a lively debate of ideas and literary contributions, with the poet Kellgren and the Lenngrens as driving forces. During the second half of the century a variety of literary journals were also published, creating a forum for the literature of the Gustavian Golden Age.

Dalin never ventured into the genre of the novel. However, a Swedish novel of modest artistic merit, based on English and French models, developed in the middle of the eighteenth century. In time, a light entertainment novel emerged for the simpler public taste. The only surviving classic from this time is an entertaining travel novel, *Min son på galejan eller en ostindisk resa* (My Son on the Schooner or an East Indian Journey), 1781, written by the ship's pastor, Jacob Wallenberg (1746–78), which mixes fresh, objective reportage with essays in the moralistic spirit of the weekly journals. All this is held together by an original structure, for which Henry Fielding's *Tom Jones* played a certain role. Wallenberg was probably also familiar with Laurence Sterne, the international prototype for this type of fictional travel book.

The aphorism, a genre popular at the time, is best represented by the international adventurer Johan Oxenstierna (1666–1733)—not to be confused with the Gustavian poet Johan Gabriel Oxenstierna (see p. 65). The former lived on the Continent the greater part of his life under rather obscure circumstances, and with his collections of aphorisms and moral philosophical essays, *Receuil de pensées 1–5* and the posthumous *Bouquet de diverses fleurs*, he attained a significant international reputation. Probably no other eighteenth-century Swedish writer attained such fame abroad—not least because he wrote primarily in French. His books were also translated into most of the other European languages, and he earned the epithet "the Montaigne of Scandinavia." The Marquis de Sade wrote a drama about him. His aphorisms are witty and libertinely sceptical in the spirit of the times, but he was not an original thinker. His international reputation contrasts remarkably with the silence that generally surrounded his name at home.

The letter was also one of the favored literary forms of the age. The foremost exponent of the refined art of letter writing was the prominent politician, Carl Gustaf Tessin (1695–1770) who, as a teacher of the future Gustav III, wrote a large number of elegantly witty letters to his young pupil, with the aim of instructing and entertaining. These were published in 1756 under the title *En gammal mans brev till en ung prins* (An Old Man's Letters to a Young Prince) and reached foreign audiences through translation into many languages.

Linné and Nature

Swedish prose developed in one further area at the middle of the eighteenth century, namely in nature and travel writing, largely due to Carl von Linné (1707–78). His contemporaries saw him as a scholar and not as a significant author, and today he is famous as a systematizing botanist and as one of the outstanding natural scientists of all time. The discovery that he also harbored a writing talent is of a later date, and Linné is now also recognized as one of the foremost Swedish writers of the eighteenth century. He started a significant and characteristic tradition of nature writing in Swedish literature that took on a unique character by growing out of an intimacy with the rich and varying nature of the Swedish countryside.

The reason why the natural scientist became something of a writer is perhaps mainly due to the environment in which he grew up. Linné was born into a clergyman's home in Småland in southern Sweden, and his experiences of the beauty of the Småland countryside were fundamental for his interest in nature. His home environment also made him especially responsive to the Bible and its language. It was from there that he took his stylistic models when he gave expression to his enthusiasm for the wonders of nature and sang praise to the Creator, whom he thought to see everywhere in the natural world. But there is also another, more realistic side to his authorship that reveals the writer's ability to give swift and precise expression to the reality he saw and which stands in harmony with the Enlightenment's appetite for reality and its utilitarian view of nature.

Linné naturally wrote his great scientific works in Latin. This is the case for the important ones he wrote during the three busy years he spent in Holland in the middle of the 1730s and which signalled his international breakthrough as a botanist. Foremost among these works can be mentioned *Systema naturae*, 1735, which he would continue to revise and complement for the rest of his life, forming a comprehensive and epoch-making work on the categorization of the natural world. His style is original and personal in a way that was highly unusual in scientific writings at this time, and it can be said that his Latin has in many respects the same qualities as his Swedish.

Nevertheless, it is naturally on his Swedish writings that his literary fame rests, and then mainly on the great travel books. The first of these, *Lapplandsresan (Lachesis Lapponica, or a Tour to Lapland)*, was written as early as during his period of study in Uppsala. Having succeeded in obtaining a sum of money for travel purposes, he set out alone on the hazardous journey up through the Lapland wilderness in the early summer of 1732 and began to keep a journal on his travel route, experiences and observations. 1732 is the same year that Dalin began to publish *Argus*.

Carl von Linné. Portrait by Alexander Roslin, 1775.

Swedish prose also began to flourish in Linné's travel diaries. His personal, observant and poetically inspired prose style is already fully chiseled out in this youthful work, in fact, it is even superior to the later travel descriptions in visual freshness and linguistic vitality. No matter whether Linné was writing cultural-geographical observations of the Lapps and their lifestyle or describing landscape, vegetation and animal life, everything appeared to him as something essential and brilliantly new. His style is both that of the scientific discoverer and the creative artist. Part of what is fresh and new in his style is the spontaneity and the frequent use of dialect words. There is always life and activity in his depictions, and in addition there is a personal, unexpected angle that results in surprising effects all the time. The visual observations are precise and lead directly into a warm admiration for the mysteries of nature that often find expression in lyrical hymns in a biblically inspired prose, as in the introduction to the travel book: "*Småland* gave birth to me/ *Sweden* I have traveled through/ the *Earth's* 450 ell long entrails looked at."

The Lapland journey remained unpublished during Linné's lifetime. An English translation came out in 1811, and it was not until the end of the nineteenth century that the first Swedish edition of this work, which is now a classic of Swedish literature, appeared. The travel descriptions Linné made during his period as a professor in Uppsala: *Öländska och gotländska resan* (The Journey to Öland and Gotland), 1745, *Västgötaresan* (The Journey to Västergötland), 1747, and *Skånska resan* (The Journey to Scania), 1751, all of which were published, have also preserved much of his original and personal style. Even though, as a prominent scientist, he took secretaries on these trips, certain parts are indisputably written by Linné himself, such as the famous dedication to the Scanian journey: "The crofter takes delight in his green tenant farm,/ the Hottentot rejoices over his like-looking children,/ the author is flattered by his conceited work." Since there are several different versions of this dedication, scholars have been able to follow how Linné worked towards the final wording. Thus, there was a conscious author in him, and much of what can seem to be spontaneous and improvised in his writings is surely the result of conscious stylistic deliberation.

In Linné there was both a logical systematician and a poetic nature mystic who everywhere "saw the unchanging, omniscient and omnipotent God before him as he walked on." He had a sense both for the precise observation of detail and for the great continuity; he could be both exact and full of fantasy. In some of his later writings in Latin his insights into the balance and interplay of nature led him to a view that foreshadows the ecological perspective of our own time. We find the more mystical side of his personality in the notes he made in his last years, that go under the title *Nemesis divina* and which mainly consist of anecdotes intended to illustrate the divine laws of retribution which Linné, an oversensitive and somewhat bitter old man in spite of his successes, found everywhere. This is a peculiar epilogue to his authorship which was not published in full until our own time.

Linné's activity at Uppsala University represented a high-point in its history. His lectures were heavily attended, and not less than 186 theses were debated under his supervision, most of them also written by him. For the first time in the history of a Swedish university, foreign students came to participate in the master's teaching; earlier the educational traffic had been a one-way street out of Sweden to the Continent. Linné also taught a young generation of natural scientists, whom he sent out on long and arduous journeys around practically the entire world. In their travel descriptions, these "disciples" continued the Linnean travel-book tradition, and their many works resulted in this becoming a favorite genre in Swedish eighteenth-century literature. Today, these works are sought-after treasures, highly valued on the antiquarian book market. Linné's legacy was kept alive to a certain extent also after his death, even if the scientific activity he started quickly subsided and his scientific estate was senselessly sold to England. However, during the nineteenth century the legend about the divinely gifted "flower king" grew, and, as mentioned earlier, the twentieth century has also discovered his literary significance. Many later Swedish writers such as Strindberg and Harry Martinson took inspiration from his nature descriptions.

Swedenborg and Mysticism

Together with Linné, Emanuel Swedenborg (1688–1772) is the most prominent writer-personality in the cultural history of the Era of Freedom. Neither one of them really belongs to literary history as a writer; both actually worked on the periphery of what is normally considered to be the literary field. But while Linné was a writer by virtue of his ability to make realistic observations and his original style, Swedenborg was that through the strength and the rich inspiration of his spiritual visions. In spite of the exclusivity of his mystical conception of the universe—or perhaps thanks to it—no other figure in Swedish cultural history has attracted such international attention in the area of literature as Swedenborg—even Strindberg can hardly contend with him on this point. As a founder of a religion he is unique in Sweden; at the same time he can be said to be typically Swedish in his solitary and visionary mysticism.

Swedenborg was the son of the seventeenth-century visionary mystic, the hymn writer Jesper Svedberg (see p. 37). Thus, there were apparently both inherited and environmentally conditioned prerequisites for his later religious development and its strong character of speculative vision. He received a very thorough humanistic education, but in choosing a career he was strongly influenced by the winds of the Enlightenment and began to study natural sciences and technology. He undertook a long journey to England and the Continent and published a number of works in the area of natural philosophy and biology that aroused considerable attention abroad. He was actively involved in the improvement of industry and technical enterprises, particularly in the mining industry.

During the course of the 1730s, however, he abandoned his materialistic and Cartesian views and developed in a more theosophical direction. He saw God's presence everywhere in nature. Existence, according to Swedenborg, consists of a soul climbing stage by stage up to ever higher perfection. This spiritual state emanated originally from God, and Swedenborg's aim was to bring man back to God. At the same time he developed his famous doctrine of correspondences which was to play a significant role in the future development of literary history. His belief was that everything on the earthly plane also has an exact counterpart on the spiritual and the divine planes. This correspondence is manifested in the linguistic and figurative expressions for things. "One will swear that the physical world is only a symbol for the spiritual," wrote Swedenborg in one of his works, and added: "and this to the degree that if one wants to express any natural truth whatsoever in physical terms and prescribed language and only changes these terms for the corresponding spiritual ones, there will be evident a spiritual truth or theological dogma in place of the natural truth or rule." Swedenborg distinguished between harmonic correspondences that exist between matter and the senses or intellect, allegorical correspondences that refer to biblical parables, and "fabulous" correspondences that comprise the myths of antiquity and symbolic poems, as well as the world of dream images. To a high degree it is the correspondence doctrine with its esoteric, symbolic language that has attracted later writers.

Swedenborg now left his natural sciences and technical preoccupations for good, and set out on a longer foreign sojourn in order to study the structure of spiritual life more deeply. In Amsterdam he suffered a severe spiritual crisis when he was afflicted by violent dreams, visions and states of ecstasy. A couple of years later, in London, he received a vision from God and the spiritual world that was to decide his future course. For the rest of his life he was active as a religious preacher and depictor of the spiritual world in a large number of works. In the so-called *Drömboken* (The Journal of Dreams), which was not printed until the middle of the nineteenth century, he gave some account of the dreams and visions he experienced during his profound crisis and tried to interpret them and see them as a spiritual guidance that would show the way out of the inner darkness. As mentioned already, Swedenborg conceived the images of the dream as correspondences. These arose when a channel opened between the soul and the intellect during sleep, but they then required an intellectual analysis when awake in order to be understood. In *Drömboken* he revealed the irrationality and fickleness of the dream in a way that to some degree can be said to foreshadow Strindberg in *Ett*

Emanuel Swedenborg. Portrait by Per Krafft the Elder.

drömspel (A Dream Play) and to have surrealistic features. His dreams constitute useful material for a modern interpretation of dreams, in particular their association with his daily scientific work. As in the following dream: "...how I later walked where there were abysses on all sides and that I turned around. Then I came into a quite magnificent grove covered everywhere with the most beautiful fig trees in the finest shape and order; on one there seemed to be left withered figs. The grove was surrounded by graves, though not on the side I was on. I wanted to go over a bridge that was on high ground and with grass on it, but I did not dare because of the danger; saw a little way from there a large and quite beautiful palace with wings where I wanted to take lodging. Thought I always had a view of the grove and the graves; a window far out on the wing was also open where I thought I wanted to have my room. This means that on Sunday I should be in the spiritual, that is the marvelous grove; the palace ought to be the design of my work which aims at the grove which I intend to see with it." From the crisis years also comes the work *De cultu et amore Dei*, 1745, a prose paraphrasing epic of creation that is Swedenborg's only real literary work. With great poetic, visionary creativity he depicts Paradise and the birth of the first man from the world egg that is fertilized by divine reason.

The later works, also written in Latin, where Swedenborg presents his religious philosophy, are of a more descriptive nature, even if they are also filled with visions of the mysteries of the spiritual world sublimely rich in detail. This holds above all for *Diarium spirituale*, his extensive spiritual diary kept over many years, in which he steadily recorded his new insights into the spiritual plane. This was published posthumously. Swedenborg's world of ideas with its anthropocentric stamp is revealed in full in these late works. Man on the earthly plane corresponds in the higher continuity to The Great Man, and God appears as an anthropomorphic being. The spiritual plane is in detail a pure copy of the earthly, and the dead spirits live in an existence filled with the same social duties as during life on earth, but in a pure and sublimated form. Life on earth is a preparation for the spiritual life, and man himself, according to the strict moralism Swedenborg developed, chooses which level he will be placed on in an existence beyond: heaven or hell. Heaven appears as an ideal society where the spirits are ceaselessly occupied doing useful things. Not for nothing does it take on the character of an enlightened utopia marked by utilitarianism and inexhaustible philanthropy. As a mystic, Swedenborg is paradoxically enough somewhat of a man of the Enlightenment, a logical systematician and an apostle of humanitarian common sense. Hell, though, he depicts in darkly brutal colors, and its empty and desperate world of pleasure is pictured with a visionary passion that has been compared with Dante.

On the basis of Swedenborg's doctrines a new religion was born, represented by *Den Nya Kyrkan* (The New

Church), spreading especially in England and America. Of greater significance, however, is the almost boundless influence that his mysticism has exerted on writers and other artists right up to our own days. The first reactions in the late eighteenth century were certainly sharply negative; the philosopher Kant, for example, wrote a virulent diatribe against "the crazy spirit beholder." But with the beginning of Romanticism, Swedenborg made a breakthrough. In England, the great visionary William Blake was inspired by him in his art and writing, and in France he acquired an enraptured admirer in Balzac, who called him "the Buddha of Scandinavia." Later on, Emerson, Baudelaire, Strindberg and Yeats would draw inspiration from his doctrines, and just as many followers can be found in the twentieth century. During recent years, the Argentinean Jorge Luis Borges, as well as several younger Swedish writers, have been inspired by his visionary strength. This powerful and broad influence shows that Swedenborg, in spite of the bizarre element in his philosophy, had a human and artistic force of attraction, an ability to give spiritual, psychotherapeutic and fantasy-inducing inspiration of an unusually high degree.

Gustav III's Cultural Policy and the Flourishing of the Theater

It was largely to the king's own credit that the Gustavian epoch became a culturally brilliant period. Just as Kristina created a cultural upswing in the seventeenth century, Gustav III stands at the center of this new high point in the development of Swedish culture. Through his literary interests, and through the active cultural policy he pursued after his *coup d'état* in 1772 (which made his power more or less absolute), he gave Swedish cultural life a much-needed injection which produced lasting results. Gustav III was most interested in the theater. He brought back impressions from abroad—during his sojourn in Paris at the beginning of the 1770s he applied himself with boundless energy to visiting the theater. However, it was a Swedish opera and a Swedish theater he wanted to create. He surrounded himself with the foremost writers of the time, supported them in all sorts of

ways and gave them the task of writing libretti and plays.
Practically every contemporary writer of note sooner or
later became involved in his opera and theater plans. At
times, these came to nothing; at times, works were created
that at least temporarily gave luster to Swedish cultural life.

Signs of a renewal of theater life were already to be found
earlier in the eighteenth century. In the autumn of 1737, the
Royal Swedish Theater opened and began to put on Swedish
plays with Swedish actors at Bollhuset near the royal castle
in Stockholm. Dalin's dramas, for example, were staged
there. In 1753, the troop of Swedish actors was replaced by
a French theatrical company. The Prussian-born Queen
Lovisa Ulrika, the mother of Gustav III, promoted French
theater, mainly at court. A new theater was erected at Drottningholm, just outside Stockholm, which came to take on
great significance for theater life up to the end of the century. After a long period of disuse during the nineteenth
century, the Drottningholm Theater has now been restored
and has become a great tourist attraction as the oldest theater
in the world still in use. French theater became important at
the court, mainly because it awakened the young Crown
Prince Gustav's interest in theater, an interest that during his
reign would grow to a real passion which, at times, seriously
encroached on his political commitment.

Having returned from his Paris sojourn, Gustav III concentrated first on forming a Swedish opera. For want of a
more creative native musical life he called on composers
from abroad: Kraus, Naumann, Uttini. The first Swedish
opera was staged in 1773 at Bollhuset. In 1782, a special
opera house was built at Gustav Adolf's Square in Stockholm. There, in 1786, the opera *Gustav Vasa* was produced.
In many ways it can be said to be the apex of the development of the Gustavian theater. The main features of the
opera had been sketched by the king himself, while the poet
Kellgren versified the libretto. The music was written by
Naumann. The subject had been chosen not least for
national and propaganda reasons: the king wanted to appear
as a worthy successor to the founder of the realm. *Gustav
Vasa* by Gustav III—there was a deeply patriotic point in
this and the opera did indeed become a considerable success,
not least the hymn-like chorus: "Noble shadows, revered

fathers,/ Sweden's heroes and knights!/ If you still enjoy its bliss,/ give freedom life again!"

In the area of drama, Gustav III first encouraged French drama in Swedish translation. In 1781 he called in a famous theater troop from France under the direction of the energetic and charismatic de Monvel, who provided theater life with a considerable stimulus. In the 1780s, the king also began to write plays himself—in order to nurture a native Swedish dramatic tradition. These plays were characterized by a good understanding of the demands of the theater and by an easy prose that reveals the influence of the new bourgeois drama form of the time. The king chose mainly historical themes, such as *Gustaf Adolfs ädelmod* (The Noble-Mindedness of Gustaf Adolf), 1782, *Gustaf Adolf och Ebba Brahe*, 1783, and *Siri Brahe och Johan Gyllenstierna*, 1787. The last one became a particular success, remained long in the theater repertoire and has been produced at the Comédie Française in Paris. The king now concentrated his efforts on creating a national theater, and the Royal Dramatic Theater was founded in 1788. Gustav III had thus created permanent institutions in the fields of both opera and theater.

A popular theater also developed during the Gustavian era. A Swedish theater troop played Corneille, Molière, Voltaire and Holberg at a theater in Humlegården in Stockholm as well as in the provinces. They also offered a native repertoire of popular comedies and musical comedies, of which several were considerable, if short-lived, successes. A whole series of respected authors of simple theatrical diversions of this type emerged at this time, while the period's more important poets also contributed to the theater. However, the other side of the Gustavian theater coin is that this whole illustrious epoch failed to produce a single Swedish classic, neither tragedy nor comedy. Its achievement was rather the creation of the institutions which would develop Swedish theater in the future. Drama, however, is an art for the present, and the Gustavian "present" would go down for posterity as a golden age for dramatic art, which developed an astounding vitality in all the many areas of the theater, all revolving around a theater-mad king who, in 1792, by an irony of history would fall victim to an assassination attempt during a masked ball in the Royal Opera of his own creation. Thus theater and reality became one, as they perhaps always were in the king's world of ideas.

Gustav III made a permanent contribution in another field also, namely by founding the Swedish Academy. Kristina's attempt to form an academy at court had, as we have seen, come to nothing, but during the eighteenth century Swedish cultural life was more strongly knit together by the founding of academies and societies of various types. In 1739, the Royal Academy of Sciences was founded for the natural sciences, with Linné as its first president, while for the humanities, the Royal Academy of Letters, History and Antiquities was established in 1753 by Lovisa Ulrika. After being discontinued for a spell, the latter was re-established in 1786 by Gustav III at the same time as its linguistic and literary tasks were transferred to the Swedish Academy, founded the same year. The model for this was the French Academy, but the number of members was limited to 18. Its task was to promote Swedish language and Swedish literature. Its motto, typical for the time, was "genius and judgment." Among its duties was that of awarding a prize for poetry and eloquence, an activity that has been considerably strengthened in the modern era since the Academy acquired the task of awarding the Nobel Prize in Literature, thereby attracting world-wide attention.

Bellman

It was exceptional talents like Linné and Swedenborg who put their stamp on the cultural life of the Era of Freedom. Such a talent also appeared in the world of poetry, in the shape of Carl Michael Bellman, whose song writing emerged during the final declining phase of the Era of Freedom. Bellman succeeded, however, in building a bridge over to the Gustavian Golden Age, of which he was undoubtedly the brightest star, at least in the eyes of future generations. Through Bellman, Swedish poetry can be said to have achieved its declaration of independence. That is not to say that he was the first of his kind. He consciously tied in to a native tradition—as represented by Lucidor and Dalin—and to the French opera, vaudeville and musical comedy tradition that had become enormously popular in Sweden at the middle of the eighteenth century. But he had sufficient independent artistic force to be able further to develop these borrowings and turn them into an individualistic and important art that was admired by his contemporaries and even more so by future generations. In Bellman's hands, song writing took on a personal and genuinely artistic form of unique character, and he has become Swedish literature's most living and cherished classic, who at long last is beginning to acquire a reputation outside Sweden.

Bellman (1740–95) came from an upper middle-class Stockholm family of German ancestry. His educational career was not crowned by any successes, nor was his time as a young civil servant. Instead, he was drawn into the era's hectic and dissolute life of pleasure and got into so much debt that for a time he was forced to flee to Norway. Already in his youth, though, he had displayed considerable poetic skills, and after his return to Sweden he began on a grander scale to develop his talent for song writing through simple, Bible-parodying drinking songs based on French models. Several of these early songs quickly became popular—an ageless popularity as it happened—and by the end of the 1760s Bellman was a well-known writer and a favorite entertainer in Stockholm society.

Bellman's poetry developed along two lines at this time: parodical poems about the fictive Bacchi Order, which he invented as a humorous pastiche on the system of orders, and the poems revolving around a permanent cast of figures that resulted in *Fredmans epistlar* (Fredman's Epistles). The former were popular at the time but would prove to be rather ephemeral, while the latter would turn out to have the greater vitality and universality. Fredman was a character whom Bellman took from the Stockholm of the day: a legendary and highly successful watchmaker, whose life foundered in heavy alcoholism. Bellman started to make the character a mouthpiece in his own drinking songs and surrounded him with a number of permanent figures as fellow stars in this bacchanalian delirium and in episodes and situations of various kinds. These characters were the love priestess Ulla Winblad and other prostitutes, drop-outs like Father Berg and Father Bergström, Jergen Puckel, Mollberg and Movitz, together with the ladies who ran Stockholm's numerous taverns. It was originally Bellman's intention to allow Fredman to play the role of a bacchanalian apostle and evangelist, a "Saint Fredman," and indeed the songs took on the form of Bible-parodying epistles along the lines of Paul's letters. But he soon dropped this idea and continued to write on the Fredman theme without any closer connection to the epistle fiction. He had plans for a poem cycle of one hundred epistles, but when the collection finally went to the publishers in 1790, it comprised 82 numbers. The publicist and fellow poet, Johan Henrik Kellgren, helped him with the editing and also wrote an enthusiastic preface to the edition. The following year, a large collection of songs came out under the title *Fredmans sånger* (Fredman's Songs); in general these have no connection with the main character of the epistles.

By this time, Bellman had long enjoyed an upturn in his social standing. After Gustav III's accession to the throne he had honored the king with flattering poems. With his cultural-political ambitions in mind, Gustav seized Bellman, made him court secretary and put him in his customary theatrical "national service," an activity in which Bellman was, however, less successful. Bellman's life ended bleakly. After the murder of Gustav III the poet's position weakened considerably. He became ill, got into debt again and was placed in a debtors' prison in the royal castle for a time. After his friends bailed him out, he developed tuberculosis and died in 1795. The main part of his writing was then still unpublished and lay in private collections. Only gradually have parts of this remaining production been published, though still not in full.

The drinking song, the bacchanalian song, is the centrifugal force from which Bellman's entire artistically significant writing springs forth. He tried many other genres: the religious song, the lullaby, lyrical pieces and others, but the dynamic center of his writing is nevertheless the drinking song. He exploits its clichés: the camaraderie of the drinking society, exhortations to drink, toasts, distance from the misery of the world around. Bacchus is worshipped as a god in an intoxicated kingdom of happiness, where what is important is to grasp the occasions for celebration as they arrive and to pursue a philosophy of spontaneous hedonism. But Bellman burst the usual confines of the drinking song genre. Through milieu sketches and episodic descriptions he widened its frame and gave it an original and richly varied shape. For him, the drinking itself took on an import far beyond mere cheerful carousing. His characters pursue their alcoholism with a furious and ecstatic intensity that goes considerably beyond the norms of the bacchanalian genre. They live asocially and lay waste to their lives with destructive possession. With occasional shocking realism, Bellman conveyed the destitution and misery and physical decay that accompanies alcoholism. He did so matter-of-factly, with-

Carl Michael Bellman. Ink drawing by Johan Tobias Sergel, 1792.

out moralizing overtones. The uncertain economic situation at the end of the Era of Freedom, which led to a moral decay and wide-reaching social consequences, is the social background for the failed and drifting characters of the epistles. From the drinking songs a social reflection of the times rings out—a reflection of considerable acerbity. Amid the immoralism there is room for a certain social criticism and a warm sympathy for the socially unfortunate and re- jected.

In Bellman's bacchanalian poetry, drinking is intimately connected with eroticism and death. The eroticism is just as orgiastic as the drinking—and likewise observed without the least moralizing. The eighteenth century's sexual outspo- kenness was striking and in Bellman it reached a dramatic culmination, in which he depicted a promiscuity that was as socially uninhibited as the carousing. Just as the epistles' main characters drink everywhere and at every opportunity, so do they make love everywhere and at every opportunity with the same wholehearted lust. Sexuality is strongly linked to death and the drive to destruction: "A thousand deaths sing around you;/ Still in your love hour/ You must perceive a death./ The worm, hidden in bloom, foreshadows the flower's death." With Bellman, the drinking song's tradi- tional awareness of death has swelled to the proportions of Baroque poetry. In the tavern, Death often lurks nearby. Beside the wine glass Death has placed its hourglass, the symbol that the course of a man's life has been measured out. Death trickles in drops from the wine god's glass, goes one of the epistles; in another, Fredman, sitting in a tavern, hallucinates how the ferryman Charon fetches him in his boat for a last journey on the river of death.

But Bellman's bacchanalian poems are also filled with music and song. In the many tavern scenes, which he brings to life with verbal artistry, someone invariably plays some instrument and strikes up a life-affirming and grotesquely exhilarating dance. In these scenes Bellman rendered life and movement with great skill: the play of lines and details, the play of sound and the brilliance of color—everything pre- sented at a lightning tempo and with breakneck leaps from one episode to another. Such depictions of the age are good reason for seeing Bellman as a poetic counterpart to

Hogarth, the eighteenth-century English artist. Yet more life and movement are found in his lyrical images when he goes out into the throng of Stockholm's streets and observes everyday life. With sure instinct for situation comedy he depicts episodes and events, whether it be boat trips, fires or funeral processions. However, Bellman's lyrical art celebrates its finest triumphs when he lets Fredman and his companions make their way out into the countryside, where he gets the opportunity to render his impressions of nature, with his sure sense for precise detail, movement and color. Some of the epistles are usually called picture epistles because of their visual sharpness. One such example is No. 48 "wherein is painted Ulla Winblad's journey home from Hessingen in Mälaren one summer morning in 1769." It gives a rural and idyllic picture of the Stockholm of the time and its surroundings:

> *Kon i vassen skylt sin kropp,*
> *Snärd i våta tågen,*
> *Bruna oxen kastar opp*
> *Himmelsblåa vågen.*
> *Ängen står i härlighet,*
> *Kalven dansar yr och fet,*
> *Hästen tumlar stolt och het,*
> *Svinet går i rågen.*
> */—/*
> *Tornens spetsar blänka ren,*
> *Kors och tuppar glimma;*
> *Morgonrodnans klara sken*
> *Syns i vattnet strimma.*
> *Barnet leker glatt vid strand,*
> *Samlar stenar i sin hand,*
> *Slungar stenen dit ibland,*
> *Där som gässen simma.*

> The cow in the reeds has covered up its body,
> Caught in the wet rushes,
> The brown ox throws up
> Sky blue billows.
> The meadow stands in glory,
> The calf dances giddy and fat,
> The horse frolics proud and hot,
> The pig goes in the rye.
> /—/

The towers' tips are shining,
Cross and cocks gleam;
The clear light of the morning reddening
Seems to streak into the water.
The child happy plays at the shore,
Gathers stones in his hand,
Throws the stones now and then
Where the geese swim.

The Bellman world and its realistically portrayed human destitution is surrounded in a paradoxical way by a poetic aura that lifts it above the gray reality that is depicted. As a contrast to the realism there are also effects that today would almost be called expressionistic—impressions that spring not from the senses but from an inner creative, hallucinatory vision. The poet has "the jaws green with bile" shine forth on the members of the drinking society and Fredman visualizes Charon's ferry as a "coal black bier" that "rocks forth on the river amid smoke and dust/ and the shrieking of ghosts." Myth and image also contrast with the realism. From art and the theater he has derived a broad arsenal of mythical and emblematic attributes of traditionally classical character, and the classical myth spins its web over the alcoholized and prostituted characters. The epistle "Blåsen nu alla" (Sound the Horns) is a rococo pastorale that presents Ulla Winblad as Venus surrounded by Neptune and his tritons in a way that is reminiscent of Boucher's painting "The Triumph of Venus," which Bellman knew well.

But with Bellman music is, naturally, more important than myth and image. The poems were set to music and were intended to be sung. Words and tunes are strongly integrated. The poet took his melodies from French songs and musical comedies as well as from well-known composers like Haydn and Mozart. He set texts to existing melodies in a parodical way that allowed a free treatment of the melody. In some isolated cases he seems to have composed his songs himself, the best known example being the evening song "Träd fram, du nattens gud" (Step forth, you God of the Night). From contemporary sources we know that Bellman accompanied his songs on the lute and gave them an extra auditory dimension by imitating musical instruments and other sounds from the poem.

Bellman was a brilliantly artistic poet, but as a personality he is fairly anonymous. The picture that formed after his death depicted him alternately as a vulgar and bohemian wag and as a deeply tragic human being. Neither says anything essential about his person. The strong artistic talent we meet in his poetry is his personal mark. Unique and independent—on an international level also—he has created a peculiarly Swedish song tradition that has had many imitators. Swedish and universal at the same time, typical of the age and yet ageless, his poetry has a rare kind of poetic radiance.

Gustavian Lyrical Poets

Bellman is not the only poet who made the Gustavian epoch a lyrical heyday. Just as in the Baroque era, a whole series of outstanding lyrical poets emerged who wrote a classical poetry of a quality that had earlier been inconceivable in Sweden. Already during the Era of Freedom, some poets who emerged from the *Tankebyggarorden* literary society had purposefully worked to make Swedish poetry more classical in language and diction. Among them was Hedvig Charlotta Nordenflycht (1718–63), who wrote a subjective and emotional poetry in which she confessed her sexual torment. But she was also a highly educated and philosophically schooled woman who wrote learned, contemplative poems. In a philosophical letter in verse to her Danish fellow writer, Holberg, she struck some socio-critical chords at roughly the same time as Rousseau, whose thesis about a return to nature she—not entirely without reason—thought she had anticipated! Among the members of the literary society were also the Counts Creutz and Gyllenborg; it was above all their poetry that became a linguistic and metrical guidepost for the Gustavian epoch's great poets. Gustav Philip Creutz (1731–85) wrote among other things *Atis och Camilla*, a pastoral verse epic typical of the time, and then unexcelled in Swedish poetry in its poetic elegance. Gustaf Fredrik Gyllenborg (1731–1808) was more oriented towards contemplative poems in the stoic spirit and wrote a "Vinterkväde" (Winter Lay) whose harsh Nordic strains were as much influenced by the old Gothicism as by Montesquieu's doctrine about the effect of climate on culture. During the Gustavian epoch, Creutz and Gyllenborg were both prominent names in cultural life and involved in Gustav III's feverishly active cultural policy. However, the most dominant figure in Gustavian cultural life after the king was Johan Henrik Kellgren (1751–95). He was versatile and had an immense intellectual range. A classicist, an educational aristocrat of the Enlightenment, he wrote sparklingly intelligent satire as well as the most convincing preromantic expression of feelings in the Swedish poetry of his time. He was a passionately engaged polemicist and social critic, as well as a sentimental opera lover. He was the first Swedish writer who could lay claim to the designation "intellectual"—he was also the first to use the word in its modern meaning. As a literary and theater critic he showed a keenness and sensitivity unknown to the time. Symptomatically enough, it was he who first, in spite of initial reservations, perceived Bellman's indisputable poetic and musical brilliance.

When Kellgren came to Stockholm in the 1770s after studies at Åbo University in Finland, he conquered its cultural life in several respects. He became involved in the king's theater plans, an activity that culminated in the versification of the royal libretto for the successful *Gustav Vasa* (see p. 52). He became the leading figure at the newly started *Stockholms Posten* and quickly made it the country's leading literary organ. As a literary critic, he started by directing his energies towards cleaning up the wild growth of crude and amateurish poetry that flourished on the Parnassus, thereby stimulating an improvement in the quality of the poetic craft. He was involved in a fierce literary debate, the first in the history of Swedish literature, with his fellow poet Tomas Thorild. He attacked the dominance of Latin in the schools and the conservatism hostile to the Enlightenment that existed at the time. As a poet, he made a rapid breakthrough, with, among others, the two poems "Mina löjen" (My Smiles) and "Våra villor" (Our Errors). In this youthful poetry he was strongly inspired by French and English poetry of the Enlightenment. He refers to both Voltaire and Pope in "Mina löjen," where he delivers an elegant and challengingly radical criticism of society, and with arrogant recklessness he jests with the nobility and the clergy, with the scholars and with women. In "Våra villor" he defends the illusion and its ability to give man ideals to strive for in life. In the middle of the 1780s, when Kellgren had advanced to royal secretary and to member—the only non-aristocrat—of the newly established Swedish Academy, his struggle against the reactionary forces of the time sharpened. In order to combat the forms of mysticism, charlatanism and occultism which seemed to threaten the ideas of the Enlightenment, he formed the society *Pro Sensu Communi*. The Society's theses, published in *Stockholms Posten* in 1787, were a major defense of the belief in reason against the obscurantism of the time. The fight continued with the poem "Man äger ej snille för det man är galen" (You're not a genius because you're crazy), where Kellgren heckled the fanaticism of the Swedenborgians, Rosicrucians, dream interpreters, alchemists and cabbalists, and maintained that "all virtue is of the light." In his remarks to this poetic piece he expressed an idealistic belief in the calling of the poet and his responsibility to society, which represented a breakthrough for a more modern view of the role of the author. When he turned here to a young author and appealed to his sense of "truth, virtue, justice, the fatherland, humanity," he was no longer only a pupil of Voltaire but also, to an even higher degree, of Rousseau, and his Romantic emotional commitment was in keeping with the revolutionary ideas of the time. He struck his last great blow on behalf of the ideas of the Enlightenment with the poem "Ljusets fiender" (The Enemies of Light) from 1792, when the French Revolution had gone into a more problematic and destructive phase and opinion had begun to turn against the revolutionary ideology of the Enlightenment. He defended here the light of reason against its dark slanderers, only now as a more moderate friend of the Enlightenment.

Towards the end of his life, Kellgren also wrote some love poems of a sort until then unique in Swedish poetry. The best known of these is "Den nya skapelsen" (The New Creation), for which Rousseau provided the original inspiration, and which was printed in *Stockholms Posten* in 1790. With the musical dynamics in perfect harmony with the movement of feelings, the poet depicts how the sight of the beloved changes his view of the world and nature: "You, who from beauty and delights/ a pure and heavenly vision give!/ I saw you—and from this day/ I see only you in the world." The poem has been characterized as a "morning star of Romanticism" in Swedish poetry and attests to a remarkable emotional revitalization. The poet's later years were darkened by a lung ailment that led to his death. "It is with Swedish genius as with the Swedish sun," he wrote in one of his late aphorisms, "we have some summer days just as beautiful as those of the southern lands, but everything else is fall and winter." His literary bequest to posterity is not especially great, but during his time his voice enjoyed an unequalled artistic and emotional, intellectual and moral authority which continues to impress.

Anna Maria Lenngren (1754–1817) was also active as a co-worker at *Stockholms Posten*; she was the daughter of an academic in Uppsala and married to one of the paper's editors. With realistic zeal she defended the ideas of the Enlightenment in her journalism as well as in her poems, which are especially characterized by the satirical epigram on the model of Martialis. These poems have made her the epoch's most popular poet after Bellman. Her satires give a brilliant picture of the crumbling aristocratic society, as in "Porträtterna" (The Portraits), and mock the pride of inherited social privilege and class barriers. Her epigram on the same alcoholic proletariat to which Bellman's characters belong is marked by ironic objectivity and warm sympathy and humor. She also wrote idylls typical of the period, such as the well-known, Rousseau-inspired poem "Pojkarne" (The Boys), where youth, with its innocence, freshness and democratic attitude toward life, contrasts with the cool careerism of adulthood. On women's questions she rather assumed a conservative attitude and persistently defended a sexually conditioned anonymity for women in cultural life, in spite of the fact that in reality she occupied a position of rank there, in particular during the period after Gustav III's death.

Also among the era's great poets was Carl Gustaf Leopold (1756–1829) who was very close to Gustav III and whose poetry is marked by his strongly English-oriented educational background and Enlightenment ideology. With *Skördarne* (The Harvests) and *Dagens stunder* (The Hours of the Day) by Johan Gabriel Oxenstierna (1750–1818), eighteenth-century classical and English-inspired landscape and seasonal poetry reached its Swedish perfection. The adventurous, bohemian Bengt Lidner (1757–93) wrote a sentimental and religiously fanciful poetry that, typical of the period, is preromantic in its emotional bombast. Also preromantic was the poetry of Tomas Thorild (1759–1808), who was the era's leading revolutionary and radical in poetry and in politics. He wrote a philosophical hexameter epic, *Passionerna* (The Passions), which gave expression to a metaphysical conception of nature, partly inspired by Shaftesbury's pantheism, and which was the cause of the vehement debate with Kellgren. He defended the right of the genius to invent his own artistic rules and the right of the author to be judged by literary criticism in the light of his special nature. In political terms, he tried—especially in England—to realize his revolutionary and utopian plans in a world republic. In his extreme, anarchistic-revolutionary standpoint he is something of a precursor and pioneer for the democratic ideas of the nineteenth century, and both Geijer and Strindberg were inspired by him. In the tradition of politically radical literature in Sweden he stands out as a bold pioneer.

Neoclassicism—Ehrensvärd

The French-schooled classicism of the Gustavian epoch met the ideals of the new era not only in the revolutionaries and sentimental preromantics, but also in the movement that is usually called Neoclassicism and that tried to renew the ideas of classical times by seeking to return to a truer Greek antiquity of clean lines and great simplicity. Several of the epoch's great poets translated the classical writers into Swedish and tried new, classical verse forms. An original contribution to this Neoclassical movement was made by Carl August Ehrensvärd (1745–1800). He combined his position as a high-ranking naval officer—eventually the highest commander of the Swedish fleet—with a devoted and deeply independent writing in works like *Resa till Italien 1780,*

1781, 1782 (Journey to Italy 1780, 1781, 1782) and *De fria konsters filosofi* (The Philosophy of the Free Arts), 1786. In an original, aphoristic form he contrasted classical antiquity with his own time and argued the artistic superiority of the former. Influenced by Montesquieu's doctrine about climate, he also polarized the southern classical against the northern barbarian and time and time again tried to show that art and culture are at home in the south, while they lack the right conditions for growth in the north: "Nature has created the nationalities so poorly and so crudely toward the north that nothing can ripen in their hands," "you cannot expect true art or taste in the northern climates." Such a cultural inferiority complex, certainly typical for a lesser language area knowing itself to be on the cultural periphery, has played an important role in Swedish literature ever since, and many writers have made reference to Ehrensvärd. But, as already pointed out by his contemporaries, he had gone a long way toward disproving his own theses about Nordic inferiority, and this holds for the entire Gustavian period. Romanticism would also take exception to the assertion that great literature could not be created in the Nordic countries.

THE NINETEENTH CENTURY
ROMANTICISM AND BOURGEOIS
REALISM

During the first decade of the nineteenth century a certain decline and stagnation set in after the great cultural explosion of the Gustavian Golden Age. Gustav IV Adolf's conservative regime, which was fond of censorship, had a restrictive effect on the cultural climate. A spirit of cosy, isolationist society writing, symptomatic of a repressive social climate, hovered over these years, while behind the scenes, new currents lurked in the making. When in 1809 the king was deposed by a *coup d'état* and a constitutional monarchy was again introduced, it also brought about a thawing of the cultural ice. In Swedish literature, the breakthrough of Romanticism coincided almost exactly with this sweeping national upheaval, just as it coincided with the last blow to the Swedish Great Power Empire: the loss of Finland after the war against Russia in 1808–09. The years around 1810 became a period of obvious literary and cultural renewal in a strongly changed social climate. The new winds came mainly from Germany. Especially receptive to the attractions of the new German philosophy and literary Romanticism were the academic circles in Uppsala, which became the stronghold of Swedish Romanticism. In Stockholm, a new Romantic form of Gothicism found a home in *Götiska Förbundet* (The Gothic Society), whose political aspirations were relatively modest but whose cult of the Old Norse legacy proved to be very fertile for literature. After the *coup d'état*, plans for a hymn-book reform gathered momentum under the inspired and energetic leadership of the poet and cleric, Johan Olof Wallin. The result was the hymn-book of 1819, a selection of hymns modernized to give a more personal and emotional religiousness and artistically more positive forms of expression.

Swedish Romanticism had many points of contact with

the Romantic currents in the rest of Europe. Philosophical idealism in the spirit of Plato, which was itself the kernel of the new German tendencies, was thoroughly established and permeated all areas of cultural life during the entire period from 1810 up to the modern breakthrough around 1880, when its dominance was broken. In spite of differences over political or artistic conceptions, the epoch's writers were nevertheless broadly united in a common, idealistic view. The new nationalism took on a special character with the new Gothic boom that broke out after the defeat by Russia. It was largely formed as a national, moralistic program in a supposedly Old Norse spirit, but on a basis rather out of touch with reality. Symptomatic of this movement is that one of its most active proponents, Per Henrik Ling, author of huge and now unreadable epics and tragedies with Old Norse themes, is today remembered as "the father of Swedish gymnastics." During the course of the nineteenth century, nationalism tended to pass over into Scandinavianism, the idea of a more strongly united Scandinavia. Especially at the middle of the century, the boundary disputes between Germany and Denmark added fuel to such sentiments, which, however, resulted more in rhetoric than in action.

Even if most of the young Romantics had their roots in the political radicalism of the late eighteenth and early nineteenth centuries, a rather conservative atmosphere permeated Swedish cultural life. With the late Napoleonic wars and the strong political reaction after Napoleon's fall, a feeling of shattered illusions dominated and a retreat to aesthetic, natural-philosophic and mystical speculations took place. But in the 1830s, more radical political winds again began to blow as liberalism attracted increasing interest. Newspapers flourished once more, not least as organs of opposition during Karl XIV Johan's regime, while in the field of literature the new climate was chiefly accompanied by a realistic writing of greater social relevance. During the 1840s, strong revolutionary and utopian currents ran through Swedish cultural life. These returned, at least periodically, during the later part of the period 1810–80, culminating in the literature of the modern breakthrough. In particular during the prelude to the important representation reform of 1866, when the old parliament of the four estates was replaced by a bicameral parliament, the climate in many areas was marked by political radicalism. However, the effects of the reform failed to be realized in society during the following decade, something which had a repressive impact on the literary climate.

During Romanticism, interest in popular writing increased strongly under the influence of German cultural life. Collections of ballads and folksongs, folktales and legends were published. This interest in folk literature is reflected very clearly in the literature of Romanticism—even if it is often a matter of a rather nostalgic enthusiasm from above for the culture of the ordinary people as a symbol of the Rousseau legacy. This interest was maintained by the more realistic writers in the middle of the century, who imbued it with a new and strong element of sympathy and political pathos, in keeping with the democratic ideas of liberalism. On the social plane, these cultural endeavors were expressed in part in the 1842 folk school act. This introduced compulsory schooling for all children and, at least in the long run, improved reading and writing skills in the country. Thus, not only did literature spread to the lower strata of society, but also a solid foundation was laid for a lively popular and proletarian writing in the future.

However, it was obviously an educated middle-class public that supported literature throughout the nineteenth century. The broad abundance of poetry that flowed during the whole epoch—not least the popular verse cycles and verse narratives that characterized the genre at the time—addressed itself especially to a middle-class circle of readers. But above all, the period meant a remarkable breakthrough for the novel as a genre in Swedish literature. It quickly became the favorite genre of the middle-class readers and attained, especially as serialized intrigue and adventure novels of the French and English sort, an immense popularity. In the political and social struggle, the realistic social novel of indignation played an important role; it too had mainly English prototypes. Drama, on the other hand, declined during this epoch. It was not until the modern breakthrough and Strindberg that it was awakened from the lethargy it had fallen into after the flowering of the theater during the Gustavian Golden Age.

The Romantic Poets
Tegnér, Atterbom, Stagnelius

When Romanticism broke through in the years around 1810, it was poetry that manifested itself as its highest form of expression. The period's foremost literary figures were poets, and three names especially stand out as epoch-making: Tegnér, who was active mainly in radical Lund; Atterbom, who became the leading figure in the high Romantic and conservative phalanx that emerged in Uppsala; and Stagnelius, a solitary and sick man, who remained outside any literary school and who led a short but lyrically productive life in Stockholm.

Every national literature has its national literary monument, and it fell to Esaias Tegnér to bear this heavy honor in Sweden. He is the classicist *par excellence*, and it is difficult to dispute his position as the unequalled master of the classical, idealistic vein of Swedish writing. However, the designation "literary monument" is hardly very appropriate, since Tegnér remains very much alive today, thanks to his poetry and above all to the extensive correspondence he left, in which he emerges as the first real personality in Swedish culture. His good and bad sides embrace a wide range of characteristics and inner contradictions, from visionary enthusiasm to bitter and melancholic misanthropy, from the forced pathetic to the wily humorous, from bold defiance to weak compliancy, from revolutionary idealism to querulous conservatism. His charming mixture of erudition and naiveté is somewhat incongruous with his role as literary idol. The strength of his literary achievement, though, lies mainly in the rhetorical clarity and the brilliant poetic art of his writing. As a thinker, he stands on the ground of Kantian idealism, but his world of ideas is really neither profound nor original. It is rather its splendidly artistic form that gave his writing a sort of weight and authority and classically monumental status.

Esaias Tegnér (1782–1846) was born in Värmland, the province in western Sweden that would also at a later date be known for its many literary talents. This was foundry country, but there was also a manorial culture there that cultivated literary interests, with emphasis on the classical as well as the contemporary, and that harbored a spontaneous sympathy for the ideals of the French Revolution. From this educational environment, which was radical for its time, Tegnér came to academic Lund, where the young students greedily imbibed the ideas of the new German philosophy. Tegnér studied philosophy, aesthetics and classical languages and read the new popular philosophers, Kant and Fichte. He had a brilliant academic career and became professor of Greek language, finally crowning his achievements with the bishopric of the town of Växjö in Småland.

Parallel with this successful career went a growing reputation as a writer. Tegnér's poetry spans cerebral, political, aesthetic and personal lyric poetry. The political element in his writing was very strong from the start. As a fiery young revolutionary he enthusiastically supported Napoleon, and in a verse dialogue between France and England he allows his French sympathies to shine through when, with striking indignation, he heckles England's imperialistic brutality: "The negro is lashed to death, alas, in order to sugar your tea." When Napoleon's despotism and policy of violence became apparent a few years into the nineteenth century, Tegnér turned away from his earlier idol. In "Det eviga" (Eternity), where cerebral and political poetry merge, he gives an unusually clear picture of Platonic idealism, filtered through the new German philosophy and poetry. In Napoleon's world, which is a world of violence and evil, the eternal values of truth, justice and beauty are alive, still immortally present in man: "If evil finally conquers all the world,/ then you can still desire justice." The poem seems to urge rebellion against Napoleon's reign: "Justice gets arms, truth gets a voice,/ and people stand up to change." The poem belongs among the great masterpieces of rhetoric in Swedish poetry, which takes on renewed urgency as soon as difficult times threaten. After the Swedish-Russian war of 1808–09, Tegnér wrote the long Gothic poem "Svea." In its original form, this can be interpreted as an exhortation to a war of revenge against Russia after the humiliating defeat. For political reasons, certain changes had to be made, which gave rise to the famous formulation: "to win back Finland within Sweden's borders." This gave the poem a more peaceful but also a blurred, compromising character. The poem, original in terms of form, starts with a Gothic exposition where Svea's, i.e. Sweden's, condition is depicted as a debasement unworthy of the Old Norse legacy. This is followed by a Romantic, visionary and dithyrambic section, where the poet, transported by divinely inspired enthusiasm, hallucinates about a battle executed in the Old Norse manner, which restores Sweden's lost honor. "Svea" is a magnificent rhetorical piece, symptomatic of the new nationalism, the strengthened national consciousness, that emerged with the nineteenth century.

Political motifs were also central during the second decade of the nineteenth century. In the days of adversity, Tegnér revised his view of Napoleon, who now in the Romantic spirit is seen as a hero, as the great, strong man who acts as an implacable force in the service of historical transformation. With Napoleon's return from captivity in Elba, Tegnér hailed him as "the awakened eagle." The poem "Nyåret 1816" (New Year 1816) was an angry satire on the political reaction after Napoleon's final fall at Waterloo, in which the dark streak in Tegnér's poetic nature emerges with bitter keenness and destructive melancholy. This poem shows us a modern, disillusioned, splintered view of life. In the contrasting poem "Nore"—written on the occasion of the Peace of Kiel in 1814—Tegnér presents us with his visionary faith in the future. In Gothic terms this poem tries to evoke a sense of union and harmony between the countries of Scandinavia, and thereby anticipates the idea of a Scandinavian union that would grow stronger around the middle of the nineteenth century.

Otherwise during the second decade of the nineteenth century Tegnér wrote poems with an aesthetic, Romantic theme. It is in these that he really emerged as a Romantic. He celebrated Skidbladner, the ship of the Old Norse mythology, as a symbol of the poet's feeling of freedom. The poet takes on the character of a prophetic preacher, a "priest of eternity" and a "citizen of the world," who in enraptured hymns celebrates the sun and the divine light. But he also reacts sharply against the exaggerations of Romanticism, and in a speech on the occasion of the great Luther jubilee in 1817 he made a brilliant cultural synthesis of the eighteenth century's belief in the Enlightenment and the world of ideas of Romantic philosophy—a boldly conciliatory compromise between intellect and feeling, between religion and reason. The same balance between the opposite poles of the ideas of the time is found in the great "Epilog," that he wrote for the conferring of Masters' degrees in Lund in 1820. Romanticism's Platonic world view is here conveyed by the Greek myth of how the god of light, Apollo, tried in vain to capture the ideal of purity in Daphne, who was transformed into a laurel tree before his eyes. In blindingly strong visions of light, poetry appears as a crystal temple in which there is no room for darkness.

Around 1820, Tegnér's interest in verse epic was stimulated, among other things, through reading Lord Byron. First came the hexameter idyll *Nattvardsbarnen (The Children of the Lord's Supper)*, 1820, that depicts a confirmation at Pentecost in a Swedish country church. It is a work that inspired H. W. Longfellow, who translated it into English. But Tegnér's great success in the sphere of verse epic was *Frithiofs saga (Frithiof's Saga)*, 1820–25, a Gothic-Romantic poem cycle based on an Old Norse saga. It became his best-loved poem and the work in which he was most successfully able to unite his talent for popularization with a thoroughly worked-out idea structure. The work quickly won acclaim at home and abroad and was translated into several languages.

From an Old Norse saga that Tegnér had read as a young boy, he created the dramatic story of the young blond Viking, Frithiof, who seeks in vain to win Princess Ingeborg's hand, who sins by desecrating Balder's temple and who, after many years as a plundering Viking, atones for this sin by building a new temple, thereby showing himself to be worthy of the beautiful Ingeborg. The main idea lies in the final poem "Försoningen" ("Reconciliation"), that lays out a syncretic doctrine of atonement which itself is the kernel in Tegnér's mature view of life and in which classical, Christian and Gothic ideas are integrated. A firework display of verse forms treated with great virtuosity runs through the 24-poem cycle, and the style changes from folksong-like cliché to supreme, creative perspicacity in the dramatic course of events. The idealized image of the Viking era seeks in part to build on Old Norse models but is strongly permeated by contemporary literary ideals, and the hero Frithiof is portrayed as both demonic and weakly sentimental in the spirit of Byron.

During the mid-1820s, after being appointed bishop, Tegnér entered a period of crisis. The poem "Mjältsjukan" (Ode to Melancholy) that with furious energy presents a black, melancholic view of life in which reality, poetry and man have lost all value, is usually seen as a symptom of this crisis. During the latter part of his life the poet was often plagued by illness and poor mental health. His activities were mainly directed towards his official duties as bishop, and he devoted only occasional attention to writing. One example of this is the song for the fiftieth anniversary of the Swedish Academy—a classical panorama of the Gustavian era and the great writers of a cultural Golden Age. In spite of the official éclat, an atmosphere of decline clouded Tegnér's later years, and his political ideas became conservative.

In his autobiographical notes, Tegnér characterized himself as a not very profound person of a sceptical disposition, a picture that contrasts strongly with his public image as a prophet of reason and religion. The sceptical, spontaneous and close observer of reality emerged most clearly in the extensive correspondence that was published posthumously and which dramatically changed the prevailing picture of him as an unimpeachable national literary saint. In his letters, which are now collected in ten volumes, he is open and frank, soberly realistic and objective, crass and cynical, unmercifully critical of people and phenomena he detested but just as emotionally loyal to friends and relatives whom he loved. It is a rich and many-sided picture, captivating in its openheartedness but disquieting in its psychological complexity. As a letter writer, Tegnér stands alongside Strindberg as the foremost in Swedish literature, and his letters are a national literary treasure almost as important as his poetry.

It was largely due to the work of one man, Per Daniel Amadeus Atterbom (1790–1855), that the international Romantic movement, mainly of a German brand, made a breakthrough in Swedish literature. Atterbom emerged as the clear leader of a high Romantic phalanx that had its seat in Uppsala and that not only wanted to be a Swedish branch of German Romanticism but also claimed to be a separate

Scandinavian Romantic school with an independent profile and with a special mission to fulfill in the development of literary history. An extensive literary polemic was carried on with the remains of the Gustavian culture. This movement was, for the most part, a quite isolated and unrealistic phenomenon in Swedish literary history, but without a doubt it has a certain cultural-historic significance. Out of its ambitions arose the most impressive literary work of Swedish Romanticism: Atterbom's fairy-tale play *Lycksalighetens ö* (The Isle of Bliss).

Atterbom came from Östergötland, a province that would prove to be an equally fertile ground for Romanticism as Värmland. Using impressions of nature from his adolescent environment and early experiences of popular literature, Atterbom reacted against the Enlightenment's one-sided belief in reason. In Uppsala he studied the latest German philosophy, was one of the founders of the new literary society *Auroraförbundet* and started its literary monthly journal *Phosphoros*. With the goddess of the dawn, Aurora, and Phosphorus, the morning star, as their polestars, these young Romantics intended to make literary history. And it was they who coined the Swedish term "fosforism," which came to signify this Uppsalian high Romanticism. Guided by the new German natural philosophy, Atterbom and his fellow-believers saw art and poetry as the highest form of spirit to come from nature. They claimed that this high, religious form of expression of poetry had been neglected in eighteenth-century aesthetics and that it was necessary to return to the "romantic" period, which roughly comprised the late Middle Ages and the Renaissance, to recover it—just as it was necessary to return to the writings of classical antiquity and Old Norse. With the intention of creating literary history they aimed at founding a new Romanticism in the tradition of the literary golden age constituted by the Middle Ages and the Renaissance. Hence the designation "Neoromanticism," that is somewhat inappropriate from a modern literary-historical angle, since it culminated during the epoch we now call Romanticism. This literary initiative led to a literary feud that lasted more than a decade between the old school (the remaining Gustavians) and the new school (the phosphorists in Uppsala, together with a few sympathizers in Stockholm). It turned into one of the great, legendary literary debates in the history of Swedish literature, in which literary satire flourished as never before.

The *Phosphoros* initiative was also accompanied by a poetic renewal. Atterbom's poetic diction is characterized by free and diverse verse forms, a rich, sensual imagery, a musical sonority in language and a boldly speculative symbolism that make his cerebral poetry dark and obscure. More accessible are, however, the series of shorter poems, "Blommorna" (The Flowers), which belong to the more lasting in his production and which earned him the epithet "poet of the flowers." His literary fame still rests mainly on the masterpiece *Lycksalighetens ö* (The Isle of Bliss), which was published in two parts 1824–27. He took the fairy-tale motif from the translation of a French folktale that he adapted freely for his own artistic purposes. The story tells how Astolf, king of the northern realm of the Hyperboreans, wanders off during a hunt, finally ending up on the Isle of Bliss, where he is united with the beautiful Queen Felicia, the genius of poetry. Beyond time and space, they experience three hundred years of happiness until Astolf wakes up and wants to return home. When he returns, he finds that a constitutional republic has been established, and the fourth adventure of the play is a sharp satire directed at the political ideals of liberalism. Unable to contribute to this new realm, Astolf wants to return to the Isle of Bliss. On his way there he is overtaken by Time and dies. The Isle of Bliss perishes, and Felicia is led by her mother Nyx (Night) back to the heavenly sphere, whence she originally came.

The symbolic fairy-tale action is, however, not all there is to this work. Its some eight hundred pages contain a welter of motifs and ideas, which reflect the entire, many-faceted world of ideas of Romanticism. The wealth of formal and stylistic variation is great: besides the main meter, a skillfully handled blank verse, there is a whole variety of verse forms such as the Italian *ottave rime*, Scandinavian ballad imitations and sections in completely free verse form. The Romantic fairy-tale character is also rendered in such a way that all of nature is animated and participates with repartee and songs. The serious is mixed with the comic, the lyrical with the satirical, the ethereal with the grotesque; not least, the humor of the work is striking throughout.

At the center of this drama of ideas is Atterbom's conception of Scandinavian poetry's special task and his view of the mission of the Romantic writer. Both Astolf and Felicia have betrayed their respective callings by staying on the Isle of Bliss, which is the symbol for southern, sensuous poetry. Astolf has neglected his social duties in his northern realm, while Felicia has abandoned the heavenly sphere to which her surname, Astralis, the star born, connects her. Therefore the Isle of Bliss must perish, and poetry return to its transcendental origin, to be able thereby to satisfy the innermost yearnings of the soul. For his social treachery Astolf finds himself without a function in the republic of the new era and he must pay with his life. The fairy-tale play can to a certain degree be read as a tragedy on Scandinavian poetry, and even in an international perspective it is a tremendously impressive work. If Tegnér's *Frithiofs Saga* became the most popular work of Swedish Romanticism, Atterbom's fairy-tale play is artistically the most accomplished and profound; it presents Romanticism's world view in a nutshell. But in its own time, as the winds of liberalism began to blow more strongly during the 1830s, it soon appeared archaic and conservative.

The third of the great Romantic poets, Erik Johan Stagnelius (1793–1823), did not attain any position of note in society, but in time he was to stand out artistically as the foremost of these poets. He spent his solitary life as a humble civil servant in Stockholm. This life seems to have taken an increasingly tragic, bohemian turn which was to provide the fuel for myths and legends. He was unable to make any enduring social contacts in the capital, mainly because of his alcoholism, which became worse over the years. In addition, he suffered from a congenital heart defect. In all probability, this illness was also the direct cause of his untimely death at the age of thirty. This darkly unsettled life, with all the characteristics of the rejected and misunderstood Romantic genius, gave much of his writing a personal, existential authenticity that makes it more alive and tangible than most of the epoch's literature. During his short life Stagnelius produced an œuvre which, in the modern standard edition of his collected works, amounts to some fifteen hundred pages. Only a fraction of this large amount of poetry and drama was published during his lifetime. Large portions of his extensive literary remains were published after his death, rapidly earning him fame.

Stagnelius' poems spring forth from the classical legacy. He translated Propertius and Horace, among others, into Swedish and he achieved many of his finest poems with Propertius' elegiac distich. But to this classical background also came strong influence from the new Romantic winds of the time. Alongside Atterbom he emerges as the most Romantic poet in Swedish literature—even if he did not have any contact with the latter or with the *Phosphoros* circles in Uppsala. Impressions of nature from his childhood on the island of Öland play an important role in his writing, and his characteristics as a cosmic, natural lyricist are significant from the beginning. The religious strain is also very apparent right from his early poetry; in his Öland childhood home, where his father was a clergyman, later to become bishop of Kalmar, he received a good religious and literary education. Early on he was also attracted to erotic motifs, which he filled with a characteristically sensual, morbid longing and contrasted with loneliness and nocturnal anxiety. In its often well-executed symbolism, Stagnelius' youthful poetry already defines the psychological contours of his adult writing: alienation and maladaptation to reality, strong but unsatisfied sexuality, longing for death and compensation through intense religious experiences.

However, Stagnelius made his real literary debut with the hexameter epic *Vladimir den store* (Vladimir the Great), which was published anonymously in 1817. The motif is taken from the Russian Nestor chronicle and is a free adaptation of the story of the prelude to Russia's Christianization. The unexpectedly strong Russian patriotism which radiates from the work, and which leads to the hope that the Russian tsar will play the role of spiritual prince of peace over all of Europe, stems from Stagnelius' political and religious ideas in the second decade of the nineteenth century. The verse epic is carried forward by a strong Christian conviction in the depiction of how the Russian Prince Vladimir captures and marries the East Roman Empire Princess Anna, who is exhorted by an angel to accept the proposal to

Erik Johan Stagnelius. Drawing, probably by Lars Gustaf Malmberg, one of Stagnelius' few friends.

be the mother of the new Russia. However, the presentation is marked in a striking way by a charged, sensual exoticism, and the oriental-romantic coloring culminates in brutal and blood-curdling battle depictions unprecedented in Swedish literature.

In the years around 1820, Stagnelius' writing showed a new religious orientation with strong streaks of mysticism. It is possible that a personal crisis spurred him to pursue his religious search by studying philosophy and mystic literature of various types. The Neoplatonic tradition comes through in his mystic way of viewing things, but equally strong are oriental traditions such as gnosticism, Pythagoreanism, cabbalism and astrology. There are also Swedenborgian elements, as well as Schelling's Romantic natural philosophy. This tidal wave of new mysticism resulted in an intense period of poetry writing, the results of which were published in a poetry collection, *Liljor i Saron* (Lilies of

Sharon), 1821. In this collection there was also a religious drama, *Martyrerna* (The Martyrs), with motifs from the late Roman Age.

Behind Stagnelius' world view lies the idea that modern man has lost the knowledge of God, man and nature which had once been his. Only in fragments of older philosophies has it been preserved, and only "the divine torch of genius" can retrieve these fragments of knowledge "from the ruins." Central to this original vision is the doctrine of the fundamental opposition between mind and matter. Matter is a negation of God. The human soul fell from God's heavenly sphere and became a prisoner in this world. Entangled in the yarn of sensuality, it remembers the original heavenly purity and longs to return to its divine origin. Only through "the sense of beauty and religious contemplation" can the true church be created that can conciliate man in his humiliating condition of sin and give him the hope of regaining his lost bliss. With a great poetic-mythic apparatus of ideas and in evocatively dark formulations, Stagnelius varied these lines of thought in the poems in *Liljor i Saron* and other late poems. Above all, he celebrated the forlornness of the soul, heavenly memories and the longing to escape this earthly life. He depicts spiritual alienation with unusual psychological clarity and derives consolation from the thought of the eternal creator: "Therefore be happy, o friend, and sing in the darkness of sorrow:/ Night is the mother of day, Chaos is God's neighbor." The idea of reconciliation is strongly present in many poems. In the classical, didactic poem "Suckarnas mystär" ("The Mystery of Sighs")—one of the foremost didactic poems in Swedish—all of nature sighs under the laws of existence, but man alone has the power to strive for reconciliation:

> *Mänska! Vill du livets vishet lära,*
> *o, så hör mig! Tvenne lagar styra*
> *detta liv. Förmågan att begära*
> *är den första. Tvånget att försaka*
> *är den andra. Adla du till frihet*
> *detta tvång, och helgad och försonad*
> *över stoftets kretsande planeter*
> *skall du ingå genom ärans portar.*

O Man! Wouldst thou learn life's wisdom,
o, hear me then! The laws are two that rule
this life. Power to desire
is the first. Constraint to renounce
the second. Ennoble unto liberty
this constraint, and sanctified and reconciled,
over the orbiting planets of matter,
shalt thou enter through the gates of honor.

Stagnelius' very last poems, though, seem to move away from mysticism. In "Näcken" (The Water-Sprite) and "Endymion"—both among his best-known—a metaphysical mistrust seems to have returned. The water-sprite stops playing his fiddle at the brook because he has learned that he can never become God's child. "Endymion" retells the Greek myth of how the goddess of the moon visits the sleeping shepherd Endymion during the night and interprets it in a way that seems to attest to a feeling of emptiness after the heaven-storming metaphysical intoxication. Among Stagnelius' late writings is also the drama *Bacchanterna eller Fanatismen* (The Bacchantes or Fanaticism) which treats the ancient myth about how the bacchantes destroy the singer Orpheus. This was printed in 1822 and is one of the poet's most accomplished works. Here, Orpheus' ascetic and sublime fanaticism is contrasted with the Bacchus cult's destructively orgiastic intoxication of the senses. The moral is that one must distance oneself from all kinds of fanaticism: man has merely to await death with stoic calm.

It is, however, as Sweden's foremost mystical lyric poet that Stagnelius takes his place of rank in Swedish poetry. He belongs to a long tradition of mysticism in Swedish literature which runs from Saint Birgitta, through the mystics of the Great Power Era's Renaissance to Swedenborg, and afterwards on to the young Almqvist and the late Strindberg, and to Gunnar Ekelöf and many other poets of the twentieth century. In terms of poetry he occupies a special position in this mystic tradition through the intense beauty of his precocious and chaotic vision, while in artistic terms, the lyrical peaks in his production have scarcely been surpassed by later poetry.

Liberalism's Breakthrough
Geijer, Almqvist, Rydberg

Romanticism was a mainly conservative trend—even if several of the Romantics had their roots in the revolutionary climate of the turn of the nineteenth century. Both Atterbom and Stagnelius held a conservative view of culture and society, and Tegnér, who at the end of the 1810s could still maintain a radical viewpoint on social questions, became quite conservative as a member of parliament in the 1830s and a target for the arrows of the liberal opposition. During the course of the decade, this opposition grew in strength and directed vehement attacks against Karl XIV Johan's stagnated policies and despotic tendencies. In particular the king's efforts at censure aroused much bad feeling in publishing circles and contributed indirectly to radicalizing the political and cultural climate. *Aftonbladet* (The Evening News) had been founded in 1830 by the liberal politician Lars Johan Hierta, and through its modern, rapid supply of news and its harsh polemics in political questions it quickly became the leading newspaper in the country. In the liberal spirit it worked for freedom of the press and the liberty to pursue a trade, for the education of the people and a more humane legislation. During the politically active period 1835–40, sometimes called "the period of rabid radicals," the paper was suspended on repeated occasions, but always returned under new names such as *Det nya Aftonbladet* (The New Evening News), *Det fjärde Aftonbladet* (The Fourth Evening News). The fight against the power of suspension strengthened its position in the long run. During the 1840s and 1850s when, periodically anyway, the radical voices were further sharpened, it was an extraordinarily strong forum for liberal interests, for which an increasingly radical literary Parnassus diligently produced debate articles on social questions, socio-realistic serials, and travel features.

The years around 1840 hosted a remarkable breakthrough for radical ideas in literary life, which can be traced back to a tradition from Thorild (see p. 65) and to some extent Kellgren, as well as the young Tegnér. However, this was the time when radical ideas first started to occupy a dominant position in cultural life, a tradition that, with short breaks, has been kept alive in Swedish literature, where the traces of radicalism are just as clear as those of mysticism. At the middle of the nineteenth century, in the wake of the 1848 revolution, this radicalism was fertilized by the ideas of social utopianism, and there was a large number of writers with a politically radical voice—most of them today just names on the margins of literary history. However, most of the era's leading literary figures were found in the liberal and utopian movement that dominated the Parnassus from around 1840: Geijer, who after a Romantic past made a sensational defection in 1838; Almqvist, the Romantic genius who united an artistic amoralism with a passionate social indignation; Fredrika Bremer with her pioneering efforts for the emancipation of women, and somewhat later the young Rydberg, with his fight for religious freedom against the Church's hegemony.

After 1838, Erik Gustaf Geijer (1783–1847) became the grand old man of Swedish liberalism. In spite of a Romantic and conservative past there were elements in his background that seemed to point in a radical direction. Like Tegnér, he came from the Värmland foundry culture where the ideas of the Enlightenment and the ideals of the French Revolution were highly valued. As a young student he had sympathized with progressive social and cultural ideas, and in 1809, as a tutor, he had undertaken a journey to England which in time proved to have provided experiences important for the development of his social views. As a writer, however, he belonged to an increasingly conservative Romanticism. He was one of the leaders of the Gothic Society, a union of young Stockholm public servants, founded in 1811. The group met under jovial, ritualized forms of "Gothic" affectation and, in the light of the newly awakened nationalism of the time and revanchist trends against Russia, worked to revive the old "spirit of freedom, manly courage and honest disposition." The movement had its deepest ideological roots in the eighteenth century's world of ideas—in Montesquieu's climate doctrine and Rousseau's gospel of nature—and its forms of expression became more artistically than politically effective. As the Society's driving force, Geijer became editor of its journal *Iduna*, where he published his Gothic poems. Some of these are classic pieces of Swedish poetry, even if they today seem fairly modest in artistic terms. Best known are "Vikingen" (The Viking) and "Odal-bonden" (The Yeoman Farmer), the former portraying a seafaring adventurer, the latter a farmer. Also well-known is the Goethe-inspired folksong pastiche "Den lille kolar-gossen" (The Charcoal Burner's Son), written somewhat later.

Geijer's lyrical production is not very significant in terms of quantity or quality. In the 1820s and 1830s, though, he wrote a number of short, personal poems that have had a certain lasting value, not least because of the musical accompaniments he wrote for them; perhaps he was more talented as a self-taught composer than as a poet. One of these small, subjectively sentimental poems is called "På nyårsdagen 1838" ("On New Year's Day 1838") and expresses Geijer's anxiety about the future in a phase of his life when he had abandoned his conservative friends and openly declared his faith in liberal ideas:

> *Ensam i bräcklig farkost vågar*
> *seglaren sig på det vida hav,*
> *stjärnvalvet över honom lågar,*
> *nedanför brusar hemskt hans grav.*
> *Framåt!—så är hans ödes bud;*
> *och i djupet bor som uti himlen Gud.*

> Lone in his frail bark seaward blowing
> The sailor fares on the trackless wave.
> O'er him the starry vault is glowing,
> Grimly below roars his ocean grave.
> "On!" bids the voice of his destiny,
> "Here, as in the heavens, God watcheth thee."

Geijer's step was a bold one. As a cultural personality with a conservative reputation he had occupied a position of rank in Swedish cultural life, which he now jeopardized by taking up this new, liberal standpoint. As a professor of history from 1817 on he had revived history writing in Sweden and played a vital role in Swedish intellectual life generally. His historical works include *Svea rikes hävder* (Annals of the Kingdom of Sweden), 1825, and *Svenska folkets historia* 1–3

(History of the Swedish People), 1832–36. As a historian, Geijer espoused many of Romanticism's organic ideas and tried to identify the inner continuity of historical events. He improved the standards of research work and demanded a more profound understanding of the views and values of bygone times. Historical involvement, which characterized Romanticism's view of history, colored his way of working to a high degree. He felt strong sympathy for the kingdom and the king's significance for Swedish history. He also found that the farmers more often served the national interest than the aristocracy. His historical works are written in a pithy, laconic prose with an indisputable personal authority. We meet more of the warmly personal radiance, which was esteemed by his contemporaries, in *Minnen* (Memories), 1834, which provides a vivid picture of his Värmland adolescent milieu and his childhood home.

The solidly balanced personal image Geijer had built up was undeniably threatened by his espousing of liberal ideas. The about-face in his political views in 1838 has also traditionally been described as a defection. However, in more recent times this view has increasingly been questioned, given the continuity that is found in his ideological development and the radical fibers that, in spite of everything, can nevertheless be discerned. In his new journal, *Litteraturbladet*, he now openly announced that he sympathized with liberal ideas, and his writing and journalism subsequently took on a more progressive and creative character. He developed a new personal philosophy that began with the maxim: "not an I without a Thou." Personality, according to Geijer, arises and develops in a social environment, where it is refined in free interplay with other free personalities and through a strong faith in God as the provider of ethical norms and as the force from which all love flows. This Christian democratic personality ideal also characterizes the stand he took on various political questions of the time. Geijer's earlier criticism of the aristocracy was now applied also to the claims to economic power emanating from the new capitalist middle-classes. He became more and more involved with the new working class and was interested in the labor movement and the utopian socialism that emerged in France. Hegel had already influenced his ideas in the

1830s, and he shared the young Hegelians' interest in the dynamics of history. In several ways his development is parallel with that of Karl Marx at this time, who, moreover, read with interest Geijer's history in German translation. More recently, people have increasingly recognized Geijer's keen awareness of the unresolved conflict between capital and labor which was to arise later, as well as his central place in the history of ideas of Swedish democracy.

It was as a historian and socio-philosophical thinker that Geijer made a contribution of significant independence and depth. In fact, he is one of the few independent and international figures in the history of ideas in Sweden. His ideal of personality, with its stress on the social unity between an I and a Thou is a central educational tradition in Sweden, which had a strong impact that can be traced far into our own time. His view of history and politics grew increasingly democratic over the years and was in line with his philosophy of personality. He himself emerged during his lifetime as a harmonious and powerful personality whose headstrong independence and need for freedom made an impact on those around him; among other things he refused to teach at the court or to enter the Cabinet because of his need of an independent position. It is this principle of a strong and free personality that, in spite of his relatively light literary baggage, made Geijer's legacy into a living and significant chapter in the history of Swedish education and literature.

There were close contacts between Geijer and Carl Jonas Love Almqvist (1793–1866). Almqvist's transition to radical, socially-oriented writing was roughly contemporaneous with Geijer's defection to liberal ideas and was in part inspired by this. Like Geijer, Almqvist had a Romantic past with certain Gothic strains. Yet there is a deep abyss between them, reinforced by their personalities. Contrasting with the stable Geijer is the darkly disturbed, artistic Almqvist with all his unstable amoralism. He is a fascinating transitional figure between Romanticism and Realism, filled with tensions and contradictions. No Swedish nineteenth-century author other than Strindberg can be measured with him in terms of intellectual range and artistic originality. No Swedish author's fate is as tragic as his, nor was any Swedish poet's production of ideas from this time as fertile. From both an aesthetic and a political point of view there is something bold, radical and provocative about his figure that sharply breaks with the ideas and norms of his age and points forward to the values of the future. In the sheltered nineteenth-century atmosphere of a small and peripheral cultural area he was necessarily something of a strange bird, and for a long time the social catastrophe of his life prevented a full recognition of his brilliance. Only towards the turn of the century, when he was called "Sweden's most modern writer" in an essay by the author Ellen Key, did the greatness of his achievement begin to be accepted and appreciated in full. His literary renown as a living classic has steadily strengthened during the twentieth century.

Almqvist's middle-class upbringing had been strongly influenced by the Moravian Brethren and Swedenborgianism. He himself said that he inherited an "accountant's soul" from his father and a "poet's soul" from his mother. After academic studies in Uppsala he had entered the same public office as Stagnelius. At the same time, in a fit of Romantic zeal, he had become involved in the newly formed *Manhemsförbundet*, a religious-patriotic society with certain Gothic roots. He also founded the *Mannasamfund* (Society of Man) and thereby succeeded in creating a circle of faithful admirers around himself, to whom he preached, with a certain charismatic bravura, a message far-removed from reality. The literary production of his youth is extensive but little known, except for the one work that deserves to be called a masterpiece, *Amorina* from 1822. In its original version, which was never published, this work had the subtitle "The mad girl's life and uncommon exploits" and was dedicated to "the great insane asylum." It is a remarkable work that mixes poetry, prose and drama in the spirit of Romanticism. Almqvist himself called it a poetic fugue with reference to its musical structure. At the center of the chaotic, bewildering plot is the cleric's daughter Amorina who, after bringing about her mother's death, goes out among the people as a zealous preacher, only to end up in a madhouse. Another melodramatically overstrung figure is Johannes, who against his will and nature becomes a murderer. Almqvist's social pathos is clearly expressed here when he pleads for a more understanding view of the criminal. As an artistic whole *Amorina* is not as impressive as Atterbom's *Lycksalighetens ö* (The Isle of Bliss) or Tegnér's *Frithiofs Saga*; however, in individual effects, its lyrically fresh and capricious language and its Romantic mixture of high and low, of poetic and realistic, *Amorina* is still today one of the most evocative works of Swedish Romanticism. It stimulates the imagination and is wholly unique.

Almqvist abandoned his civil service existence in order to settle down in Värmland as a farmer in the Rousseau-Gothic spirit; however this undertaking also failed. He aired his aversion to the life of the civil servant in the story *Ormus och Ariman*, whose Persian mythological theme he transformed into an exhilarating and crushing satire of the bureaucratic world. Ormus, who represents the principle of goodness, tries to establish a world run on common sense by promulgating a long series of regulations and edicts, born of a rationalism far-removed from reality. Ariman, on the other hand, is the embodiment of evil, whose abode is the realm of night and of loneliness, a typically Romantic creature, who in his demonic confinement to nature laughs at Ormus' zeal to establish laws. There are strains of Almqvist's personality in both characters, and the story ends in a sense of disintegration and despair: "Why is the good man stupid—why is the wise man evil—why is everything a tattered rag—."

In the literary salons of Uppsala and Stockholm which Almqvist, and also Geijer, frequented, he presented short poems that he had set to music himself. Here too the parallel with Geijer is remarkable, although in this respect Almqvist was undoubtedly the more fertile and stimulating of the two. He called these poems *Songes*, and they were intended to be presented, for example, with flute accompaniment and certain dramatic effects. The short poems are in general of a mystic character, simple and naive but intensely impressionistic. Like Geijer's short poems, they have retained their popularity, in particular in song form. One example is "Marias häpnad" (Mary's Amazement):

> *Lammen så vita på ängen beta;*
> *men barnet Jesus utmed dem går.*
> *Häpen Maria stannar och ropar:*
> *"Jag ser en strålring omkring barnets hår!"*

The lambs so white graze in the meadow;
but the child Jesus is with them there.
Amazed Mary stops and calls:
"I see a halo round the child's hair!"

Toward the end of the 1820s, Almqvist had also begun to write historical novels in the style of Walter Scott. He was the first author of note in Sweden to take Scott's historical novel form and apply it to Swedish history. In the novel *Hermitaget* (The Hermitage), he took the motif from the period of Swedish medieval history depicted in *Erikskrönikan* (see p. 21). Almqvist learned historical color and evocative depiction of nature from Scott, but the art of poetic formulation is entirely his own. Originally enough, the story ends in Scotland (where the hermitage is located), thereby announcing the coming of Scott's historical novel to Swedish literature. Almqvist's most significant historical novel, though, was *Drottningens juvelsmycke* (The Queen's Jewel), 1834. Its motif is taken from the Swedish history of the 1790s, and it blends epic prose narrative with dramatic and lyrical sections. At the center of the action is the androgynous main character, Tintomara. She is a ballet dancer at the Opera in Stockholm and was there on the dramatic night when Gustav III was shot. Her bisexual being attracts men and women alike; she is a lyrical revelation beyond all the contradictions of existence. She is innocently drawn into intrigues, gradually becomes their victim, and is executed. This ambiguous creature no more allows herself to fit into society's conventional slots than did her creator. The novel's motto hints that her purity is linked with demonic forces: "Tintomara! Two things are white: innocence and arsenic." The evocatively melodramatic course of events is rendered with a wealth of variation and intricate artistic skill, and the work represents the artistic highpoint of Almqvist's Romantic phase.

During the 1830s, Almqvist entered a period of feverish literary productivity, and he began to collect his writings into a wide-ranging work published in two different series under the title *Törnrosens bok* (The Book of the Wild Rose). He gave the book a frame story in which a circle of literary enthusiasts at a hunting lodge in the forests of central Sweden narrate the tales to each other. During the course of the decade, contemporary social motifs clearly entered more and more into Almqvist's books. His political views were obviously moving towards liberalism and social utopianism, and he began to study social thinkers such as Charles Fourier, Louis Blanc, Robert Owen, and others. His liberal social leanings corresponded with Realism in the literary sphere. Contributing to this development was the fact that during the 1830s he was a frequent traveler in the Swedish provinces, where he acquired a considerable knowledge of the lives and living conditions of the people and the individual character of the different provinces. In 1838 he wrote his famous study *Svenska fattigdomens betydelse* (The Significance of Swedish Poverty), where he analyzed the peculiarities of the Swedish national character. This is characterized by poverty, he claims, and by poverty he means the ability to fend for oneself. Without a doubt there is a great deal of idealistic glorification of poverty in Almqvist, as well as a lot of Rousseau. The way in which he draws parallels between Swedish nature, Swedish climate and Swedish national character is a Gothically-exploited legacy of Montesquieu's climate doctrine. Yet the piece has the character of a Swedish national essay, reinforcing a cherished myth about a peculiarly Swedish, nature-influenced national character, poor, rugged and hard-working, in a way that made it a living tradition for a long time to come.

The ideas in *Svenska fattigdomens betydelse* took literary form in a long series of portraits of the lives of the people that tell of simple folk's toil and abysmal living conditions. In *Kapellet* (The Chapel), which gained some recognition outside Sweden through a German translation, he tells of the fishing communities along the Småland coast and their struggle for survival. Other stories depict how young people from the lower levels of society create a better existence for themselves through enterprise and enthusiasm, without thereby abandoning their sense of belonging. The stories are idealistic declarations of love for the simple people, their healthy lifestyle and strong will to work. Almqvist stressed the positive in his characters and the conditions in which they lived and demonstrated a thorough knowledge of their simple everyday life. With these stories he created a new

Carl Jonas Love Almqvist. Portrait by C. P. Mazer, 1836.

genre in Swedish literature and a long tradition of popular, realistic, narrative art in which the working people stand at the center.

The most important number in this series of realistic stories was the short novel *Det går an* (It Can Be Done, translated into English under the title *Sara Videbeck*), 1838. This was the work which attracted most attention during Almqvist's lifetime. Artistically, it is not remarkable. It is a novel of travel and conversation, about two passengers, a glassmaker's daughter called Sara Videbeck, and Sergeant Albert, who take the Mälar boat Yngve Frey from Stockholm and continue by coach to Västergötland. The trip itself is masterfully depicted, displaying an unquestionable familiarity with the area and the lyrical objectivity which more and more became Almqvist's artistic signature. During the journey, the two travelers begin to discuss marriage and woman's position. With a radicalism that shocked his contemporaries, Almqvist has Sara speak out on marital freedom as a bold program for new forms of cohabitation. She polemicizes against marriage and against communal property and cohabitation and envisages a free relationship between man and woman, built on an inner communion but with separate finances and homes. This utopian program was directed against the dependent status of women and emanated to a high degree from Almqvist's own marital experiences. Such a criticism of western marriage was, however, stepping on hallowed ground at this time, and a comprehensive and aggressive *Det går an* debate ensued, with a long series of polemical letters. The great commotion that the novel aroused damaged Almqvist's reputation and hopes for a continued social career. He was now forced to relinquish the position of school principal that he had held during the entire 1830s, and where he had made far-sighted and remarkable pedagogic contributions. All that remained to him was journalism and writing for his daily bread.

Almqvist's international orientation at this time is just as clear as his interest in the life of the Swedish people. In 1838 he wrote a treatise advocating reform, *Det europeiska missnöjets grunder* (The Causes of European Discontent), which was published only in part at the time and did not appear in its entirety until 1850. In twelve fictional and conversational letters he lays out here his social and political radicalism vis-à-vis the great questions of the time. He pleads for revolutionary action to remedy the misery that characterized the European way of life. Here also he takes up the process of marital liberation and the right of every individual to "right of ownership and right of use of what that individual possesses and acquires." In other contexts too he debates "the European problem" and discusses the need for revolution. In the field of literature, he pleads for politically conscious, tendentious novels in the essay "Politik och poesi" (Politics and Poetry) from 1839. The essay "Om poesi i sak" (On the Poetry of Facts) from the same year is a realistic program to counter a Romantic ideal, that is seen as "poetry of words only." "Poetry's restoration" is presented here as an important link in "society's rebirth." Further, in 1840–41, he undertook a study trip to England and France that broadened his international perspectives greatly. He could now follow the French internal political game and the manifestations of social dissatisfaction at closer hold. In newspaper articles and in letters to his family he gave lively descriptions as a socially and politically engaged tourist. From London, for example, he sent some articles allegedly written by a certain Quincy Parriot, which indicates that he was familiar with Dickens' *Sketches by Boz*. Almqvist draws a dark picture of the poverty in England and provides a strategy for how it ought to be fought.

The Paris stay also resulted in a novel, *Gabrièle Mimanso*, 1841, that took its motif from the attempted murder of King Louis Philippe in the fall of 1840. It therefore contained highly topical material, but it is above all a novel of adventure and intrigue in imitation of Eugène Sue and Alexandre Dumas. Almqvist's writings during the 1840s rendered the tendentious novel an attractive, easily accessible form of entertainment. In this late and less noticed writing he was able to plead for polygamous love and combine the dramatic intrigue of the bandit novel with a philanthropic theme, built on Fourier's socio-utopian "phalanstères." In another late novel he launched the concepts "upper class" and "lower class" in Swedish.

But it was as a newspaperman that Almqvist made his greatest contribution during the 1840s. He got involved in the editing of *Aftonbladet* and became its leading radical writer. He challenged reactionary forces with unhesitating outspokenness and his pen was feared and detested. With the experiences from his foreign travels, he spoke out against the fact that Swedish society too was characterized by social injustice and shocking class differences. He pleaded for increased political and social democracy, and he made committed contributions to the question that more than any other occupied political debate in Sweden at this time: the reform of parliamentary representation. He pursued this committed journalism in an increasingly socially exposed position. He became the object of fierce attacks from the conservative press and was regularly involved in bitter controversies. It is clear that he was driven out onto the social periphery over the years, where asocial shadows darkened his life. Catastrophe struck in 1851 when financial worries led him into shady monetary transactions and, accused of trying to poison a money-lender, he was forced hastily to flee the country to escape the law. It is difficult to imagine what was behind the accusations. Later attempts to clear him have failed to lead to convincing proof of innocence, and it will probably never be possible to attain any complete clarity. But Almqvist never returned to Sweden. For the last fifteen years of his life he lived in exile.

Almqvist fled via Bremen to America, where he settled under initially favorable social circumstances. Later on, increasing penury seems to have overtaken him. He settled in Philadelphia and married a boarding-house landlady. His function seems to have been to contribute to the entertainment by playing the piano. His literary genius lay dormant; he occupied himself mainly by writing simple, apparently bombastic poetry that he put into the voice of a well-known Stockholm writer of such verses, Seseman. Only in our time have these "poems in exile" begun to be appreciated for what they are and collected under the title *Sesemana*. In a naive, pared-down and subdued form—which at times is reminiscent of Emily Dickinson—he often talks here about the debasement of his exile existence and confirms with nostalgic irony that "only Sweden has Swedish gooseberries." In spite of attempts to return to Sweden, he was forced to remain in exile and died in Germany, thereby closing the final chapter on a life story more fantastic than any of his literary creations.

Unappreciated during his life, Almqvist has become one of the few real giants of Swedish literature. In spite of the fact that most of his works are marked by a noticeable inconsistency of quality, his authorship displays an amazing breadth and many-sidedness. His register includes both aesthetic speculation and socio-political commitment, mystic searching and realistic reports about the lives of the people, creations of the imagination and opinion-forming journalism aimed at creating a more democratic society. In both literary and social terms he was a major groundbreaker who never ceased to surprise with his radical boldness. The cognomen "shattered Romantic genius" has often been applied to him, but it is more correct to see his many-sidedness as the outpouring of an enormously rich talent and a unique genius. Besides Almqvist at Hierta's *Aftonbladet*, Vendela Hebbe contributed some boldly critical and revealing social reportage. Fredrika Bremer—of whom we will hear more later—also worked there. At *Jönköpingsbladet*, another markedly radical newspaper where Almqvist had published articles toward the end of the 1840s, the young Viktor Rydberg (1828–95) also made his first journalistic appearance with articles and serialized novels in the shadow of the 1848 revolution. He belonged to the next generation of liberals and can be said to start where Almqvist (because of his enforced exile) left off, namely as a leading progressive writer. During the period 1855–80, just before the modern breakthrough, Rydberg was clearly the central figure in Swedish cultural life. After an unsettled, insecure childhood and disrupted university studies, he developed quickly as a journalist. His heyday began in 1855 when he began to work for the *Göteborgs Handels- och Sjöfartstidning* as an editorial writer and theater and literary critic. He became increasingly known as one of the most argumentative, debate-oriented writers in the country. He became particularly involved in Church politics and theological questions, and it is here that he made his most weighty progressive contribution, through polemics against the Church's orthodoxy and dogmatic view of Christ.

Most of all, though, his activity at this newspaper is associated with the novels which were serialized there. In these early serials and novel fragments, Rydberg often followed Almqvist's recipe of combining tendentious novel and adventure intrigue. He might depict a poorhouse in the spirit of Dickens and use the novel form to put forth an active program of social reform to protect the vulnerable and exposed in society. *Fribytaren på Östersjön (The Freebooter of the Baltic)*, 1857, which also came out in book form, is about pirate adventures, political intrigues and witch trials in seventeenth-century Sweden, but it is also a novel of ideas directed against intolerance, oppression and inhumanity. While *Singoalla*, 1857, is a Romantic medieval narrative about the forbidden love between a knight and a gypsy—which made it Rydberg's probably most widely read and popular novel, *Den siste athenaren (The Last Athenian)*, 1859, became his great contribution as Romantic writer of ideas. It is the first more significant novel of ideas in Swedish literature. Its action is played out in late classical times and deals chiefly with the intrigues of the early Christian Church to strengthen its power over the disintegrating classical society. Depiction of the age and dramatic tension, though, play a lesser role here than the actual idea content, which treats the opposition between classical and Christian. The writer sees his ideals of freedom and reason realized in Hellenic society, while the growing Christian Church represents lust for power, despotism and intolerance. Rydberg's personal view, however, is that the earliest forms of Christianity incorporated much of the classical spirit. Thus he felt that it should be possible to unite antiquity and Christianity and thereby overcome the violation of the oldest traditions, which the Christian Church's seizure of power at the beginning of the Middle Ages had brought about.

In our own time, Rydberg's novels, including the late work *Vapensmeden* (The Armorer), 1891, have fared less well. Now his literary renown rests mainly on the poetry which was published in two late collections in 1882 and 1891. In his poems he often focuses on childhood and the child's world of ideas, and a commonly occurring sphere of motifs is that of searching and brooding. His obsession with the great questions of existence and with the problem of eternity culminates in the structurally magnificent cantata he wrote for Uppsala University's 400-year jubilee in 1877, which takes its motif from the Old Testament's depiction of Israel's journey through the wilderness. Out of the confusion and doubt of a universe in which time and space appear as "a frightful, infinite prison," the inner development curve of the poem progresses to a strongly idealistic conviction which reaches back to Tegnér's rhetoric: "What rightly you think, what you want in love,/ what beautiful you dream, cannot be ravaged by time,/ it is a harvest that will be saved,/ for it belongs to the kingdom of eternity."

Rydberg's two foremost poems are, however, the idea poem "Prometheus och Ahasverus" and the poem of social indignation "Den nya Grottesången" (The New Song of Grotte). The former, which of all of Rydberg's poems is richest in perspective, is one of the most distinguished of all idea poems in Swedish poetry. Ahasuerus, the shoemaker from Jerusalem who was doomed to wander eternally for refusing to allow Christ to rest during his time on Golgotha, stands for what in the history of mankind has been determined by violence and power. He represents what Rydberg in the preface to *The Last Athenian* had called the oriental-despotic principle, which demands submission to the laws of existence and the hierarchies of power. As modern arguments he may adduce Darwin's thesis about the fight for existence and Marx's thesis about the implacable class struggle. Prometheus, on the other hand, stands for the western, Hellenic principle and defends rebellion against the world system, the struggle for something better. He sees the poet and artist as fighters for the liberation of man from the world system of power. In the conclusion of the poem, the Messiah appears and seems to side with Prometheus. The ideas from *The Last Athenian* have here taken on a visionary, evocative shape, in which the myths have undergone a free and creative interpretation. So too in "Den nya Grottesången," where Rydberg took the motif from one of the Old Norse Eddic lays that tells how King Frode made the mill Grotte (treadmill) grind so hard that it fell apart. In the poet's vision, the "treadmill" represents modern industrialism and its ruthless exploitation of the human work force. It contains strong and convincing expressions of the poet's social indignation at the way in which the capitalist laws of competition had weakened the position of the already vulnerable working class and debased it further. The appalling female and child labor conditions described in the poem do not, however, correspond to Swedish working conditions at that time but have rather a more general international relevance. It is above all materialism, atheism and egotism in modern society that Rydberg attacks, and in a postscript he makes the prophecy that the socialists' Utopia will also lead to King Frode's treadmill.

It was not only as a poet and journalist that Rydberg performed a cultural achievement. He was also a historian of religion, wrote tracts on Germanic and Old Norse mythology, was a cultural and art historian with some monumental portraits of Roman emperors to his name, and as a philosopher he attempted a scientific, theoretical reconciliation of metaphysics and empiricism. Like Geijer, he was at home to an equally high degree in the history of ideas and scholarship as in literary history. He is one of the few significant poets of ideas in Swedish literature, a truly intellectual poet who nevertheless was not alien to the world of mystical experience. In his contribution to literature he powerfully gave shape to the idea crises of a transitional phase. He was a harbinger of the modern breakthrough in literature but his own roots lay in the idealistic, humanistic optimism of the early nineteenth century and liberal-democratic radicalism.

Fredrika Bremer and the Realistic Novel

The history of Swedish novel writing prior to the Romantic movement is a fairly modest chapter. Only from Romanticism on did it begin to develop distinct realistic, satirical features in the Romantic tradition, with Almqvist's early novels as the high point in this development. However, Almqvist, and even less Rydberg, can hardly be called a pioneer of the middle-class realistic novel that was to become the nineteenth century's most significant contribution to the literary genres. This role fell to Fredrika Bremer (1801–65), who established the realistic novel in Sweden around 1830 and gradually became an important cultural personality, with far-reaching ideas and a socially radical tone. Given the woman-centered themes in her books it was quite natural that she became the leading figure of the Swedish women's movement, whose modern society bears her name. In contrast to her contemporary fellow authors, she became an international celebrity who undertook long journeys and made important contacts abroad. She was a central and in many ways remarkable figure in Swedish literary and cultural history at the middle of the nineteenth century.

Fredrika Bremer came from a Finland-Swedish family that moved to Sweden during her early childhood. Her upbringing was culturally and artistically relatively progressive but also strictly patriarchal. Her writing was largely a protest against this male-dominated home environment. She made her debut in 1828 with the first installment of the series

Teckningar ur vardagslivet (Sketches of Every-day Life), which she continued to publish over the following years. Her breakthrough came, however, with the novel *Familjen H*** (The H-Family)*, 1830–31, which can be called the first middle-class realistic novel in Swedish literature. It takes its material from the contemporary upper middle-class home life of the sort the author herself knew well. At the same time, her presentation is marked by a strongly humanistic and idealistic spirit rooted in Romanticism. She then became attracted to modern English social philosophy (Bentham, Mill) on the one hand and German Romantic philosophy (Herder) and Christian mysticism on the other. Her interest in social, humanitarian idealism was strengthened through various personal contacts. Significant for her development at this time was Geijer, for example, and the view of a healthy and harmonious home life which chiefly emerged from his memoirs. During a visit to Norway she began work on the novel *Grannarna (The Neighbours)* which came out in 1837 and is among her best works. The main theme in the book is Christian-platonic conciliation, but of central importance is the contented, older woman figure, "ma chère mère," who represents a more matriarchal home ideal than the one Fredrika Bremer herself had known. With deep insight into the dark forces dwelling in man, the novel culminates in a light and warm harmony, and a sense of human self-assurance.

In her next novel, *Hemmet (The Home)*, 1839, Fredrika Bremer continued to develop this Geijer-like faith in the significance of the home and its ability to promote the best in individuals. She regarded the home as society's basic unit and calls it a "fatherland in miniature." She pleaded, though, for the liberation of individuals from the traditional home's oppressive patriarchal bonds. In particular, of course, this applied to women, whom she felt ought to be educated for a profession and a more independent position in the home and society. She did not go as far as Almqvist in her demands for women's emancipation, but otherwise the parallels between the two authors are remarkable. Both are typical exponents of the nineteenth century's strong attraction to a religiously colored social utopianism with humanitarian and idealistic features. During the 1840s, just like Almqvist earlier, she set out on journeys through the Swedish provinces which she depicted in a couple of novels. Over the years she had acquired an international circle of readers through translations of her works and these latter novels were equally addressed to a non-Swedish audience—a kind of literary tourist propaganda from an exotic country on the periphery of the western world. She tried to depict a woman's process of inner liberation in novel form, with greater stress on erotic problems than she normally allowed herself. She also depicted utopian attempts to establish a socialist collective colony, along the lines of American social experiments, as the foundation for a kingdom of eternal peace.

Over the years, Balzac's realistic technique had also increasingly come to characterize Fredrika Bremer's novel writing. In a programmatic article from 1853 she gave her view of the novel as a modern epic that gives shape to the individual's development and struggle and that shows the world from all sides, positive as well as negative. She tried to realize this idea in the novel *Hertha*, 1856, which became probably her best known work. In dark colors she depicted a home tyrannized by a brutal and dominant father. The main character, Hertha, is a young woman who tries to break out of this oppressive and debasing milieu and go her own way, independent of the laws of patriarchal society. The novel closes with a vision of a future in which all people can enjoy a free, independent upbringing. This novel, rather innocent in today's eyes, was received by Fredrika Bremer's contemporaries with great commotion and violent critical debate. In spite of her irreproachable character, Hertha's striving for women's emancipation was too shocking for the tastes of those setting the trends. Later, however, she was to play an important role as a symbol of the women's emancipation movement that grew stronger during the second half of the nineteenth century, and Hertha became the name of the women's movement's own journal.

Fredrika Bremer's writing career is marked by an ever strengthening independence and awareness. Her intellectual curiosity drove her out on the first of her long journeys. A visit was arranged to America, the country where she hoped that a new human and social ideal would be developed. She recounted her experiences and impressions from this trip during the years 1849–51 in the book *Hemmen i den nya*

Fredrika Bremer. Portrait by O. J. Södermark, 1843.

världen (The Homes of the New World), which came out in three volumes in 1853–54. As a traveler she showed an enormous appetite for seeking out people and milieus. She visited famous authors like Emerson—with whose philosophy of life she had much in common—and the Scandinavian-oriented Longfellow. She visited the worker "phalanstères" that had earlier inspired her and was alternately critical and enthusiastic. She was impressed by the vitality of American life and the many social institutions that facilitated people's lives there, and it appeared to her that women had acquired a significantly freer position and were able to develop their skills in a better way. However, she was not blind to the negative sides of American society. In the southern states she protested with obvious indignation against slavery, and in Cuba she witnessed with profound distress the inhumane exploitation of the slaves on the sugar plantations. In the Negroes' own culture she felt a strong, spontaneous joy, particularly in their song and dance, which she saw as the best expression of an independent American culture. On the way home she also visited England, where she was especially interested in the cooperative and Christian-socialist movements. Her other long journeys took her to Rome, Palestine and Greece, from where she collected her travel impressions in *Livet i gamla världen (Two Years in Switzerland and Italy, Travels in the Holy Land, Greece and the Greeks)*, 1860–62. Her aim was now chiefly to seek out the roots of western culture. She visited the Pope in Rome, and in the Holy Land she went on pilgrimages by horse to the well-known biblical sites. The ancient ruins did not inspire her with any neoclassical enthusiasm, but she did become interested in mother myths and other feminine figures of Greek mythology. In these she saw foreshadowed women's role in the progress which, with typical nineteenth-century optimism, she perceived in the course of world history.

Fredrika Bremer's social contribution has to a great extent surpassed her literary contribution. Her novels are seldom seen as classic masterpieces, and they have not attained any larger circle of readers in our time. Her intellectual breadth in combination with a lively world of feelings, however, makes her books stimulating; as a narrator she occasionally surprises us with unexpected ideas and with perfectly imitated dialogues and precise observations of everyday middle-class life. Not only did she initiate the Swedish women's movement with her novels, but she also established through her example a succession of women novelists who, to a greater degree than earlier, focused the world's attention on Swedish literature. From the middle of the nineteenth century on, it is to a large extent authors like Sophie von Knorring, Emilie Flygare-Carlén, Marie-Sophie Schwartz— now more or less forgotten, but then highly regarded— who were in demand on the international book market. The tradition culminated with Selma Lagerlöf. For a long time thereafter, Sweden's literary Parnassus, in the eyes of the rest of the world, had a female face.

Runeberg and Finland-Swedish Literature

At the signing of peace after the war of 1808–9, Sweden had been forced to surrender Finland to Russia. Finland became a Russian Grand Duchy directly under the tsar. The political and cultural unity that had prevailed uninterrupted since the Middle Ages was thereby broken. Cultural life in Finland had been almost completely dominated by a Swedish hegemony. After the separation from Sweden, Finnish cultural life went its own way to a great extent. However, for a long time to come, it was still the educated, Swedish-speaking upper class that supported culture in Finland and that was responsible for a growing national consciousness. Later too, when Finnish-speaking culture had grown strong and independent, this Swedish-speaking minority culture would continue to play an extraordinarily important role in Finnish cultural life. Thus, from 1809 on, Swedish and Finnish literature were no longer united within a national, literary-historical frame. If, on the other hand, you consider Swedish literary history as that of Swedish-language literature, then, of course, Finland-Swedish literature does rightly belong there.

In the new Russian Grand Duchy of Finland, contemporary national sentiments were concentrated at Åbo University, where the German Romantic movement strongly inspired the young intellectuals. During the course of the 1820s, some important cultural profiles began to emerge, and after the university moved to Helsinki in 1828, a circle of these literary and intellectual fiery spirits gathered there to discuss political and cultural questions with a new patriotic vision. Among them was Elias Lönnrot who collected the treasury of popular songs in Finnish which later became the foundation for the Finnish national epic, *Kalevala* (famous not least through the compositions of Jean Sibelius). A major figure was also Johan Ludvig Runeberg (1804–77), who through his poetry in Swedish did more than anyone before him to establish a Finnish national consciousness. A period as a tutor deep within the Finnish interior had left Runeberg with a lasting impression of the Finnish people and Finnish nature that would be fundamental to his future poetry. He was also to mark his Finnish independence by attacking in newspaper articles the Tegnér-dominated rhetoric of the Swedish literature from Sweden.

His debut, with *Dikter* (Poems), 1830, signified the breakthrough of a poetic Realism in Swedish literature. Inspired by Serbian folk poetry in German translation, he wrote— under the title "Idyll och epigram" (Idylls and Epigrams)— a concentrated, simple and natural poetry with several elements characteristic of folk poetry. The themes were realistic, transferred to a more Finnish form and with a special Finnish tone. They were also timeless: love and death, human toil and daily life, nature and the changing of the seasons. The overwrought Romantic mood had been replaced by a classical restraint and universality. A pithy, epic element is present in many of these poems, above all in some where the Finnish farmer steps forward to meet the reader. Best-known among these is the poem about the farmer Pavo who is struck three times by a bad harvest. This is a national mini-epic about wretched poverty, industriousness, fear of God and solidarity between people. In later collections of poems in 1833 and 1843, Runeberg widened his range of motifs. In several role poems he portrayed the masses, while a poem like "Den enda stunden" (The Only Hour) is one of the great love poems of Swedish poetry:

> *Allena var jag,*
> *han kom allena;*
> *förbi min bana*
> *hans bana ledde,*
> *han dröjde icke,*
> *men tänkte dröja,*
> *han talte icke,*
> *men ögat talte.—*
> *Du obekante,*
> *du välbekante!*
> *En dag försvinner,*
> *ett år förflyter,*
> *det ena minnet*
> *det andra jagar;*
> *den korta stunden*
> *blev hos mig evigt,*
> *den bittra stunden,*
> *den ljuva stunden.*

Alone I was,
he came alone;
past my path
his path led,
he didn't stop,
but thought to stop,
he didn't speak,
but his eye spoke.—
You unknown,
you well-known!
A day disappears,
a year flies by,
the one memory
the other chases;
the short hour
became for me eternal,
the bitter hour,
the delightful hour.

Runeberg also tried the verse epic with great success. *Älgskyttarna* (The Moose Hunters) from 1832, a hexameter idyll in nine songs, took its motif from the Finnish interior. The story is about a moose hunt and a successful courtship, but the epic action is of lesser importance. What the poet wanted to give was a lively, documentary depiction of the Finnish people in a remote, sparsely populated area of the country. His ethnographic knowledge is rendered in detail, with Finnish words skillfully fitted into the Homeric hexameter form. Runeberg put much effort into describing the social strata in the Finnish countryside; all categories of people appear here, from the well-to-do farmer to the crofter and on down to the beggar. The human portraits are marked by warmth and humor and by the poet's light, harmonious view of life and strong respect for people and their worth, independent of social position. In later idyllic epics of a similar sort, Runeberg continued to depict Finnish society, but in other environments.

In the 1840s, Runeberg sought more exotic motifs— partly under the influence of Almqvist's Wild Rose book. The most significant of these efforts is the verse epic *Kung Fjalar* (King Fjalar), 1844, a highly unusual work, where Old Norse Gothic is combined with Celtic Ossianism and classical Neohumanism. Its five songs depict how the Old Norse King Fjalar tries to promote his land's welfare, but since he does it without asking the gods for advice, he is punished by them: his two children accidentally fall in love with each other, and upon discovering that they are siblings, take their lives. Fjalar is an Old Norse Oedipus, who ignores the seer's warnings about arrogance toward the gods and who, after he is punished, is forced to acknowledge their sovereignty and then take his own life. In the socially and politically progressive 1840s, the religiously conditioned moralism in this work appears almost as a reactionary attack on the liberals' faith in man's inherent ability to create a better world for himself. It has been judged variously, but artistically it must be seen as one of Runeberg's foremost achievements through its monumental, concentrated, narrative art.

However, Runeberg was soon to return to his Finnish motifs. He was fascinated by the tales from the 1808–9 war with Russia that were still alive among the people, and he began to write a cycle of narrative poems about the legendary events of the war: *Fänrik Ståls sägner (The Tales of Ensign Stål)*, which came out in two parts in 1848 and 1860. His aim with these poems was not to write history in lyrical form but rather to present a national lyric-epic collection of legends that would reflect national moods and attitudes and stimulate a sense of solidarity. *The Tales of Ensign Stål*, which stand out as Runeberg's most popular work, are a superb example of nineteenth-century Romanticism's interest in creating a national consciousness and national myths through literature. The legends served their purpose excellently and came to play a major role in the young state of Finland's process of national liberation. The national mythology appears not least in the poem "Vårt land" ("Finland"), which was to become Finland's national anthem. It stresses the paradox in the country's poverty and its natural abundance. The elements which weld the country together are the beauty of nature, the heritage handed down by the efforts of Finland's forefathers, and the hardships in the form of war, years of famine and starvation that the people has had to withstand. The end of the poem hints at freedom and independence. Yet its aim might also be to express a national moralism of Runeberg's own stamp, as in the poem

"Molnets broder" ("The Cloud's Brother"), written much earlier, one of the high points in the collection. This depicts the passage of a Finnish youth from early egotism to love and the building of a family, and then finally, during the war, on into the national, supra-individual sphere, in which he sacrifices his life for the fatherland. The collection of legends consists largely of such portrait poems, through which consciousness of the national myth is channelled. The highest military leadership is criticized for incompetence, while the higher officers who distinguished themselves heroically in battle are painted in sympathetic colors—as are, of course, the simple people in the ranks: the naively brave soldier Sven Duva, the cheery Munter and the stalwart canteen keeper Lotta Svärd. In the twentieth century the naiveté in Runeberg's idealization of the events of war became more and more evident and was criticized, but he can still be admired for the epic force and lively, realistic clarity in his brilliantly narrated poems.

To a high degree, Runeberg corresponds to the nineteenth century's ideal of a national poet. In spite of the fact that he wrote in Swedish, he became the obvious central literary figure for the young Finnish state and its culture, and his memory has been preserved under nearly cult-like conditions. He was also important for maintaining the cultural ties between Sweden and Finland in spite of the political and territorial separation. It has not been without significance for Finnish-Swedish relations that these depictions of the Finnish people's way of life belong to the Swedish literary legacy. However, he was to an equally high degree a universal poet who came into his own above all when presenting the timeless aspects of life and nature, love and death, happiness and destitution. In his poetry one meets a timebound and patriotic Realism and a free and universal Classicism.

Runeberg was succeeded as national literary figurehead in Finnish cultural life by Zacharias Topelius (1818–98), who was active in various cultural areas. He wrote lyric poetry and drama, he was a journalist and professor of history, and he wrote historical novels in the spirit of Scott. One of these, *Fältskärns berättelser* (The Barber-Surgeon's Tales), 1853–67, also became enormously popular in Sweden. He made his most important contribution, though, in the area of books for children and young people. The geographical proximity to Hans Christian Andersen's tales created a favorable soil for children's books in all the Nordic countries, and Topelius recognized the potential. In his fairy tales and fairy plays, largely collected in *Läsning för barn* (Reading for Children), 1865–96, he found his own tone: more unreflecting and unsophisticated than Andersen's, with spontaneous warmth and humor and a feeling for nature. Topelius became immensely popular as a children's book writer, and, like Andersen's, his books reached far corners of the world and were translated into some twenty languages. With him, the children's book became an independent genre in Swedish literature, and he paved the way for the boom in children's books that arose around 1900. That a belletristic author of note could devote his talents to the writing of children's books became something of a precedent, and several of Sweden's foremost writers, such as Rydberg, Strindberg, Heidenstam and above all Selma Lagerlöf, would later write fairy tales and other works for children and young people. With Topelius as a model, Swedish children's literature thus achieved a remarkably high quality.

THE LITERATURE OF THE MODERN BREAKTHROUGH

With the so-called literature of the modern breakthrough at the end of the nineteenth century, the Scandinavian literatures entered the world's literary arena and made a lasting contribution for the first and only time in the modern era. The period around the turn of the twentieth century was in many ways a highpoint in Nordic literary history. Names like Georg Brandes, J. P. Jacobsen and Herman Bang from Denmark and Henrik Ibsen, Bjørnstierne Bjørnson and Knut Hamsun from Norway became international celebrities, of whom at least Brandes and Ibsen had an intense and lasting luminosity. Swedish literature was also part of this Scandinavian entry into international literary life. It was in the main Strindberg, of course, who was the pioneer and giant of world-wide literary significance, but there was also Ola Hansson—and somewhat later and to a greater extent, Selma Lagerlöf.

The modern breakthrough—the term coined by Georg Brandes in 1883—was no unambiguous phenomenon. The common unifying element within this new movement was the feeling of representing something new and modern in relation to the old. Initially at least, the movement was marked by strong anti-religious sentiments, political and social radicalism, and by the idea that new literary trends like Realism and Naturalism, as well as new currents of ideas such as Positivism with its faith in reason and science, benefitted this radicalism. The belief that "modern" meant bold radicalness remained, even as the movement later entered a phase where it more strongly emphasized a combination of individuality and artistry and tiraded against Positivism as well as Naturalism. Constant renewal, the principle that would come to guide the twentieth century's many modernistic movements, was already a dynamically effective force in the modern breakthrough. Strindberg's development was the clearest proof of this mania for change in the spirit of modernity and followed quite closely the changes in the literary climate during the period from the end of the nineteenth century to the beginning of the twentieth. Behind all these changes, there remained, however, a certain continuity in the radicalness of the feeling for life and the will for literary expression.

The Swedish preconditions for a breakthrough for the new literature around 1880 were several. Literary life, which had been vital and flourishing at the middle of the century, had shown strong signs of stagnation in the 1870s. The still prevailing idealism, a legacy from Romanticism, began to appear obsolete. Cultural conservatism went hand in hand with an increasing political conservatism which was fostered and defended by the Establishment's social and economic interests. This tendency was mainly a reaction against the change of political structure to which the earlier nineteenth century's radical political movements had led. Through the representation reform of 1866—that triumph for liberal efforts—the old parliament of the four estates had been replaced by a modern, bicameral parliament. Great hopes were tied to this reform, but with franchise being limited to property-owners, hopes were dashed. Instead of the old society based on privilege a new economic class society arose, and large groups of the population, such as the working class, were without political influence. Over the representation in the new parliament, whose real will to reform society proved to be minimal, there arose strong feelings of betrayal in the radical camp; and it is to a significant extent from such sentiments that the literature of the modern breakthrough developed in Sweden. The young writers around 1880, who can be mainly said to have continued the radical efforts that characterized literature at the middle of the century and who gathered together under the designation *Det Unga Sverige* (Young Sweden), concentrated mainly on critical writings, directed against established society and its conservatism in social and political issues. On the general political level too, this polarization became very pronounced. Within the growing labor movement, social and economic injustices led to intensified activity, including several strikes. The great strike in Sundsvall in 1879 became the signal for a more concentrated and organized activity. It was in the 1880s that the Swedish Social Democratic Party emerged, becoming a national party in 1889. It was modeled on German reformist and revisionist social democracy and its leading light was the young journalist, Hjalmar Branting. The labor movement got its own daily newspaper in 1885, the *Social-Demokraten*, of which Branting soon became editor-in-chief. The union movement also finally caught on in the 1880s, both on the local and the national level, for certain categories of workers. A nationwide trade union confederation was formed in 1898. There were often clear links between this political labor movement and the young authors. Branting himself was interested in literature and had some contact with Strindberg as early as the 1870s. Thus, the modern breakthrough for Swedish literature in its initial phase was linked to political developments which, at least in part, would be continued during later phases when artistic trends were less oriented toward social and political issues.

Sweden's Nordic neighbors were also very important for the modern breakthrough. In Denmark as well as in Norway, literary ideas were ahead of those in Sweden and stimulated the Swedish literary world. From Denmark, Georg Brandes—as well as his brother Edvard—exercised an enormous influence as a literary critic with his catch-word about "putting problems under debate" and his theses about the new literary modernity. When, in a series of lectures in Copenhagen in 1888, he propounded Nietzsche's new individualism and superman theories, they quickly penetrated the Swedish literary climate and in a short time transformed the literary atmosphere. From Norway, Ibsen's drama exercised an equally authoritative influence, especially *A Doll's House*, and writers like Bjørnson, Jonas Lie, Alexander Kielland and others rapidly aroused great interest. The connections with Norway were natural, since the two countries were at this time still united. When the modern breakthrough occurred in Sweden, the personal contacts with Danish and Norwegian fellow writers were close and meaningful, both in the form of personal acquaintances and correspondence. The pan-Nordic author contacts were especially important when Scandinavian writers settled abroad and transferred their artistic activity to an international cultural sphere. The Scandinavian writer colonies in world metropolises such as Berlin and Paris played an indisputable role in laying the foundations of European Modernism during the last two decades of the nineteenth century. Spurred on above all by the international successes of Ibsen's dramas, they tried to win for themselves a stronger place in the European book market or theater life by writing directly in the great cultural languages. Strindberg especially, wrote several of his important works in French. Ola Hansson tried to launch himself into German literary life in a similar way. Nordic literature's unexpected advance could not be more clearly demonstrated than when Scandinavian writers gave up their mother tongue in their efforts to become Europeanized. Neither before nor since has Nordic literature so concretely manifested itself in an international context as during this period—even if its direct importance should not be exaggerated.

However, the factors peculiar to social, political and cultural conditions in the Scandinavian countries are hardly an adequate explanation for Nordic literature's sudden appearance on the stage of world literature. Individual successes like those of Brandes and Ibsen created an increased demand for Nordic theater and literature. Nordic literature was a sought-after novelty that aroused interest and curiosity, a sort of literary exoticism that created a boom for a short time. However, it also embraced a handful of authors who would prove to have a lasting greatness, especially Ibsen and Strindberg. If one examines content, program and means of expression, "the Nordic Renaissance"—as people sometimes called this literary upswing—shows not so much originality as participation in contemporary international idea and art trends. It appears as an energetic and independent manifestation of already extant, aggressive ideas within European nineteenth-century culture rather than as an original contribution built on national cultural features. It is to a high degree a question of an interaction, in which continental stimuli were exploited, transformed and given a creative expression that in its turn exercised a positive influence on an international literary climate. In the contemporary idea movements which laid a foundation for the modern breakthrough in literature, August Comte's Positivism, with its faith in reason and science, combined with evolutionist theories of Darwin's biological type and Herbert Spencer's historical-philosophical type and with the various strains of socialism. In the Swedish debate and literature of the 1880s, socialist and anarchistic ideas played an important role and paved the way for a strongly socio-critical stance that often bore utopian features. Literature acquired models mainly from the realistic tradition and from the new Naturalism. Dickens, who had already made an impact on Swedish literature by the middle of the nineteenth century, still played an important role, but stronger were the influences from French literature, above all Flaubert and the brothers Goncourt. Zola's Naturalism, with its unflattering social and human portrayals and its scientific claims, also left its mark. Of the great Russian writers it was only Turgenev who at this time provided impulses and inspired a more impressionistic style, while certain socio-satirical influences came from the new American literature, for example from Mark Twain.

Thus the literature of the 1880s was characterized by a socio-realistic and socio-critical attitude that also had a strikingly strong feminist element that strove for female emancipation. Toward 1890, however, strong changes took place in literary ideas. These were brought about in particular by the discovery of Nietzsche's antipositivistic reaction, his subjective individualism and superman theories and his artistic primitivism—proliferated by Brandes. In a climate with greater emphasis on art and the individual, one can distinguish a late naturalist trait, where attention is focused on the individual's emotional life and on psychological border zones. Here, Strindberg and Ola Hansson played prominent roles outside Scandinavia. In Swedish literature, however, this internationally common feature was superseded by a movement of a more national character, which in its worship of art took inspiration from Swedish nature and the Swedish provinces. To a high degree this was in keeping with the new wave of patriotism that emerged toward the turn of the century in cultural as well as in political life. Its attitude toward national motifs, saga and legend, nature and beauty, provides an argument for calling it Neoromanticism, even if its interest in the philosophy of art, nature and history was clearly weaker than during Romanticism proper. Thus the Swedish literature of the 1890s took on an entirely different profile from that of the 1880s, and by tradition the writers of the eighties with their socio-realistic attitude are usually contrasted with the writers of the nineties with their national, artistic and individualistic ideals. However, the designations "eighties" and "nineties" cannot in a later perspective be seen as strictly demarcated, since the tendencies overlap and the continuity is always very strong. Strindberg, as mentioned, very clearly followed the trends just like other writers of the eighties, while several of the writers of the nineties have significant roots in the ideals of the 1880s.

Swedish literature of the nineties has clear parallels with European Symbolism, even if a direct influence cannot be traced. Only toward the turn of the twentieth century did the literary climate become more aesthetic, in the spirit of French Symbolism, and *fin de siècle* sentiments such as decadence, mysticism and occultism were embraced by many younger writers. It is not a question of any unambiguous aesthetic turn-of-the-century atmosphere, however. A few of the new writers cultivated a somewhat disillusioned intellectualism emanating from the anti-Christian writings of the radicals of the eighties, while others experienced no difficulty in combining the new lyrical subjectivism with their contacts with political radicals and the social democratic press. The first decade of the twentieth century was a period of politically radical awakening. A civil rights movement was successfully reducing restrictions in the legislation on political franchise and the labor movement was energetically striving for increased economic and political influence. Its ambitions culminated in the Great Strike of 1909—a temporary defeat for the union movement which was nevertheless eventually followed by a significant breakthrough in the political efforts of the labor movement. Shortly after the Great Strike, in the years immediately before Strindberg's death, the so-called Strindberg feud broke out. On the surface this was a struggle for literary hegemony between the writer of the eighties, Strindberg, and the writer of the nineties, Heidenstam, but it actually came to reflect the profound conflicts between the interests of the middle class and the new working class. Strindberg and the ideas of the eighties were favored by the working class and it was they who emerged as the winners. Thus things had come full circle and it was again time for the original ideas of the modern breakthrough. However, by the years around 1910, Swedish literature was affected by new impulses from the Continent, including the emerging modernist movements, and the time had come for a new phase of literary history.

August Strindberg

There was not much in the cultural climate to indicate that a great figure of world literature would emerge in Sweden at the end of the nineteenth century; August Strindberg (1849–1912) arrived with all the explosive force of the unexpected. Yet Swedish nineteenth-century literature had earlier seen many prominent writers. There was an international dimension to the literary contributions of both Tegnér and Stagnelius, and the former acquired a certain fame abroad. Fredrika Bremer was already an international celebrity as an author during her lifetime, and Almqvist should rightly have been one—if any Swedish writer before Strindberg belongs to world literature then it is he. However, none of these had anything like the force of Strindberg, nor did they turn out to attract such lasting attention as he. Certainly his literary dimensions were only appreciated to a limited extent in the Sweden of his time; Swedish cultural life was entirely too narrow to accept such an unruly and intransigent exotic bird as Strindberg, and in his homeland full recognition of his contribution came relatively late. But in an international context his significance very soon became clear, and the following generations of great writers and modernistic pioneers, for example Kafka, Eugene O'Neill and Henry Miller, were considerably influenced by his authorship. The real period of greatness for his writing, however, did not come until the middle of the twentieth century, when world-wide interest snowballed and when above all his drama struck a chord with the sense of absurdity generated by the age. Only then did his literary status grow in Sweden, until he rose to the position of a brilliant and indisputable national literary saint.

However, Strindberg's stature has often been questioned.

For the most part the "abnormal" sides of his personality and writing have then been stressed and rejected as deviations and madness. He has also been the subject of psychiatric studies, foremost being that by Karl Jaspers. But his psychological insights have also been a point of departure for Adler's power-centered psychology, and on the whole twentieth-century man has increasingly been able to identify with the psychological experiences conveyed by Strindberg with such hypersensitive sharpness. His growing greatness lies above all in the fact that his picture of life is increasingly recognized as authentic and that in a way he appears as a pioneer in registering and expressing the sweeping changes in man's consciousness brought about by the new insights and ideas of, for example, Marxism and Darwinism, and by the growing industrialized mass society. This extreme sensitivity of consciousness, this intuitive ability to unmask man's social facade and inner psychic movements was perhaps Strindberg's foremost tool in attaining exceptional artistic results. But his significance cannot be reduced to this. What gradually surprises one about Strindberg is the immense expanse, versatility and receptivity of his talent. He was not only active in practically all areas of literature, he devoted his energy also to visual art—to a more modest extent, certainly, but again using pioneering forms. He made music and experimented with photography. He had a passionate interest in natural science that drove him to charlatan and unproductive experiments, and in the humanities he was active among other things as a cultural historian and language researcher, specializing in Chinese.

The Swedish national edition of Strindberg's work begun in 1980 will comprise some seventy volumes, a literary breadth and versatility that few other authors in the past hundred years could exhibit. His most important area of activity was indisputably drama, where he produced historical plays in the Shakespeare tradition, classically balanced idea dramas and fairy-tale plays, pioneering naturalistic contemporary dramas and equally original symbolistic works in the form of intense and absurdist chamber plays. His pioneering contribution to Swedish prose is almost equally significant and revolutionary. The main feature is a naturalistic narrative prose with easy dialogue and with stress on human and social depiction, in which socio-critical, analytical and satirical elements emerge with an unconventional and provocative sharpness. Equally strong is Strindberg's ability to convey in prose form natural lyrical impressionism and a popular grotesque, inner landscapes of symbolistic, indeed almost surrealistic, character, and historical or autobiographical plots which are as packed with facts as they are subjective. His poetic contribution is considerably less but just as progressive in its unconventional freedom of form. In addition, there are essays on literary and cultural history, travel depictions and a substantial quantity of scientific—or rather quasi-scientific—writing, together with, last but not least, an abundant correspondence of considerable literary value. A number of ideas, literary trends, and attitudes toward life emerge from within the frame of this unceasing and varied literary activity: Rousseauianism, Darwinism, socialism, anarchism, Naturalism, Nietzscheanism, Symbolism, occultism, Swedenborgian mysticism, the spirit of religious conversion—to mention just some of them. Not least because of the rapid changes within this eclectic spectrum of ideas, Strindberg emerges as a frantically searching modern author and human being.

It is perhaps surprising that this hypersensitive, tumultuous and uninhibitedly expansive talent came from a relatively simple middle-class Stockholm environment at the end of the nineteenth century that certainly provided a good cultural background but hardly more. His father was a steamboat broker who had married a waitress. This social divide at home came to play a considerable role in Strindberg's world of ideas and was the source of the title of his autobiographical novel *Tjänstekvinnans son* *(The Son of a Servant)*, which reflects his haunting lack of social self-esteem. Even if it is written in darker colors than the actual reality, it gives the reader a meaningful picture of Strindberg's own psychology and of the violent collision between a dynamically inquisitive and receptive talent and a constant feeling of social inferiority in the various social milieus he encounters. During his youth he was torn between a short-lived religious awakening, social-utopian commitment and scientific aspirations. In spite of his intellectual ability he failed to take a degree. Tutoring and teaching provided only sporadic stimulation. His attempt to establish himself as an actor was also a failure, something that seems to have left him with a lasting feeling of bitterness. His earliest attempts at writing drama also met strong resistance from theater directors and publishers, even if a couple of them were actually staged at the Royal Dramatic Theater in Stockholm. As a whole, there is little of note in Strindberg's youthful dramatic production, even if titles like *Fritänkaren* (The Freethinker) and *Den fredlöse (The Outlaw)* are early indications of the author's leaning toward radical extremes. More striking is the initial failure of the work that he ambitiously had hoped would be his breakthrough: *Mäster Olof (Master Olof)*. It was written in the summer of 1872 on the island in the Stockholm archipelago that was to be the setting for the successful novel *Hemsöborna (The People of Hemsö)*. With *Master Olof* Strindberg gave Swedish drama a play that, through its intense and living dialogue and its lively, apposite historical tableaux, broke with the rather meager native drama of the earlier nineteenth century. The inspiration for this dynamic work about the Swedish reformer Olaus Petri came above all from Shakespeare's historical plays, but Goethe and Schiller also played an important role. Historically, the freely adapted action reflects both the contemporary world of ideas and problems and the young poet's inner life. At the center stands the weak and compromising Master Olof, flanked by the pragmatic King Gustav Vasa, who ruthlessly exploits the Reformation for his own purposes, and the implacably consistent anabaptist Gert Bokpräntare, who sacrifices his life with relentless radicalism and contemptuously rejects Master Olof's half-heartedness in the final rejoinder: "Apostate!" The play's characters are characterized by a charged and aggressive dialogue that would later become Strindberg's hallmark as a dramatist, and even the lesser roles display considerable psychological credibility. After the play was refused by the Royal Dramatic Theater, Strindberg tried without success to rework it. He even versified the drama in rhyme, a version published in 1878 without success. Only in 1881, after his real breakthrough as a writer, could the original prose version be performed and published.

In somewhat desperate circumstances, Strindberg held

various jobs during the 1870s. He earned his living as a journalist for a time, thereby gaining good insights into contemporary Swedish society. His social position improved when in 1874 he was employed as an assistant at the Royal Library in Stockholm. A few years later he married the actress Siri von Essen and started a family. During the 1870s he increasingly tried his hand at prose, and wrote among other things sketches from his student years in Uppsala and from the Stockholm archipelago. The real literary breakthrough did not come until 1879 with the socio-critical novel *Röda rummet (The Red Room)*, which struck literary life like lightning and became a great success. With unrestrained satirical force the author here channelized his strong dissatisfaction with the reactionary turn social developments had taken after the parliamentary reform. The fact that he himself was forced to declare bankruptcy because of the troubled economic times had apparently contributed to the outburst. He exploited his journalistic experiences to portray environments and incongruities. Parliament and bureaucracy, economic fraud, religious deception and more are all treated with irony. Society is presented as an egotistical and unchecked conspiracy of the Establishment and those striving for power; the perspective is throughout socially radical and revelatory. The furious fighting spirit is diluted to some degree, though, by a conciliatory humor and the human weakness of disillusionment in the description of the idealist's failing in this social jungle. With its concrete, lively and intensely individual character, *The Red Room* was epoch-making both for Swedish prose and Swedish literature in general. The milieu depictions are often of a naturalistic character, even if any direct traces of Zola are difficult to demonstrate. There is, however, a clearer influence from Dickens and Twain in terms of characterization and satirical grasp. As a novel, the book is loose and episodic, as if the attack on society were more important than the artistic whole. When Strindberg some years later completed his socio-satirical attack on contemporary Swedish society in *Det nya riket* (The New Kingdom), 1882, he had given up the novel form for a more essayistic presentation with narrative features. His ability to reveal with effective, unchecked irony the humbug, power mechanisms and false facades of the social machinery culminated here. It is a rashly splendid satire with its worm's-eye view of society—and its easily identifiable personal attacks rendered it far from harmless. It made Strindberg's social position more precarious and gave rise to his leaving the country in 1883. In the early 1880s, Strindberg had returned to drama. Of greater interest, however, is his lyrical debut with *Dikter* (Poems), 1883. This collection, that also contained some poetry from his youth, represented a marked rejuvenation of Swedish poetry through its nonchalant and free form, its naturalistic motifs and its brutal vocabulary, all of which now seems fresh and natural in comparison with the period's otherwise stale, idealistic, reminiscent poetry. The writer also found a form in the arena of lyric poetry that corresponded with his radical temperament and offered him new expressive territory and new incursions into the domain of the expression of feelings. The poems have a modern feel and point ahead to twentieth-century lyrical Modernism, as for example the poem "Solnedgång på havet" (Sundown on the Sea), which ends:

> *Sverige ligger som en rök,*
> *som röken av en maduro-havanna,*
> *och solen sitter däröver*
> *som en halvsläckt cigarr,*
> *men runt kring horisonten*
> *stå brotten så röda*
> *som bengaliska eldar*
> *och lysa på eländet.*

> Sweden lies like a smoke,
> like the smoke from a maduro Havana,
> and the sun sits over there
> like a half extinguished cigar,
> but around the horizon
> stand the breakers so red
> like Bengal fires
> and shed light on the misery.

Yet it was narrative prose that mainly occupied Strindberg's interests also in the 1880s. In some works he applied a critical-radical scrutiny to Swedish history, with emphasis on cultural history. Of literary value in these historical writings are the stories in *Svenska öden och äventyr* (Swedish Fates and Adventures) that came out in three volumes, the first in 1882. These deal with contemporary ideas and personal problems in historical guise and with pronounced naturalistic features. Currents of Rousseauianism, socialism, anarchism and Darwinism run through magnificent, vividly sketched milieus. In spite of the free treatment of historical reality they often give a pedagogically effective picture of periods and social conflicts in Swedish history, such as for example the antagonism between town and country in the story "Per och Pål." Strindberg boldly broke with history writing's traditional perspective and in most cases sided with the lower classes. His criticism of civilization turned sharply against all forms of upper-class culture—to the extent that he even criticized the role of the author. In the mid-1880s, his political radicalism moved increasingly towards a utopian, individualistic anarchism. These stories came into existence after Strindberg settled abroad. In 1884, in Switzerland, he began a series of short stories where he dealt with various sexual, sex role and marital motifs as polemics against the main tenets of the women's movement. He published them that year under the title *Giftas (Married)*. In these often artistically brilliant stories he drove naturalistic outspokenness far into an area that at this time was still taboo. This short-story collection became a challenge not only to the women's movement, which regarded Strindberg's attack on "leisured upper-class women" as a betrayal of the radicalism of the eighties, but also to the conservative social establishment as a whole. The book also brought him an indictment—for blasphemous writings about Holy Communion in the short story "Dygdens lön" ("The Rewards of Virtue"), and when Strindberg came home to defend his case in court, he became the object of massive popular ovation as a radical, far-sighted author. Strindberg was acquitted but never recovered completely from this event, and his hypersensitivity, with its tendency to paranoia, increased considerably. Bitterness, not to say animosity, marks the later works in the second volume of *Married*, 1886. It is in these that his famous misogyny appears. The earlier stories still retain a humoristic and quite idyllic character, such as in "Ett dockhem" ("A Doll's House"), an almost cheerful and sociable parody of Ibsen's successful drama that was always referred to in the women's rights debate of the time. The individual psychological and pathological features in some of the later short stories, however, point ahead in Strindberg's development, and he made a progressive incursion into new territory when in one of the stories he painted an understanding picture of male homosexuality.

The new personal, psychological features are also expressed in the series of autobiographical novels with the collective title *Tjänstekvinnans son (The Son of a Servant)*, 1886–87, 1909. Its modernity lies in its auto-analytical energy and audacity, its concentration on following the psychological and social factors constituting "the story of the development of a soul." The work, especially the dark childhood reminiscences of the first part, has also, as mentioned previously, played a certain role in the formation of psychological theory, with its depiction of a socially conditioned inferiority complex and the resulting need to compensate. Rousseau undeniably played a certain role as a model of relentless ego analysis, but a naturalistic documentary technique characterizes the work too. As a novel, *The Son of a Servant* is much more than a story of mental development; it is a richly alive and sharply detailed depiction of time and milieu, in which Strindberg's unceasing anti-idealistic criticism and desire for social unmasking triumphs again and again. In its satirical, chronicle-like and analytically essayistic form with its many strongly emotional features, it is one of Strindberg's very best prose works— perhaps not least because he was able to distance himself from his self-dissection by depicting his alter ego in the third person. It made a great impact on younger writers and started a strong tradition of the autobiographical novel in Swedish literature.

Le plaidoyer d'un fou (A Madman's Defense), 1887, written in French, also belongs to the autobiographical genre. Strindberg's work was increasingly being translated by the middle of the 1880s, and he now chose to write directly in a foreign language. The work was published in French and came in German translation during the 1890s, not appearing in Swedish until 1914 *(En dåres försvarstal)*. This delay might be explained by the fact that Strindberg depicted here his stormy marriage to Siri von Essen with brutal psychological openness, and it has always been read as a sensational *roman à clef*. The form he chose for this frank unmasking of his private life is, however, artistically remarkable. In *The Son of a Servant*, there was one single truth on the psychological plane, in *A Madman's Defense*, the psychological truth is unstable and unsure and ambiguous. Using the subjective first person form the author can create uncertainty in the mental boundary areas inhabited by the desperate protagonist; here he discovers how the contours of his earlier homogeneous "I" are dissolving. *A Madman's Defense* is a bold literary leap into a modern, relativized conception of personality.

In the state of mental anxiety and feverish productivity in which Strindberg found himself at the end of the 1880s, he oscillated between themes. With nostalgic affection while under self-imposed exile abroad, he returned to the Stockholm archipelago of his youth in the novel *Hemsöborna (The People of Hemsö)*, 1887, a naturalistic, Darwinist drama with popular, humorous features set in a barren coastal environment. This sturdy depiction of everyday life is one of his best novels—and incomparably the most popular. It has become something of a Swedish national novel. A freely dramatized version of the story, which went still further in popular burlesque humor, did not acquire nearly as great a popularity. The archipelago motif is also found in the stories in *Skärkarlsliv* (Skerrymen's Lives), 1888, of which "Den romantiske klockaren på Rånö" (The Romantic Parish Clerk at Rånö) is the best known. With boldly visionary means Strindberg depicts here a dreamer who seeks refuge from harsh reality in music, which becomes his true life. This story attests to the new, more aesthetically oriented literary climate at the end of the decade, while the historical short story *Tschandala*, 1889, attests to other features in the new artistic winds; it is characterized by Nietzscheanism and radical lines of thought. However, the influence of Nietzsche, with whom Strindberg corresponded and whose philosophy he discovered at a time when his utopian socialism had cooled significantly, is most obvious in the archipelago novel *I havsbandet (By the Open Sea)*, 1890, one of his most remarkable works in an international perspective. The naturalistically sketched archipelago milieu has here been transformed into a symbolic setting for the barren and hallucinatory drama of fate that constitutes the novel's action, and in which a psychologically frail intellectual aristocrat, the fishery superintendent Borg, goes under in the harsh, naturebound archipelago life when he steers his boat right out to sea in the direction of the constellation Hercules. With both *A Madman's Defense* and *By the Open Sea*, Strindberg created novels that can be designated pioneering contributions to the emergence of the modernist, twentieth-century novel.

However, Strindberg's foremost contribution at the end of the 1880s was in the field of drama. His naturalist "tragedies" were milestones in international literary history and dramatic art. Very conscious of his medium, he tied in to classical drama and classical demands for unity, while allowing the modern action to be permeated by the naturalistic and psychological theories of the time. His first great contemporary drama, *Fadren (The Father)*, 1887, a charged depiction of how a man is mentally broken down by the suspicion that he is not the biological father of his children, is reminiscent of both classical tragedy and works such as Shakespeare's *King Lear* and *Othello*. Linking up with his earlier sex role theme, the woman is depicted as the driving force behind this mental murder, while at the same time the drama illustrates the undermined position of the patriarchal society. The work was translated into French, with Strindberg receiving a congratulatory letter from Zola himself. The next naturalistic play was *Fröken Julie (Miss Julie)*, 1888, his best known and probably most frequently performed drama. He observed here the classical unities of time and space while also, in line with modern psychology, aiming at presenting the main characters not as complete personalities but as fragments, as accidental products of inherited and social circumstances. At the same time, something unmistakably Swedish—with traits of sturdy Swedish popular comedy—hovers over this midsummer night. Julie, the emotionally deprived young noblewoman from the manor house, allows herself to be seduced by the cynical and ambitious servant, Jean. Incapable of following her instinct to the bitter end, Julie is urged to take her own life. In this well-composed and dreamlike one acter, the popular idyll of the midsummer night is effectively contrasted with the implacably tragic event over which the main characters have no control. *Fordringsägare (Creditors)*, 1889, gives a tragicomic version of the same triangle relationship dealt with in *A Madman's Defense* and takes up the contemporary psychology of suggestion and the demonized view of women typical of the time.

Strindberg's inspiration ebbed for a time during the 1890s. However, his personal life provided plenty of drama, and on the inner plane he went through some remarkable changes that came to influence his later writing in a decisive way. After having spent the years around 1890 in Sweden, he moved abroad again in 1892, more precisely to Berlin. He was driven there by loneliness after his divorce and by a literary atmosphere at home that he found hostile and distasteful. He was also encouraged by his fellow writer Ola Hansson, who had begun to establish himself as a writer in Germany. In Berlin he led a stormy, bohemian life, typical of the time, among German, Polish and Scandinavian artistic circles. These included the Norwegian artist Edvard Munch. Strindberg got married, for a second time, to an Austrian journalist, a marriage, though, which was not long-lived. Disillusioned with literature, he devoted himself mainly to rather dilettantish and unproductive scientific experiments and speculations. Fruitless ambitions to establish himself as a man of science and alchemist also characterized his stay in Paris, where he moved in 1894. However, several of his dramas were staged there, including *Miss Julie* and *The Father*, and for a short time he attracted significant attention and made contacts with French cultural life and artist circles. However, for the most part he lived in a mentally taxing solitude that led to a series of mental crises, the so-called Inferno crisis. This was marked by strong elements of occultism and mysticism—documented in the diary Strindberg kept during these crisis years—and led to an upheaval in his view of life which resulted in a greater religious element in his writings. This path led him via the problem of Orestes' guilt and revenge, to Dante's wandering through hell and above all to Swedenborg's correspondence idea and spiritual visions of life as an institution of penitence and correction. His spirit of revolt and zeal for world improvement were transformed into submission to a belief in a strict world order where every being is punished for his self-assertion and for his spiritual crimes and where only the insight that these crimes must be atoned for leads to improvement and trust. Strindberg first formulated these crisis experiences in the prose work *Inferno*, written in French and published in Swedish in 1897. Considered a novel of spiritual development, this work is original in its free formulating of psychic experiences and by the role given to chance in a reality whose contours increasingly begin to dissolve and be replaced by a many-layered myth structure. Its bold modernity has exercised a significant influence on more recent writers. The stories in *Legender (Legends)* were written shortly thereafter. This collection of religious examples presents a series of portraits of conversion, intended to illustrate how divine world order intervenes in people's lives.

However, Strindberg gave his foremost literary expression of the Inferno experiences in drama form. With the trilogy *Till Damaskus (To Damascus)*, 1898, 1904, he created a work that can be said to have launched expressionist drama. In spite of a certain realistic depiction of milieu, the action here is entirely set on an inner plane, where roles as well as stage-properties are symbolic projections of the consciousness of the main character (The Unknown). The three dramas depict his dreamlike wandering through a hell-like existence, punctuated by the intervention of divine providence which will lead him to conversion and atonement. The scenes change with the whim and hallucinatory sharpness of a dream, while the drama's artistic unity is achieved with accomplished symmetry. *Advent (Advent)*, also from 1898, is a fairy-tale and mystery play in tune with Strindberg's new ideas, where the naive idyll contrasts with a brutal presentation of the nature of evil. In *Brott och brott (There are Crimes and Crimes)*, 1899, the theme was presented in the form of French comedy, while *Påsk (Easter)*, which appeared in 1900, is a medieval morality play in a modern Swedish small-town environment. The setting was based on the university town Lund, to which Strindberg had returned after the most severe of the crisis symptoms had eased, and before he settled down in his childhood Stockholm for the rest of his life. In *Easter*, the dark themes of crime and guilt make way for a more conciliatory resolution. The medieval fairy-tale play *Svanevit (Swanwhite)*, 1901, a distant, chivalric ballad written in a style typical of the time, is close to the symbolic drama espoused by Maeterlinck. A brutal contrast to this drama is *Dödsdansen 1–2 (The Dance of Death 1–2)*, 1901, to a certain degree a return to the naturalistic drama with its unity of time and place, but at the same time a furious and absurd unmasking of a static marital hell that takes on the stamp of the unreal. It points ahead to modern absurdist drama and has been greatly acclaimed in the post-war period.

Ett drömspel (A Dream Play), which was completed in 1902, represents the summit of this busy period of playwriting. It is Strindberg's perhaps most remarkable work, and he himself called it, with some oft-cited words, "my most loved drama, the child of my greatest pain." In this drama about philosophies of life, he succeeds better than earlier in integrating his new drama form with his view of life, which combined Schopenhauer-like pessimism with heroic harmony. The play assumes the unpredictable movements and transformations of the dream and requires constant scene changes and metamorphoses on an open stage. The language is lyrical and irrational and the action marked by unexpected appearances. An evocative and magical unreality is fused with the uncheckable course of events characteristic of the dream. The work can be seen as a long dramatic poem that in elegiac form expresses resignation to the sufferings of existence, conveyed in its best known and oft-repeated line: "Man is to be pitied." The main figure in the drama is the daughter of the Indian god Indra, who descends to earth in order to participate in human life. Everywhere she finds torment and shattered illusions: in the cheerful and naive officer patiently waiting in the autumn of his life for his sweetheart, the actress Victoria; in the poor lawyer with humanitarian leanings; in the perceptive poet. Behind the manifold incarnations and settings characteristic of the dream lie constant, subtle allusions to Strindberg himself and his life. The play ends in an Indian-style mysticism of suffering, in which suffering is seen as redemption and death as the liberator; Indra's daughter leaves her temporary earthly guise in order to take the people's lamentations before the eternal being. It is not without interest that this is delivered in a Shakespearean blank verse:

> O, nu jag känner hela varat's smärta,
> så är det då att vara människa...
> Man saknar även det man ej värderat,
> man ångrar även det man icke brutit...
> Man vill gå bort, och man vill stanna...
> Så rivas hjärtats hälfter var åt sitt håll,
> och känslan slits som mellan hästar
> av motsats, obeslutsamhet, disharmoni...

Oh, now I feel the agony of existence!
So this is to be mortal.
One even misses what one did not value.
One even regrets crimes one did not commit.
One wants to go, and one wants to stay.
The twin halves of the heart are wrenched asunder
And one is torn as between raging horses
Of contradictions, irresolution, discord.

After his crisis, Strindberg went through a period of astonishing literary inspiration, where he managed to write a long series of historical plays. He revived the Shakespearean historical drama by integrating his own theme of penitence in many forms into his diversified presentation of historical personalities and settings. *Folkungasagan (The Saga of the Folkungs)*, 1899, gives a darkly evocative picture of the Swedish Middle Ages, where the problem of penitence is centered around King Magnus Eriksson and Saint Birgitta. *Gustav Vasa (Gustavus Vasa)*, from the same year, gives a popular, powerful picture of the founder of the Swedish kingdom, where the painting of history is executed in lighter colors and where the main character in effect does not make his first entry until the third act. In *Erik XIV (Erik XIV)*, also from 1899, Strindberg found a psychologically weak hero with whom he himself could identify. Theatrically, *Gustav Adolf (Gustav Adolf)*, 1900, belongs to the most remarkable of these historical dramas, due to its epically narrative theatrical technique which can be said to fore-shadow Brecht's epic theater. However, because of its considerable length—it takes some six hours to perform—it has never attained any theatrical success. *Kristina (Queen Christina)*, 1903, gives an unhistorical but interesting portrait of the cultured queen which has certain similarities with Miss Julie. By 1901, when Strindberg wrote *Karl XII (Charles XII)*, his dramatic art had shifted more and more towards the moods and first person reflections of symbolist drama. This was most clearly noticeable in the historically and psychologically bold portrait of *Gustav III (Gustav III)*, 1903, which deviates strongly from the traditional, idealized picture of the glorious "charmer king." These later historical dramas rejuvenate the genre by presenting the action as a dreamlike event and by the typical Strindbergian symbol machinery working to full effect in the historical course of action.

But Strindberg also found time to devote his attention to the other genres during this later period. His new poetry, collected under the title *Ordalek och småkonst (Word Plays and Miniatures)*, 1903, has a more symbolic, musical character than earlier and coincides thereby with the much stronger lyrical stamp that he gave his late dramas. Dramatic sketches also lie behind large-scale creations like "Trefaldighetsnatten" (The Night of Trinity) and "Holländaren" (The Dutchman). However, the main number in this poetry is the subjectively elegiac sequence "Chrysaetos," which arose from his feelings of isolation after the failure of his third marriage—to the actress Harriet Bosse. A strongly effective symbolic art makes this poem sequence deeply moving and manifestly original. During these years, moods of loneliness and forlornness often hover over Strindberg's work, as for example in the meditative little prose book *Ensam* (Lonely), 1903, where the Stockholm exteriors take on a magical, dreamlike character through an impressionistic prose with symbolistic affinities. In a slim volume he also devoted his attention to the fairy tale—in imitation of Hans Christian Andersen, but with clear personal and timebound *fin de siècle* features. From 1904 on, when the theatrical situation became less favorable for Strindberg's drama, he again went over to social depiction with Balzac as a model. It

August Strindberg. Portrait by Richard Bergh, 1905.

was now more permeated by his new spiritual-mythical conception of reality, and the satire is marked by a lowering sombreness. *Götiska rummen* (The Gothic Rooms), 1904, was intended as a companion-piece to *The Red Room*, and some of the persons in the earlier novel return here in an ever more mercilessly penetrating light. The most outstanding in this new series of social depictions is the novel *Svarta fanor* (Black Banners), which did not appear until 1907 although it was written much earlier. It became Strindberg's perhaps most notorious work, maybe chiefly because of the fact that the figures were easily identifiable from real life. His vehement misanthropy, his bitter antipathy to the disguises and power struggles of social man, his unchecked impulse to unmask and dissect reach a peak here. In the eyes of posterity, when it is no longer seen as a sensational *roman à clef*, this novel appears as modernly innovative in its resolute and surrealistic representation of life as a socio-biological machinery behind illusory facades. The two short novels *Taklagsöl* (Roof Framing Feast) and *Syndabocken (The Scapegoat)*, 1906, are also highly original. Strindberg himself called them chamber plays in prose form. *Taklagsöl* in particular is a prosaic dream play in its presentation of an ailing man's confused inner monologues, in which life is an elusive riddle, a series of ghost-like fragments. *The Scapegoat* is a more unified, small-town story of earthly suffering which calls to mind the biblical story of Job. Also belonging to Strindberg's late prose are his "blue books," collections of disparate memoranda on various subjects, perplexing ideas in the field of natural science and occultism, interspersed with impressionistic prose poems. These are still largely terra incognita in Strindberg's immense œuvre, the mysterious terrain of which has not yet been adequately mapped.

However, Strindberg made his last really significant contribution in the area of drama, with the so-called chamber plays: *Oväder (Storm)*, *Brända tomten (The Burned House)*, *Spöksonaten (The Ghost Sonata)* and *Pelikanen (The Pelican)*, all from 1907. The birth of these boldly innovative dramas is closely associated with that of the Intimate Theater in Stockholm that year. Here he found a theater that was willing to try to realize his pioneering dramatic ideas. In some open letters to the theater he tried programmatically to set out his view of the modern theater and its potential. It was a scaled-back drama form that preoccupied the writer and which he strove to realize in the chamber plays. Characteristic of these is that environment and stage-properties play the main role, rather than the characters. These rather appear as lost and unreal aliens in a symbolically charged setting, the meaning of which is fully clear while the characters themselves are elusive and without meaning. This reduction of the personality often leads to deformation of human characteristics, as with, for example, the mummy in *The Ghost Sonata*. The language becomes apparently illogical and disconnected, as if its ability to render a meaningful picture of reality were challenged. However, the chamber plays are all very different. While *Storm* is a desolate, subjective mood picture, *The Burned House* has clear points of contact with *A Dream Play* in its resigned lack of illusion. *The Pelican* is a last surreal study of hate in woman's psychology. *The Ghost Sonata* stands out as the foremost and most pioneering of the chamber plays; its influence on the modern development of drama has been almost as great as that of *A Dream Play*. The difference between the two works lies mainly in the fact that *The Ghost Sonata's* mercilessly painful and naked pessimism is without the filter of resignation, so that the work is characterized by a lack of relief and a disharmony. Strindberg's last drama, *Stora landsvägen (The Great Highway)*, 1909, "a drama of wandering with seven stations," attests to a softer placability, where suffering mankind's solitary road is pictured in heightened lyrical visions. This drama—a kind of deeply experienced swan song that can be compared with Shakespeare's *The Tempest*—has been overlooked by posterity in spite of its beauty.

The very last years of Strindberg's life witnessed a decline in his literary production. During the so-called Strindberg feud (see p. 139), he was again provoked into taking up a political position, characterized by both popular socialism and a broadly humane and artistic anarchism. Since he was not considered for a Nobel Prize by the Swedish Academy, his admirers on the Left collected money for an "anti-Nobel Prize" for him, and at his funeral great bands of workers rallied and paid homage to the old barricade fighter. Thus, paradoxically, the solitary mystic came again to be seen as the champion of the masses. But Strindberg's contribution cannot be summed up simply through such contradictions. It is above all the tumultuous diversity of his work that continues to fascinate readers and theater-goers all over the world. His gigantic literary production cannot be put into formulas or given easy labels. In its enigmatic, many-faceted and apparently inexhaustible vitality, and with its absolute candor, it will undoubtedly continue to attract readers and studies for a long time to come. It is a dynamic testimony to the revolutions the human consciousness was to undergo during the twentieth century and which the century's later writers would continue to tackle in line with the tradition established by Strindberg, that sensitive pioneer.

Young Sweden
Victoria Benedictsson, Ola Hansson

In the shadow of a giant like Strindberg, the other young radical authors of the eighties had trouble in asserting themselves. In the rather loose grouping that appeared under the banner Young Sweden there were, however, a number of talented writers who willingly listened to the new signals of a modern breakthrough and who more or less faithfully adopted the complex of ideas that can be summed up under terms like socialism, Darwinism and Naturalism. Their works represented a breakthrough on a broad front for a de-idealizing depiction of reality and a critical social commitment, and they were involved in lively and acrimonious debates with the social establishment, for example, on questions of women's rights and morality. Like newly formed student alliances such as *Verdandi* in Uppsala and *DUG* (*Den Unga Gubben*—The Young Old Man) in Lund, Young Sweden reflected the radical waves of the time, even if its adherents quickly oriented themselves in other directions during the last years of the century. Many of them had their roots in the Swedish countryside, and their new Naturalism was above all expressed in depictions of everyday life with strong social accents. The social opposition of the eighties was thus infused with an obvious provincialism and also—in the spirit of Brandes and Ibsen—by a strong emphasis on the liberation and development of the personality. In spite of its interest in socialism, the eighties constituted an ideologically very individualistic movement that received a dynamic thrust from the interest in Nietzsche which broke through around 1890. This is especially noticeable in the striking number of women authors of the time, for whom the emancipation of women was central. Especially interesting was Anne Charlotte Leffler (1849–92), who for a time was considered an equally important representative of the young literature as Strindberg, and whose everyday, realistic works with such typical titles as *Sanna kvinnor* (*True Women*) and *Kvinnlighet och erotik* (Femininity and Eroticism) mainly take up the problem of women's rights. Through translations her work acquired a foreign readership, and she had international contacts, for example with

Karl Marx's daughter Eleanor in London. Gradually, through marriage to an Italian duke and professor, she made contact with intellectual circles in Italy. Like the pervasive themes in her books, her life thereby came to represent a liberation from the narrow women's roles of the time.

However, Young Sweden—if you except Strindberg—produced little of lasting artistic value. Two interesting profiles with somewhat looser ties to the group, though, eclipsed the rest: Victoria Benedictsson (1850–88) and Ola Hansson (1860–1925). The former became known under the male pseudonym Ernst Ahlgren, and from her Scanian hometown she wrote stories about everyday life in which Realism was no mere program but based on her own observations. For the women's emancipation theme in her two novels, however, she used her own experiences. When very young she had thrown herself into an ill-matched marriage to an older widower with five children. An attempted suicide during pregnancy had deprived the child she was carrying of life, and an ensuing illness left her an invalid. Against this background her human and literary struggle for independence becomes a more than admirable achievement. *Pengar* (Money), 1885, is a novel of female development, and the psychological nuances of the main character have a certain inner affinity with the author. It ends in a highly personal plea for truth and represents an attack on western marriage. Her other novel, *Fru Marianne* (Mrs. Marianne), 1887, is a kind of dream of an ideal marriage. Her depiction of a pampered, novel-reading woman has often been compared with Flaubert's *Madame Bovary*, but it is rather a novel of personal development, in which the protagonist eventually becomes a model country housewife. In spite of the tendency to overexplicitness, the novel is written with considerable psychological credibility. Her literary successes brought Victoria Benedictsson into closer contact with the leading circles of cultural life in Stockholm and Copenhagen. There she became acquainted with Georg Brandes, an acquaintanceship that on her part became passionate love. She subsequently broke down under the mental strains to which she was subjected and committed suicide. Her own story, therefore, has taken on the character of a tragic legend. Her personally most committed works were the diary sketches she made during her last years, collected for example in the so-called *Stora boken* (The Great Book), and in the autobiographical fragments that were published after her death. In their unchecked self-revelation they are a significant document of her struggle for personal liberation during these critical years.

Ola Hansson also came from Scania. After his student years in Lund, he too began to write stories and sketches about everyday country life in the spirit of Turgenev. But he made his real debut—and his first significant contribution—as a lyric poet. In general, the authors of the eighties had distanced themselves from lyric poetry, associated as this genre was with Romanticism. However, besides Strindberg, a couple of Scanian poets, of whom Ola Hansson was the foremost, attempted a more naturalistic form. In collections like *Dikter* (Poems), 1884, and *Notturno*, 1885, he used the poem both as the poetry of social indignation about the poverty and misery of country people and as a sentimental landscape painting in musically gentle verse. The landscape of the Scanian plains with its verdant foliage and autumnal mists sang out here in a simple, melodic diction that, as much as Strindberg's poetry of the eighties, represented something new in Swedish poetry and formed a new tradition there. In character it is related to the mood painting of French Symbolism, and it gives expression to a mystical affirmation of life of quiet intensity.

However, Ola Hansson left poetry for a while and embarked upon late Naturalism, with psychologically penetrating sketches of life guided by emotion and instinct. In the short stories in *Sensitiva amorosa*, 1887, he gives subtle, advanced analyses in erotic psychology which often dwell upon the deviant and the unconscious and which are based on studies in contemporary psychology. The book was seen as decadent and an offense against morality and was subjected to outspoken criticism. Later, though, it was appreciated for its polished and nuanced expressiveness in descriptions of elusive mental states. A corresponding study in criminal psychology gave rise to the prose sketches in *Parias* (Pariahs), 1890, one of which was dramatized into a one-act play by Strindberg. Ola Hansson was also at this time very active as a promoter of modern international literature, especially French, and without a doubt he stands out as the most individualistic and inventive literary essayist, with an aesthetic-analytical prose that was way above the average during the epoch. Misunderstood by contemporary critics, he sought contact with Strindberg, with whom he shared a devotion to Nietzsche's individualism and superman preaching. For Hansson's part, this new acknowledgement of life—which at the same time was a departure from naturalistic domains—resulted in the Nietzsche-influenced collection of prose poems *Ung Ofegs visor (Young Ofeg's Ditties)*, 1892. Furthermore, he stated his new literary position in the polemical pamphlet "Materialismen i skönlitteraturen" (Materialism in Literature), one of the period's most interesting literary manifestos, where he stresses the importance of intuition and the inner life in general.

About this time, Ola Hansson left the hostile climate in Sweden and settled in Germany, where he quickly established himself as a writer and literary critic. He encouraged Strindberg to do likewise, and the Swedish writers' colony they founded in Berlin became for a short time a lively cultural center that was visited by many German writers, such as Gerhardt Hauptmann, Richard Dehmel and Max Dauthendey. During this brief heyday, Hansson enjoyed a renown that was at least equal to that of his illustrious countryman. However, in 1906, when his success diminished, he left Germany and settled in France. Thereafter followed a restless existence, moving from country to country without being able to establish permanent roots anywhere. He became the true cosmopolitan of Swedish literature, but as in several other cases of Scandinavian emigrant literary romanticism at this time, his life took on increasingly tragic overtones. Isolation from his homeland caused his mental health to waver and his literary production to decline in quality. The conflicts between ruralism and roving cosmopolitanism, between a naturalistic conception of reality and psychological mysticism created interesting tensions in Hansson's writing. In spite of its indisputable dimensions—people have not failed to point out that to a certain extent he anticipated Freud's depth psychology and Henri Bergson's doctrine of intuition—something abortive and unfinished hovers over his authorship as a whole.

Poetry at the Turn of the Century
Heidenstam, Fröding, Karlfeldt, Ekelund

The change that occurred in the literary climate around 1890 resulted above all in poetry gaining a stronger position than previously. After the relatively modest contributions that the eighties made in the field of poetry, a lyrical boom period now followed that can be said to correspond to the poetic heyday under Romanticism at the beginning of the century. At that time, Tegnér, Atterbom and Stagnelius emerged as brightly shining stars on the Parnassus; now Heidenstam, Fröding and Karlfeldt took their places as luminaries in poetry's heaven. Lyricism manifested itself not only in an increased number of high quality poetry collections; it also pervaded narrative prose and gave it a brilliant poetic stamp. It was above all in these two genres, poetry and prose epic, that the writers of the nineties worked.

The changes in literary interests at the time certainly favored poetry. The stress now came to lie on the inner life rather than on the depiction of social reality, on the imagination rather than on detailed observations of reality, and finally on aesthetic evocation and mysticism rather than on political tendency and message. In other respects, for example in the interest in national provincialism, the nineties were more closely tied to the preceding decade. However, while the provincialism of the eighties paid attention to people's lives from a social standpoint, the nineties' depictions of nature and everyday life had a stronger national and aesthetic character, where the study of people's lives acquired a value as an ethnographic manifestation of all that was most Swedish. Even if, to some extent, the radical political efforts of the eighties continued, a conservative spirit gradually became increasingly pervasive. This was expressed in a more nationalistic view of history and in a renewed emphasis on religious values—in both cases with greater stress on aesthetics than on actual political and religious conviction. Instead of social problems, the individual and his conflicts of conscience and self-realization became central. Since many of the points of view that belong to the modern breakthrough were maintained simultaneously, the changes generally meant a widening of motifs, but at the same time a tempering of the social passion that marked the modern breakthrough in its introductory phase.

As pointed out earlier, many of the writers of the eighties heralded the new literary climate around 1890; both Strindberg and Ola Hansson can lay claim to having initiated it early on. However, by tradition people usually point to Heidenstam as the real standard-bearer, partly with the poetry collection *Vallfart och vandringsår* (Pilgrimage and Wander-Years), 1888, partly with the program *Renässans* (Renaissance), 1889. Here, in direct polemics against eighties' Naturalism, Heidenstam pleaded for idealism, joy of life and individualism. Within a short time he acquired a supporter from Young Sweden's ranks, namely Oscar Levertin (1862–1906), who in the eighties had distinguished himself as a fine novelist in line with the radicalism of the period, but at the same time as aesthetically discriminating. However, no new struggle between the new and the old schools arose; the change in climate came about too smoothly for this. On the other hand, Heidenstam's and Levertin's personal hegemony in the literary world was strengthened, and on the whole the book publishers tended—with Strindberg and Ola Hansson in self-imposed exile on the Continent— strongly to favor the young writers. These acquired their own literary organ in the still extant journal *Ord och Bild*. In the daily press they had a forum in *Svenska Dagbladet*, which on the initiative of Heidenstam underwent a progressive reorganization, resulting in a revitalized cultural page. The paper's most brilliant reviewer was Levertin, who made his foremost contribution in the area of literary criticism. But he was also one of the epoch's most esteemed and typical poets, with collections such as *Legender och visor* (Legends and Songs), 1891, and *Kung Salomo och Morolf* (King Solomon and Morolf), 1905. These were characterized by aesthetic motifs and evocative word music, by a romantic-exotic coloring but also by a certain linguistic uncertainty. His somewhat narrow artistic range has caused his poetic star to dim considerably with time.

The new decade's real lyrical figurehead was rather Verner von Heidenstam (1859–1940). All his poetry is pervaded by the aristocratic view of life that was a legacy from the environment in which he grew up, and in many ways he stands

out as a late representative of the manorial culture that had
seen its best days at the turn of the century and was already
becoming anachronistic. After a period of his youth spent in
the Orient and in Rome, wavering between painting and
writing, he made his appearance in the eighties as a typical
radical in both politics and literature, in many ways a kinsman of Strindberg. He was in contact with the latter in
Switzerland, and there arose a lively exchange of ideas
between them, in which Heidenstam's views came increasingly to support individualistic self-fulfillment. A certain
political radicalism nevertheless pursued him from this time
on and did not disappear completely until the so-called
Strindberg feud around 1910, when the once intimate friends
locked in battle. This debate finally drove Heidenstam over
to the conservative camp, where he increasingly took on the
tragic mantle of the dethroned aristocrat.

After eleven years abroad, Heidenstam returned to Sweden in 1887 and made his literary debut the following year
with the collection of poetry *Vallfart och vandringsår* (Pilgrimage and Wander-Years). In its blend of life-affirming
fantasy and naturalistic clarity, it signalled a remarkable
rejuvenation of Swedish poetry. Many of the lively, narrative poems have oriental motifs and are based on various
ideas the poet had acquired during his sojourn in the Orient.
They celebrate lust for life, hedonism, or, as in the well-
known "Moguls kungaring" (The Mogul's Royal Ring), the
game of chance with human existence. The exotic drapings,
however, often conceal a discussion of ideas that is closely
connected to the favorite themes of the eighties. The cycle
"Ensamhetens tankar" (The Thoughts of Loneliness) consists mainly of short mood poetry of the sort Geijer and
Runeberg introduced into Swedish poetry and where
Goethe emerged as the master. These poems can give expression to a nostalgic longing for the childhood home: "I long
for the soil,/ I long for the stones where I played as a child,"
but also to subjective contemplation about the mysterious-
ness of the ego or the transience of love. It is above all with
these short poems and their universal themes that Heidenstam made a lasting contribution.

Heidenstam created one of the nineties' most original
works in the lyrically intense novel of ideas, *Hans Alienus*,

1892, where verse and prose are imaginatively mixed. To a significant extent it is a visionary, historically-loose fantasy in time and space, with an often obscure Symbolism supporting the central idea. Heidenstam's typical poetic prose appears here, hieratic and ceremonious in character; the artistic value of each formulation seems to have been carefully weighed and the episodes are often shaped as static tableaux, as lyrical examples. In this boldly expressive and aesthetically overloaded form, the protagonist embodies the poet's own desire to leave modern western culture's pragmatic consciousness and seek his way as a pilgrim to a fantasy kingdom of beauty and inner contemplation. However, all this is pervaded by an awareness of the unfashionableness of the ideals.

A similar conflict between art and reality permeates many of the poems in the collection *Dikter* (Poems), 1895, where the poet's "neoromantic" renaissance assumes artistically convincing expression. In "Tiveden"—Heidenstam's native region in central Sweden—he gives an extravagantly imaginative depiction of nature while also pointing out that the area of his birth stands clad "in rags and poverty." Idealism appears false, and there is more disdain and contempt in Heidenstam's attitude toward life than earlier. In this emotionally broad and contradictory register the poet's position appears as a sort of Romantic "split." The collection reaches its lyrical and most humanly pure expression in the poem "Jairi dotter" (The Daughter of Jairi), with its longing for the "beyond." However, as a whole, these new poems are more nationally than exotically oriented, and Heidenstam's development during the 1890s steadily approached a much stronger national traditionalism. In his poetry he increasingly assumed the role of popular-national mouthpiece. In the essay "Om svenskarnas lynne" (On the Swedish National Temperament), 1897, he attempted—somewhat in imitation of Almqvist—to sketch a Swedish national character. He was resentfully ironical about the Swede's attraction to everything modern and foreign, "the Germanic race's most cosmopolitan and modernized nation," and about his inability to create his own traditional roots. In the poem sequence "Ett folk" (A People), published in *Svenska Dagbladet* in 1899, he openly appeared as a political tribune, displaying an ideological pluralism in his range of ideas. "Sverige" (Sweden) is intended as a nature and tradition-oriented national anthem; "Åkallan och löfte" (Invocation and Promise) strikes pure Gothic chords in its desire for a war to return the homeland to the greatness of former times, while "Medborgarsång" (Civic Song) takes a clear stand for universal suffrage in the contemporary right-to-vote movement which aimed at abolishing the remaining restrictions: "It is a shame, it's a stain on Sweden's banner/ that civil rights are named money." The ambiguous drift in Heidenstam's public personality appears clearly in this remarkable alloy of the radical and the reactionary.

Heidenstam's historical writings, which began with the lengthy narrative collection *Karolinerna (The Charles Men)*, 1897–98, with motifs from Karl (Charles) XII's Russian campaign at the beginning of the eighteenth century, can be regarded as a manifestation of the new patriotic spirit. In the Swedish hero-king the writer saw the great man who, with strong self-will and not without tragic consequences, represented his people's interests. But the main role is, nevertheless, not played by the king but by the Swedish people themselves, with their will to endure privations during difficult famine years. The somewhat loosely tacked-together collection of stories, with its various perspectives, forms a sort of national-cultural monism, whose heroic patriotism is in harmony with the period's view of history and need for historical consciousness and for outstanding historical figures. It has been Heidenstam's most popular work, and also won acclaim internationally, its nationalism being of a universal type. His historical writing continued with *Heliga Birgittas pilgrimsfärd* (Saint Birgitta's Pilgrimage), 1901, another story about a great and strong personality and its conflicts of conscience. The time-setting of this novel about the Swedish medieval saint and her journey to Jerusalem returned in the novel series *Folkungaträdet (The Tree of the Folkungs)* which consists of *Folke Filbyter*, 1905, and *Bjälboarvet (The Bjälbo Legacy)*, 1907. With the pithy, stylized and symbolically visionary prose that characterizes Heidenstam's stylistic art, he depicted here medieval Swedish society and its growth in a way that made this historical novel cycle into one of his most artistically accomplished works. Primarily for school use, the author also wrote the stories in *Svenskarna och deras hövdingar (The Swedes and Their Chieftains)*, 1908–10, a historical counterpart to Selma Lagerlöf's more geographically-oriented and better-known *Nils Holgerssons underbara resa genom Sverige (The Wonderful Adventures of Nils)*.

After the Strindberg feud, Heidenstam entered a more purely conservative phase, where an anti-democratic aristocracy went hand in hand with cultural pessimism and an advocacy of national defense. On the literary plane, he sought a classically simple poetry of feelings that resulted in the collection *Nya dikter* (New Poems), 1915, generally ranked as his best. In mostly short poems he expresses private emotions far removed from political and other public positioning, and yet with deeply moving, universal themes. He celebrates human life as an incomprehensible miracle in the eternal night, and the memory of life is both intensely joyful and distanced, like an aesthetic impression. Many of these poems belong to the classics of Swedish poetry, for example "Vi människor" (We Human Beings):

> *Vi, som mötas några korta stunder,*
> *barn av samma jord och samma under,*
> *på vår levnads stormomflutna näs!*
> *Skulle kärlekslöst vi gå och kalla?*
> *Samma ensamhet oss väntar alla,*
> *·samma sorgsna sus på gravens gräs.*

> We, who meet some short hours,
> children of the same earth and same wonders,
> on the headland of life surrounded by storms!
> Should we go unloving and cold?
> The same loneliness awaits us all,
> Same sad sighing on the grave's grass.

A poem "Himladrottningens bild i Heda" (The Queen of Heaven's Picture in Heda), which is based on a twelfth-century Swedish church sculpture, clothes its faith in and veneration of life in religious terms; "Gustaf Frödings jordafärd" (Gustaf Fröding's Funeral), written for his fellow poet's funeral, gives a grand and moving portrait of a friend. Heidenstam wrote very little after *Nya dikter* (New Poems).

During the last 25 years of his life, he occupied the position of unproductive writer-prince. In 1912 he was elected to the Swedish Academy, and in 1916 he was awarded the Nobel Prize in Literature. He built a magnificent residence, Övralid, near Lake Vättern, from where he reigned over a Swedish cultural life that had long since renounced his ideas: a literary monument to a past golden age, lacking the strength to realize his creative ideas. At his death he left a few poems, *Sista dikter* (Last Poems), 1942, and some fine autobiographical fragments, *När kastanjerna blommade* (When the Chestnuts Blossomed), 1941.

While Heidenstam and Levertin can be counted as the traditional and conservative cultural skalds of the nineties, Gustaf Fröding (1860–1911)—just like Karlfeldt—has a stronger popular and spontaneous force which has continued to attract readers during the twentieth century. From a more popular cultural standpoint, Fröding can be said to be the foremost national Swedish poet. He was also the poet of the nineties with the strongest footing in the ideas and cultural climate of the eighties. His anti-rhetorical and hypersensitively open poems expressed his warm commitment to the ordinary people and their conditions, while he knew how to compensate for his own sickliness and inadequacies with grand Nietzschean dreams of the superman and a richer realization of life. On closer scrutiny, though, Fröding—just like Karlfeldt—is an erudite poet who in his work moves unhindered over vast traditional fields and obscure associations. In his mental anguish and his social vulnerability, he is a literary kinsman of Verlaine and the other *poètes maudits* who appeared in France at the same time, but he is far from being any easily defined representative of the period—it is the universally humanly naked that lives on in his poetry. All these contradictions make him an unusually exciting poet, whose many different roles are held together by an unmistakably personal, lyrical harmony characterized by scepticism and tenderness, by inner vulnerability and visionary passion, by warm humor and bitter misanthropy.

Fröding belonged to the Värmland foundry environment where Tegnér and Geijer had also had their roots and where Selma Lagerlöf grew up at about the same time. Threads ran between all these illustrious literary families, and in Fröding's case there was also an unhappy legacy of degeneracy and mental illness that clouded virtually his entire adult life. As early as his exceptionally unsuccessful student years in Uppsala, the first signs of brooding, depression, alcoholism and mental disturbance appeared—and Fröding was to spend large parts of his poetic career in mental institutions. As a young student he was mainly attracted to the social radicalism of the eighties, and Strindberg was his great literary discovery. Later on, German nineteenth-century poetry (e.g. Goethe, Heine) would also strongly influence him. In a way typical for the time, he compensated for an adolescence marked by evangelism with a hedonistically dissolute student life that soon consumed an ample inheritance. However, he acquired a certain social stability through employment as a journalist at the politically radical *Karlstadstidningen*, and he became a good newspaper writer, whose chatty articles often contained a certain personal freshness. His literary debut did not come until 1891, when the collection *Guitarr och dragharmonika (Guitar and Concertina)*, in large part compiled during a stay at a German mental sanitarium, appeared to an unusually strong public response. In this there was a long series of appositely humorous poems about everyday life in Värmland, now popular classics in Swedish poetry—"Vallarelåt" ("Herding Song"), "Det var dans bort i vägen" (There Was a Dance on the Roadside), "Jan Ersa och Per Persa" ("Jan Ersa and Per Persa"), "Äktenskapsfrågan" ("The Matrimonial Problem"). The tone of the Song of Songs can be traced in the image of a Värmland girl—in a poem that is influenced by Edgar Allen Poe's lyrical composition technique. But ripples of international culture spread from this Värmland landscape. The eclecticism embraces poems about Xenophon's Anabasis, Apelles in Abdera and Publius Pulcher, Tersites, Mephistopheles and Tolstoy! He uses a clever Persian poetic form, such as in "En ghasel" ("A Ghasel"), where the poet depicts himself as excluded from existence by an inner barrier, and elegantly ironic Baroque pastiches. His imitation of style is masterly and the word-music boldly evocative.

In the next poetry collection, *Nya dikter* (New Poems, largely tr.) 1894, there are poems from Värmland as well as "biblical fantasies" and poems "from near and far." Among the first-mentioned are a Byronesque pastiche of the small town idyll such as "Balen" (The Ball), with its affectionately comical collision between dream and reality, a folkloristic humoresque such as "Bergslagstroll" ("Mountain Trolls"), and a social poem like "Den gamla goda tiden" ("The Good Old Times"), that depicts the hard conditions endured by the foundry smiths. In the popular and dialectal poems, just as earlier, there are echoes of a native popular tradition and of Robert Burns, who was highly admired and translated by Fröding. In other poems the author waxes ironical over the literary dispute between idealism and Realism, and he gives a splendid portrait of Esaias Tegnér, straying in a bishop's sermon into the pagan hedonism of Greek mythology. He wrote a pastiche of Nietzsche's *Zarathustra*, and in the poem "Atlantis" he presented a vision of social collapse in which he juxtaposed contemporary class oppositions with the fate of the legendary sunken island:

Guldet fick makt att förtrycka,
rikmännens kast, en förnäm myriad,
stal millionernas lycka,
åt och drack och var glad,
vann sin förfinings
segrar, och nöden
växte med segrarnas rad.

Så efter mäktiga öden
sjönk och förgicks Atlantidernas makt,
folket, som självt gav sig döden,
ligger i gravarna lagt.
Härligt begåvat,
sjunket förfallet,
sist till sin undergång bragt!

Havet har prytt med koraller
dödsdrömmens stad, där de hänsovne bo.
Solljus likt stjärnskimmer faller
matt över gravarnas ro.
Algernas fiber
grönskande näten
kring kolonnaderna sno.

En gång, ja en gång för oss ock
slocknandets kommande timme är satt.
En gång, ja en gång på oss ock
faller väl slummer och natt,
vagga väl vågor,
lyser väl solens
sken genom vågorna matt.

Gold gat the power for oppression:
Lordlings of Mammon the empire seized,
Stole all the millions' possession,
Squandered in riot and feast.
Luxury's conquests
Won they, and Ruin
Grew as the tale increased.

Then, as the high Gods fated,
Vanished and sank in the gulfing waves
A people to death dedicated—
Sank to their ocean graves:
Splendidly gifted,
Sunken and perished,
Whelmed in the sunless caves.

Thick-set corals are gleaming,
Paving the city of dreams and of sleep:
Sunrays like starlight seeming
Fall on the soundless deep:
Weeds of old ocean,
Twining their fibres,
Over the columns creep.

Some day, ah some day for us too
Dawneth our hour for the quenching of light:
Some day descends upon us too
Sleep and eternal night—
Waves rolling o'er us,
Sunlight that filters
Dim through the waters bright.

With *Stänk och flikar* (Splashes and Rags, largely tr.), 1896, Fröding created his most remarkable and most progressive collection of poetry. In the title poem he gives a kind of program for his poetry, where he stresses the importance of fragmentary impressions. The collection is also full of visionary poems, behind which the poet's hallucinations during his periods of illness can be detected. In "Drömmar i Hades" ("Dreams in Hades"), for example, a broad pagan material is evocatively woven into a primitive symphony of magical chants. Parallel with these images from mental border zones, there are fresh nature scenes, as in "Strövtåg i hembygden" ("Homecoming"), and lively pagan scenes, as in "Gudarna dansa" (The Gods Dance). This Nietzschean vitality culminates in the utopian depiction of a glorious realm of the senses in "En morgondröm" ("A Morning Dream"). The strong erotic openness of this poem, unusual for the period, provoked a scandal and led to an immorality charge of which he was, however, acquitted. The radical and provocative in Fröding's attitudes appears here as a direct continuation of the rebellious cultural position of the eighties. But there is also room for an inner mysticism in these poems, as above all in "Sagan om Gral" ("The Story of the Grail"), where the poet in a hallucinatory vision expresses a sort of monistic mysticism for which the Grail becomes a unifying symbol. Fröding further develops this mystical Grail theme in the remarkable little collection *Gralstänk* (Grail Splashes), 1898, where the poems are condensed and abstract, filled with theosophic speculation and obscure, violently clashing associations, stylistically bold and unconventional. Here Fröding is no longer a popular and accessible poet, he is esoteric, modernistic, dark and tentative, moving in the fringes of human consciousness, such as when he fuses the figures in Shakespeare's *The Tempest* into a "Calibariel" or when he explores a new concept of God in the sequence "Gud?" (God?): "Is there a universal I,/ eternally unchangeable?/ Or just a life all,/ all-spirit?"

The originality was intentional with Fröding. In a poem about the winged horse Pegasus in the collection *Nytt och gammalt* (New and Old, largely tr.), 1897, he gives an in part purely modern, expressionist manifesto for his poetry: "I want to compose boldly, free as the fancy," "my verse will venture what may not be ventured,/ and roll ahead where no one at all may roll." During a period of illness he later wrote the remarkable "Mattoidens sånger" (The Songs of the Mattoid), which were first printed posthumously. In these "sub-human songs," inspired by Indian myth, he tried to reach down to an elemental and lower consciousness in nature: that of the snail, the ant, the wolf, the snake, even that of the green leaf or granite. In form these poems are boldly pioneering in a modernistic way, and naively and sensuously fresh in their basic, immediate perspective. Fröding's writing career was largely over by the turn of the century. He left an extensive literary estate, however, that gives new accents to his writing. Though only slightly more than fifty at his death, he was old and worn out, yet his poetic legacy to the twentieth century was rich and has something to say to everyone. He was both a people's and a poet's poet.

Erik Axel Karlfeldt (1864–1931) had the same dual-footing in popular and in erudite culture as Fröding. Most of his poetry emerges from the peasant culture of his native province of Dalecarlia. Its popular and song-like accents give a universality to the sketches of peasant life, with their closeness to nature and to the changes of life and the seasons. His academic training, which led to posts as a teacher and eventually a librarian, gave his poetry a scholarly perspective, manifested above all in magnificently ornamented Baroque diction, which gives his poems an evocatively archaic ring. As a poet, Karlfeldt is an old-fashioned celebrator of the traditional farming society that had begun to disappear at the beginning of the twentieth century. He appealed strongly to the nationalistic sentiments that defended the life styles and values of agrarian society against the advance of modern industrial society. In time his poetry lost considerably in significance and came to appear as rather exotic even in his own country, but its popularity has hardly diminished over the years. Strong in color, sturdy and close to nature, it stands out even today as the most Swedish of all Swedish poetry.

His debut collection, *Vildmarks- och kärleksvisor* (Songs of the Wilderness and of Love) from 1895, is characterized by a simple lyrical tone and by themes of nature and the countryside that reveal the lyrical craftsman. The introductory poem "Fäderna" ("My Forefathers") takes on a more personal character by stressing the continuity of peasant life through the generations. The poet feels he has betrayed this, but he hopes to be able to compensate with his rural poetry. In other respects his lyric poetry is marked here, as later, by a certain impersonality and paucity of ideas, characteristic of the genre the poet worked in, where the intense feeling for life and nature are central and given a more universal expression. In the poetry collections which followed, *Fridolins visor och andra dikter* (Fridolin's Songs and Other Poems), 1898, and *Fridolins lustgård* (Fridolin's Pleasure Garden), 1901, Karlfeldt expressed his world of ideas through a protagonist who gives vent to the poet's innermost feelings and wishes. Fridolin is an academic who returns to his native soil to become a farmer. He has an exuberant, virile joy of life and a melancholy strain that is not without a certain affinity with the *fin de siècle* climate. He commits himself to the agrarian way of life with an almost hedonistic pleasure with dark undertones and is obviously enchanted by the folkloristic culture by which he is surrounded. Love plays the most important role in Karlfeldt's world of ideas; a long series of poems with erotic motifs, "Intet är som väntans tider" ("Time of Waiting"), "Nu öppnar nattglim sin krona" ("The Jasmine Unfolds"), "Dina ögon äro eldar" ("Your Eyes Are Flames of Fire"), belong to some of the very best love poems in Swedish. The folklore motif culminates with the "Dalecarlian wall paintings in rhyme," appearing in the latter of the two collections. These are based on popular paintings with biblical motifs, "Elie himmelsfärd" ("The Assumption of Elijah"), "Jone havsfärd" ("The Voyage of Jonah"), and the poet has tried with subtle humor to reproduce the naiveté of the original, where the biblical is fused with the Dalecarlian landscape and peasantry:

Här åker sankt Elia upp till himmelens land
i en kärra så blänkande ny.
Han bär gravölshatt och skinnpäls, han har piska i sin hand,
och mot knäna står hans gröna paraply.
/—/

Och nu rullar vagnen uppåt, och Elias breda hand
vinkar avsked åt hans jordelevnads bygd;
och vi se det är ett stycke av vårt eget dalaland
i de drömmande furubergens skygd.

Behold the good Elijah setting out for Zion's land
In a bright new cart so fine to see,
With Sunday hat and leather coat, a stout whip in his hand,
And a green umbrella by his knee!
/—/
So up the wagon's rolling, and the prophet's outspread hand
Is waving toward the earth a last good-by;
And we see that it's a portion of our own Dalecarlia land
That nestles in the wooded mountains nigh.

The Fridolin world is to a certain degree a sort of rural counterpart to Bellman's world of Fredman, filled with an elemental and intense feeling for life, even if more socially stable and closer to the soil. However, after the collection *Flora och Pomona*, 1906, Karlfeldt's poetry became more exclusive and esoteric with a more obvious link to Baroque poetry's figurative splendor. His interest in the Baroque had clear parallels with contemporary French Symbolism and Latin-American Modernism and foreshadowed the re-evaluation of the ideal of Baroque style that occurred during the twentieth century. At the same time his association with the turn-of-the-century's neoromantic and decadent moods became more marked. In poetic roles he represented himself as "the last knight of the lily" and as "the dancer who across the boards spreads the strewn purple leaves with his foot," while the sequence "Häxorna" (The Witches) gave expression to an occult, demonic eroticism of a brand typical of the time. But in these new poems, where the typical tone usually associated with Karlfeldt's poetry has become deeper and darker, the earlier motifs still dominate. He celebrates the past and nature, and in the poem "Träslottet" ("The Wooden Castle") he reshapes his childhood milieu with the sharpness of hindsight. In archaic turns of phrase folk wisdom appears in a perspective that becomes more profound through the study of the folklore of peasant culture.

With the collection *Flora och Bellona*, 1918, Karlfeldt—

after a period of silence—appeared as a critic of the times against the background of the First World War and the Russian Revolution. He saw the war as an appalling consequence of the age's rootless industrial civilization, and he energetically defended his own lyrical territory: "What do we care about the tsar?/ Look at the starling, look at the starling!" He wrote a raging diatribe against the wanton acquisition of land that destroyed the old Swedish villages, while behind the facades of the new democratic society he detected pure demagogery. Thus in his agrarian isolationism he took a strongly conservative stance of hostility to the modern age. The parallel with Heidenstam is clear, but unlike the latter, Karlfeldt remained poetically active to the end. In his final collection of poetry, *Hösthorn* (The Horn of Autumn), 1927, he turned against modern youth and their musical preference for jazz over traditional folk music, while returning to his Dalecarlian motifs and to new songs in praise of nature and the home region. Some of his most powerful lyrical creations appear in this last work: "Sub luna," where the Latin variations on the timeless themes of life, love and death reveal Karlfeldt the scholar, and above all "Höstpsalm" (Autumn Hymn) and "Vinterorgel" ("Winter Organ"), which display a stronger religious faith than earlier. The same is true of the poem "Psaltare och lyra" (Psalter and Lyre) from 1929: "Give us a faith to end with/ secure in dark death."

Karlfeldt had already been elected to the Swedish Academy in 1904, and in 1912 he became its permanent secretary. As such, he came to occupy an official and international position. Karlfeldt's posthumous Nobel Prize may have appeared to be the result of dubious internal politics, particularly since his poetry, from an international point of view, has a relatively narrow, provincial focus with its very specific Swedish folklore. However, behind the many showy picture postcards of nature and countryside and the anachronistic footing in a long-dead peasant culture's customs and values, there is in Karlfeldt a strong and universal feeling for life, a belief in life's eternal fundament that carries far beyond the typical range of provincial poetry. His love poems and his nature motifs have a profound human character whose local footing in time appears accidental. His poems also take the form of a rare, genuine handicraft, as if prompted by an affinity with the peasant culture he was at one with. Karlfeldt's lyrical diction is filled with ringing beauty, metaphorical wealth, novel word formations and archaisms, all molded into a surprisingly varied and yet unified work of art. The seductive magic of his poetry gave rise to the expression "the Karlfeldt danger" in Swedish literature well into the twentieth century, but it is the intense alloy of joy of life, word and art in his rural world of ideas, with its emphasis on motifs of love and nature, that ensures his steady, homespun appeal and makes the fact that it is now essentially out of fashion insignificant.

Vilhelm Ekelund (1880–1949) emerged somewhat later than the poets of the nineties. Born and raised in Scania, he became the bard of the southern province. His earlier poetry revealed him as a Scanian poet in the same provincial tradition that writers of the eighties and nineties had established. Soon, however, the special nature of Ekelund's poetry emerged. Here, turn-of-the-century Symbolism, Impressionism and aestheticism made a stronger impact than earlier in Swedish poetry. He disdainfully turned his back on regional poetry, devoting himself instead to subjective solitude, impressions of nature intoxicated with beauty, and lofty ovations to great poetry and art. Starting with his real debut with the collection *Vårbris* (Spring Breeze), which symptomatically enough came out in the first year of the new century, he published at short intervals seven uncommonly fine collections of poetry, ending with *Dithyramber i aftonglans* (Dithyrambs in Evening's Splendor), 1906. What he published after that in the way of poetry is not extensive; instead he went over to other genres such as the essay and the aphorism. Written over a short period between the ages of 20 and 26, this lyrical achievement constitutes a remarkable and extremely homogeneous collection. Appealing and at the same time obscure, it is consistently marked by high spiritual and artistic temperature, classically self-contained as well as ecstatic and melodious. Ekelund did not win the public's favor as did Fröding and Karlfeldt, but more clearly than any other poet at the turn of the century he wrote a poetry that signified something lyrically pioneering and fertile for future poetry. With his free verse and his musically impressionistic diction he became a brilliant model for the twentieth century's modernist poets.

It is in collections like *Syner* (Visions), 1901, and *Melodier i skymningen* (Melodies in Twilight), 1902, that the individualistic tone of Ekelund's poetry begins to appear more clearly. Intoxicated with beauty and with soft melancholy he celebrates the forest, plain and coast of the Scanian landscape, and he sketches its light with a mild yet bold impressionistic palette. In a serene ode to beauty he gives expression to an enraptured aesthetic mysticism, but he can also complain in desperation that words cannot adequately capture the experiences of beauty; Ekelund's poems often express near silence, the unspeakable. Other poems are marked by solitude, gloom, fatigue and melancholy in the spirit of Verlaine. However, light is still the stronger element in his poetry, and his verse often has an Apollonian, hymn-like character. While the earliest landscape images came from a discovery of Ola Hansson's poetry, Hölderlin, Stagnelius and Stefan George increasingly become models for his ecstatic cult of beauty, and the countryside takes on a more intimate character and becomes the expression of a hypersensitivity and an intense and fragile mental state. In the next collections, *Elegier* (Elegies), 1903, and *In Candidum*, 1905, Ekelund developed a lyrically nuanced language of feelings in which he could give expression to his nervous vulnerability and violent swings between ecstasy and despair. These are unusually pure and clear and painfully intense expressions of feeling, especially in poems where he celebrates a platonic eroticism. But pictures of cities, stemming from trips to Berlin and Venice, also became more common and could—as in a poem called "Staden" (The City)—give rise to a collective, mystical communion.

In *Havets stjärna* (The Star of the Sea) and *Dithyramber i aftonglans* (Dithyrambs in Evening's Splendor) from 1906, a classical dithyramb form appears, solemn and archaic, but also modernly associative and condensed. The latter collection in particular represents the mature culmination of Ekelund's poetry. The classical, hymn-like tone is sometimes interrupted by an expressionistic radicalism, but as a rule forms an intense fusion of feeling for nature and cultural tradition, as in the poem "Havet" (The Sea):

O tillflykt, säkra ro!
Hur själen än har tröttnat,
du ständigt dock, o hav,
i härlighet är nytt.
Hur månget hjärta glömt
vid denna djupa syn,
Hur mången själ har stillnat!
Och mänsklighetens ädle, tankens
och sångens väldige, ha mättat sina själar,
o heliga, av dina brus, som sjunga
i morgonbrus ur Pindaros och mörkna
med Psaltaren till väldigt aftonbrus!

O refuge, secure repose!
However the soul has grown weary,
you steady though, O sea,
in splendor are new.
How many a heart has forgotten
at this profound sight,
How many a soul has quieted!
And humanity's noble, thought's
and song's powerful, have appeased their souls,
O holy, from your roar, that sings
in the morning roar from Pindaros and darken
with the Psalter to a powerful evening roar!

The strong classical orientation that appears in *Dithyramber i aftonglans*—one of the foremost collections in Swedish twentieth century lyric poetry—came to characterize Ekelund's subsequent work after he finally left lyrical poetry. Antiquity became for him a radiant vision of light and his guiding star when he gave up poetry, for whose emotional subjectivity he came to feel a strong distaste, choosing instead the essay and the aphorism as his media. Only a number of Baudelaire-inspired prose poems in the volume *Böcker och vandringar* (Books and Wanderings) from 1910 continued his deeper poetic interest—on the other hand these few belong to the foremost of their type in Swedish poetry. The prose Ekelund developed, beginning with *Antikt ideal* (Classical Ideal), 1909, has, however, also a strongly lyrical character, and many of his aphorisms have the clear stamp of modern short poems. Behind Ekelund's change of allegiance lies above all a strong Nietzschean experience, but the classical view of life he invokes in his essays and author portraits is more Apollonian than Dionysian and emanated from a bright visionary educational experience, purged of turn-of-the-century melancholy and fatigue. With his demands for spiritual will, ethical rigor and unity he writes here in neoclassical tradition, where antiquity signifies a demanding inner ideal rather than artistically conditioned mood experiences.

Ekelund's personal life at this time also underwent an upheaval. He fled Sweden to avoid a prison sentence for a relatively minor offense and went in self-imposed exile to Germany, where he endured terrible poverty, before later settling down in Denmark. During these socially and emotionally trying times his view of life became more profound, and his writing became an existential life program, an unceasing struggle for light and air, for meaning and clarity, for insight and maturity. *Båge och lyra* (Bow and Lyre), 1912, the first collection of pure aphorisms, is characterized by force, expressive lyricism and sarcastic humor, in short by a violent need for expression conveyed with unfashionable distance and with modern provocation. To a certain extent Ekelund belongs to the early modernist climate around 1910, in other respects he placed himself completely outside contemporary society and sought consolation with the classical authors and thinkers. Goethe and Emerson in time became two of the brightest guiding stars on his path toward inner equilibrium and harmony. *Nordiskt och klassiskt* (Nordic and Classic), 1914, is dominated by the polarization to which Ehrensvärd and nineteenth-century Romanticism gave pregnant expression and which Ekelund tried to resolve into a tenable alloy. During the 1910s, Ekelund's position was under constant change, most clearly noticeable in *Metron*, 1918. The demonstrations of strength, the struggle to get ahead, the play of feelings have here become unobtrusive, toned-down; a balance of the senses, moderation, inner calm, harmony in the simple and the everyday are the dominating ideals. The pendulum has swung back, in an anti-Nietzschean direction, toward a more humble and cautious view of life where the word "lowness" has taken on a positive ring.

The leaning towards cryptic exclusivity in the shaping of the language, already noticeable earlier, was strengthened considerably in the large number of collections of aphorisms that Ekelund published from the 1920s on, e.g. *Levnadsstämning* (Life Mood), 1925, *Passioner emellan* (Between Passions), 1927, *Lyra och Hades* (Lyre and Hades), 1930, *Det andra ljuset* (The Second Light), 1935, *Elpidi*, 1939. He became something of a modernist of the aphorism who, through obscure Latin and Greek allusions and quotations, makes immense demands of the reader. In spite of the fact that he always derived intellectual nourishment from the great western literary and philosophical traditions, his continuously changing system of thought took on an increasingly original stamp and progressed toward an intellectual mysticism or even an intellectual magic. He thus became something of an esoteric prophet for a small number of initiated, a sort of guru who gave enriching experiences of light, clarity, insight and mental equilibrium—a practical philosopher who conducted a constant battle for learning and laid the foundation for an everyday mental hygiene. A polemical cultural criticism shines forth from his web of special concepts, which turns against the shallow and meager cultural ideals of the period and seeks to present a fertile alternative image of more profound intellectual experience. He sought a synthesis between classical western learning and eastern mysticism, and he strove to anchor his idea of learning in "the popular-noble," in a sort of aristocracy of the simple with an understanding of the essential in life. As before, nature is for him a source of constant stimulation, as is the world of books; one of his many posthumous collections of aphorisms is called appropriately enough *In silvis cum libro*, 1957.

The conflicts are many in this self-therapeutic literature of edification. The inner monologue which the author carries on with himself is never resolved. It is the seeking itself that is the essence of the writing process, where the central concepts appear in ever new, poetically evocative constellations. With his distance and isolation Ekelund found but few readers in his own time. However, the chosen few stood out as all the more devoted and enthusiastic. Above all he has become a poet's poet; the Finland-Swedish modernists as well as the post-war modernist generation diligently drew from his almost inexhaustible sources. As a literary household god he has played a boundless role for twentieth-century Swedish literature. With his synthetic and cross-disciplinary doctrine of learning his works have an indisputably international appeal, but his inaccessibility has hitherto hindered a more extensive interest in his aphorisms. With his direct and intense world of feelings and his unusually sensitive intellect, however, he is one of the most distinctive figures in Swedish literature, both as a lyric poet and as an aphorist, and an apparently enduring attraction for new, select readers.

The climate at the turn of the century favored lyric poetry, and many other prominent poets appeared. Anders Österling (1884–1981) had his roots in the symbolist cult of beauty and in the provincial poetry typical of the nineties. With his breakthrough collection *Årets visor* (The Year's Songs), 1907, he stood out more even than Ekelund as a Scanian counterpart to Karlfeldt, with freshly sensual poems of Scanian countryside and nature. During his long life he varied his idyllic, harmonious and hedonistic motifs—without thereby forfeiting darker tones. Bo Bergman (1869–1967) had another kind of footing in the sentiments of the turn of the century. From his debut collection *Marionetterna* (The Marionettes), 1903, he appeared as a sceptic, with roots in the faith in reason of the eighties but without sharing in its hopes of development. Clarity and resignation entered a sensitive union in his musically mellow poetry, where love and nature motifs play an important role and lyrically pregnant sketches of Stockholm provide the geographic setting. The desolate determinism which existed in earlier poetry was gradually softened and replaced by a much more passionate belief in eternal values, in human community and in the private individual as opposed to modern mass man.

Selma Lagerlöf and Prose Around the Turn of the Century

Poetry became the dominant literary genre around the turn of the century, even if Heidenstam as well as Levertin were important prose writers. It was Selma Lagerlöf (1858–1940), however, who emerged as the supreme talent in this generation of writers in the area of narrative prose. She became its most prominent literary exponent and, alongside Strindberg, the only of the epoch's Swedish writers to attain world renown. With her genuine narrative talent she won a lasting fame far beyond Sweden's borders, above all through her prose narratives and legends. She is one of the most translated Swedish writers of all time. Like her literary contemporaries, she had her roots in the provinces, more particularly in the manorial culture of Värmland from which writers like Tegnér, Geijer and Fröding had also emerged. This provincial footing, the key factor in her narrative art, was, however, no obstacle to an internationalization of her motifs during her writing career, while her creative fantasy, where the supernatural plays a large role, has a universal stamp which made her themes attractive everywhere. It is not so much the nineteenth-century novel's narrative ideal that shaped her prose, as the folk tale and other oral narrative traditions: the legend, the Romantic narrative and even the Icelandic saga. Like another famous Nordic writer, Hans Christian Andersen, she stands out above all as a storyteller, and a storyteller with a specifically female profile. Her conception of reality in legend is not only evocative symbolically but also marked by an intuitive and profound understanding of people and a sort of ageless life wisdom that only superficially appears anachronistic.

Isolation and solitary fantasy worlds were the ingredients of Selma Lagerlöf's adolescence on the Värmland estate Mårbacka, which her family was later forced to leave because of bankruptcy, but which she in turn was able to buy back. There she created her own literary center with the fruits of her success as an author, and in time it became a much-visited tourist attraction. Her receptive character was nourished here by the popular narrative traditions with which the countryside teemed, and in contrast to her fellow Värmland writers she really exploited this treasure of merry tales and ghost stories for her own literary purposes. Poor health explained her preferring the world of literature to that of reality, and her early literary attempts often bore the mark of Romantic escapism. Lyric poetry was not foreign to her as a means of expression; an epic poem, "Madame de Castro," was first published as late as 1984, and she also tried the sonnet form. However, she chose the teaching profession, and during her period of training and early teaching years she came in contact with the more socially progressive ideas of the time. Like the other writers of the nineties, she had to a high degree a background in the eighties, and she was characterized by liberal philanthropy and a belief in progress. But it was still to the Värmland manorial life that she returned in literature, in particular after the catastrophe of the family's bankruptcy. Stimulated by success in a literary competition, she made her debut in 1891 with a prose epic permeated with Värmland folklore: *Gösta Berlings saga (Gösta Berling's Saga)*.

With this work Selma Lagerlöf renewed Swedish narrative art in the same way that Heidenstam had renewed lyric poetry with his first collection a few years earlier. Her lyrical and imaginative narrative style with its archaic turns of phrase, its invocations to the reader and the story's characters, and its lively emotional insights stood out as something new. Its web of fantastic events, linked apparently randomly into a more uniform whole, broke with past novel composition and the genre's demands for faithfulness to reality. The manneristic style was in part taken from Thomas Carlyle, but also from the Icelandic saga. In the main, though, this loosely connected chain of stories was simply original. Many of the stories are relatively detached in relation to the overall course of action, others have a tenuous connection with the main action. But from the welter of events and persons an ever clearer conceptual whole emerges, in which fantasy and art are juxtaposed with work and usefulness, and where the theme constantly moves around guilt and atonement, deception and love.

The stories take place in the early nineteenth century in a Värmland where the foundries are thriving and life is a heady round of parties and balls, but where the dark forces of superstition also play their pranks on people, and where bears and wolves roam the sparsely settled area. In this Värmland landscape—lovingly animated and endowed with human voices in the manner of the Romantic tale—there arises a maelstrom of incredible, evocative events, omens and apparitions, not to mention evil, sudden death. This occurs after the drunken clergyman Gösta Berling and the other cavaliers take over the Ekeby foundry for one year and put its owner, the Major's wife, to flight, following a Faust-like wager with Evil, in the wolfskin-clad guise of the foundry owner Sintram. The wager is that they will surrender themselves to the pleasures of life and not undertake any useful work. In this Romantic spirit work at the foundry is also abandoned, and a series of misfortunes and catastrophes befalls the district as a result. In particular, the dashing adventurer Gösta Berling, who seduces women with wild abandon and lets a reckless joy of life guide his existence, contracts a guilt that can only be atoned for through a deep humiliation and through work being taken up again at the foundry. The story is a long, nostalgic homage to art and fantasy in past times, while also defending ambitious, reformist trends. The strength in this attempt to fuse the demands of artistic beauty and constructive social ethics, though, lies less in the realistic episodes where the social divisions are alluded to in a scene of revolutionary tension between the manorial life of the cavaliers and the misery of the people, than in the brilliant evocativeness with which Selma Lagerlöf portrays the vitality of this Värmland *ancien régime*, and the romantically grand dimension she gives the lives of her characters. This story is full of great dramatic events and emotions, but behind the extravagant gestures and the supernatural ghost machinery there is a rich measure of the timeless, universal wisdom of life and ambiguous symbolism of the saga.

After this brilliant debut, which did not begin to attract attention until after Georg Brandes gave it a very favorable review, Selma Lagerlöf concentrated for a while on a shorter narrative format. Already in *Gösta Berling's Saga* the high points often lie in the individual small stories rather than in the whole, and in her subsequent works too she was most accomplished on the smaller scale. The short stories in *Osynliga länkar (Invisible Links)*, 1894, belong to her foremost. They span a wide register of motifs: some tie in directly to the themes of her debut work, others to the Icelandic sagas and medieval history. One story is a portrait of Fredrika Bremer. In several cases the author here attempts a realistic narrative without saga features. Her next larger effort followed a visit to Italy. Inspired by the environment, life and popular beliefs of the South, she wrote the remarkable novel *Antikrists mirakler (The Miracles of Antichrist)*, 1897, in which she abruptly broke away from her Värmland cultural legacy. As in *Gösta Berling's Saga*, she tried here to merge modern Realism with the unreality of the legend. This fusion fitted her narrative disposition best even when, as here, she aimed at a novel of ideas tackling modern sociopolitical problems. The action takes place mainly in a nineteenth-century Sicily of great poverty and adversity. A fake painting of Christ (Antichrist) turns up there, on which it is written not: "My kingdom is not of this world," but rather: "My kingdom is only of this world." A whole series of wonders then occurs, social construction is begun, and a railroad is built. But the message on the painting of the Antichrist, which is obviously a symbol of socialism, also comes into conflict with Catholicism. How Selma Lagerlöf in this visionary story really reacted to socialism as a philosophy has been the subject of much discussion; her position is hardly unambiguous. But in the final chapter—a conversation between the Pope and a priest, which has some of the same broad perspective of ideas as the sequence about the grand inquisitor in Dostoevsky's *The Brothers Karamazov*—it appears fairly clear that she looked optimistically at the ability of socialism to create better conditions for man, and that she aimed at a sort of synthesis between socialism and Christianity. Earth and Heaven must be reconciled, Christ and Antichrist must enter an alliance. In the modern perspective of so-called liberation theology this is a prophetic and topical message, and *The Miracles of Antichrist* is also a work that aroused greater attention abroad than at home. It belongs among Selma Lagerlöf's most translated works, and it is indisputably one of her most original and richest in ideas.

In *En herrgårdssägen (The Tale of a Manor)*, 1899, there is a stronger *fin de siècle* attraction to occultism and extreme psychological states. The story of how the love of the young Ingrid cures the mentally ill Gunnar Hede is a variation of the Beauty and the Beast theme—that motif which so revels in hair-raising Gothic Romanticism, with cemetery scenes, apparent death, madness and an evocative infusion of legend. End-of-the-century psychology contributed to shaping Selma Lagerlöf's view of the nature of mental illness and split personality. The narrative style is here toned down and simple. The same combination of spine-chilling Romantic plot and subdued diction returns in the story *Herr Arnes penningar* (*Herr Arne's Hoard* or *The Treasure*), 1903, a dark and desolate story from sixteenth-century Bohuslän, reminiscent of the Icelandic saga in form and filled with evil, sudden death and ghosts. Behind the ghoulish chain of events, however, is the invariable theme in Selma Lagerlöf's stories, that of guilt, punishment and atonement.

Between these two stories, Selma Lagerlöf had written one of her largest works: *Jerusalem I–II*, 1901–02. During her years as a teacher in Falun, Dalecarlia, she had come into contact with a revivalist movement among the Dalecarlian farmers that resulted in many of them emigrating to the Holy Land. A trip to Jerusalem and Egypt brought her into closer ties with these religiously fanatic emigrants—all of which provided her with the outline for a deeply engaging peasant story with a myriad of fascinating portraits and grand, supernatural events. The first, and artistically most consummate part, takes place in Dalecarlia and depicts how the old patriarchal, agrarian society with its footing in Lutheran Christianity breaks down when modern revivalist movements pass through the district. There is particular force in her presentation of the ancient Ingmarsson family, the leading peasant family in the parish but the one which is also subjected to the most difficult trials when the traditional agrarian social pattern collapses. In the depiction of these placid farmers with their strong feeling for tradition, justice and "God's ways," the imitation of the style of the Icelandic sagas is an archaic and enormously effective medium that gives the novel a profound dimension of the ancient Nordic narrative art. Here Selma Lagerlöf's prose-epic art celebrates its greatest triumphs in terms of visual effectiveness, understanding of human nature, maturity and emotional intensity. One example of this is the opening description of how Great Ingmar Ingmarsson as a young man brings his wife, the child murderer, home from prison, spurred on by the counsels of his forefathers, which he thinks he hears in a hallucination.

Selma Lagerlöf. Portrait by Carl Larsson, 1908.

Another is the final description of how the religious emigrants leave their homes. It is clear that Selma Lagerlöf's
strongest sympathies were with the old peasant society, but
she also had a certain understanding of the boundary-breaking emotional states of religious conviction and depicted, as
always, hysterical and agitated mental states with great
insight. The second part of the novel, somewhat weaker than
the first in literary terms, describes the fanatic emigrants'
hardships and tribulations in the Holy Land, where many of
them are broken down by illness and the strains of the

climate. At the same time a desolate atmosphere hovers over their blindly faithful undertakings which result in personal and social catastrophes. At the end, some of the main characters return to their home parish in Sweden, and life on the old farm of the Ingmarssons can go on as before. Occasional melodramatic weaknesses notwithstanding, the work belongs among the absolute peaks of Swedish narrative art.

At the beginning of the twentieth century, Selma Lagerlöf returned to the legend form she had successfully cultivated earlier and wrote, among other things, her much-praised *Kristuslegender (Christ Legends)*, 1904, visionary, religiously lyrical short stories, mainly about the young Christ and the magical influence he exerted on people around him. These are permeated by her strong feeling for the religious miracle, particularly in "Ljuslågan" ("The Sacred Flame"), a story which stands somewhat apart from the rest. Here she depicts a Florentine knight who, under the most trying privations, succeeds in carrying the holy flame from Jesus' grave in Jerusalem back to his native city, a pure and timeless prose epic, charged with intensive symbolism.

Selma Lagerlöf's next larger work was of an entirely different type and became her most popular and widely read book: *Nils Holgerssons underbara resa (The Wonderful Adventures of Nils)*, 1906–07. This was originally commissioned as a geographical reader for elementary-school children, a task that Selma Lagerlöf accomplished with ingenious imagination by giving it the form of a fairy tale. Here, a mischievous young boy is transformed into a Tom Thumb pixie who follows a flock of wild geese on their spring journey up through the country to northernmost Lapland and back again when fall comes. In this way she was able to depict Swedish towns and countryside within the framework of an adventure story, while the little boy's wild escapades among gigantic animals and people gave the young readers rich opportunities for identification and not least enjoyment. In fact, the book was considerably more entertaining than instructive. The wild geese's zig-zag route across the country seems to be guided more by tourist attractions than zoological authenticity, and the story is continuously interrupted by tales about the different provinces, by legends and all sorts of yarns. The author herself even appears in one of the sections, in which the flock of wild geese on its way south passes her home estate Mårbacka and Nils Holgersson gets the opportunity to tell her about his fantastic adventures. However, it is the animals who have the main roles in this eventful, air-borne odyssey, and Rudyard Kipling's *The Jungle Book* provided the stimulation and inspiration for a rich portrait gallery of anthropomorphic creatures. As is the case with Kipling, the story is also something of a morality play, in which Nils Holgersson, by mixing with the animals, learns the power of action, manners and solidarity and can thereby be transformed into a human being again. The extensive and well-narrated work—it comprises some five hundred pages—became a great success in spite of objections from teachers, and became virtually obligatory reading in Swedish schools for a long time to come. It also won an immense popularity internationally and was the work that above all founded Selma Lagerlöf's world renown; it has been translated into more than forty languages. On the goose's back, Nils Holgersson made his triumphal procession among children the world over, and the work belongs indisputably among the foremost children's books of all time. In spite of its nationally limited purpose it proved able to stimulate children's imagination regardless of cultural or national identity.

By the early twentieth century, Selma Lagerlöf had attained a significant international reputation and become more and more an official cultural personality in Sweden. In 1909 she received the Nobel Prize in Literature, and in 1914 she was elected to the Swedish Academy as its first woman member. All this attention contributed in the long run to an abatement in her productivity and creative energy. But in the 1910s she still wrote several works of considerable interest. In *Liljecronas hem (Liljecrona's Home)*, 1911, she returned to the everyday provincial atmosphere around the themes from *Gösta Berling's Saga*. Another story from Värmland, *Kejsaren av Portugallien (The Emperor of Portugallia)*, 1914, is more a melodramatic tragicomedy than anything else, in which an eccentric old man loses his reason when his beloved only daughter fails to return home after falling victim to the jungle of the big city. In his arrogant madness he imagines himself to be the "Emperor of Portugallia" and his daughter the empress, and he refuses to recognize reality. This both tragicomic and moving story culminates in a spirit of reconciliation which bears many of the characteristics of the legend. In *Körkarlen* (*Thy Soul Shall Bear Witness*), 1912, Selma Lagerlöf's interest in the occult reached a peak. The larger part of the story takes place literally "on the other side" of life, in a state where the soul is freed from the body. In its depiction of illness and social deprivation, however, this short novel paradoxically enough has a touch of social realism. The evocative depiction of death's creaking cart travelling through the damp desolation of a New Year's Eve is supported by a remarkable union of religious feeling for life and occult mysticism that was apparently significantly more than an aesthetic game for the author. The novel's theme is the problem of evil and the need for penitence and atonement. For Selma Lagerlöf, who always believed in the victory of the forces of good over evil and destruction, this problem was strengthened by the outbreak of the First World War and the shocking catastrophes of civilization. She tried to give shape to her crippling experiences in the novel *Bannlyst* (*The Outcast*), 1918, which became her most problematic work. At the center stands a man who, during a North Pole expedition, was forced to eat human flesh and whose reclusive life of Christ-like love for his fellow man is an attempt to atone for the curse he brought upon himself.

During the latter part of her life, Selma Lagerlöf devoted her writing energies mostly to autobiographical works about her childhood and youth, as well as to the so-called Löwensköld-cycle. This consists of three parts: *Löwensköldska ringen, Charlotte Löwensköld*—both from 1925, and *Anna Svärd*, 1928; a planned fourth part was never completed. (The trilogy has appeared in English under the collective title *The Ring of the Löwenskölds*.) While the first part is a true ghost story of the Värmland brand where spine-chilling Romanticism flourishes as never before, the action in the other two parts takes place in the Värmland manorial and parsonage milieu and concentrates on the existential problems that Selma Lagerlöf always wrestled with and to which she tried to give final shape. The work's world of ideas is somewhat disconnected and confused, though the portraits of people have considerable depth and a revelatory sharpness. A liberal, life-acknowledging religiousness rings out from the sometimes quite romantically cliché-filled course of action. This appears as fundamental in Selma Lagerlöf's world of ideas. The obvious religious feeling for life is always combined with a philanthropic love for man and a positive joy of life. For later readers, Lagerlöf's predilection for the supernatural and the occult can give her writing a questionable character, but seen as sagas and morality plays her work still makes a strong impact. Her narrative talent stands beyond all question, even if she sometimes yields to stylistic mannerism and exaggeration. Her works are perhaps above all to be seen as intensely emotional literary adventures that are filled with a warmth for life and a firm—but far from naive—faith in the ability of positive forces to give meaning to the chaos of existence.

The step from Selma Lagerlöf to Hjalmar Söderberg (1869–1941) might seem long. But only four years separate *Gösta Berling's Saga* from Söderberg's debut novel *Förvillelser* (Aberrations), 1895, and he too, with his distinct profile, is a typical child of the late nineteenth century. His province is Stockholm—alongside Strindberg he is the foremost portrayer of Stockholm in Swedish literature—and his prose is characterized by lyrical musical moods that convey a typical melancholy and a post-eighties scepticism. But the differences are certainly considerable. Where Selma Lagerlöf is a vitally warm emotionalist, Söderberg is mainly an intellectual and sensualist. With Selma Lagerlöf there is still an intuitively confident faith in a good and meaningful world order and in an existence beyond the visible world, while Söderberg is an uncompromising sceptic and a disillusioned pessimist who dismisses all religious and mystical solutions, all occultism and all philosophical and political charlatanism. The legacy from the radical ideas of the eighties is considerably more alive in him, even if the fighting spirit has weakened considerably and been replaced by an ironically observing analysis. As an author, Söderberg is in many respects a Swedish counterpart to French writers like Maupassant and Anatole France (whom he translated with great skill), Russian authors like Turgenev and above all Chekhov, and Danish authors like J. P. Jacobsen and in particular Herman Bang, who was one of the most powerful reading experiences of Söderberg's youth. In spite of his intellectual attitude to life, with its melancholy and ironic underlying sentiments, eroticism is the main theme in his writing. However, it is chiefly the impossibility of love that he depicts, and his erotic narratives give a sociologically interesting diagnosis of the fixed sex roles in the middle-class society of Oskar II's time. His impressionistically but also journalistically accomplished style lacks a counterpart in Swedish prose in terms of purity and clarity and professionally conscious effectiveness, and some of the works in his quite discriminating production undoubtedly count among the pinnacles of Swedish literature.

While young, Söderberg supported himself as a journalist and wrote short stories and prose pieces for newspapers and journals before his debut with *Förvillelser*. The book provoked much scandal and debate; its erotic depictions were considered offensive to the moral ideas of the time, and the anemic vacillations of the young protagonist Tomas Weber were hardly a good model for the young. The latter roams the streets of Stockholm in a sort of passive introspection, providing Söderberg with numerous opportunities for fine, impressionistically chiseled Stockholm exteriors. Weber has several love affairs but is no more able to hold on to love than Söderberg's other main characters. He becomes involved in a foolish money swindle that leads to an unsuccessful suicide attempt. But the action is fairly unessential in this debut work; it is the moods and images that are the main thing. On the whole, the short format suited Söderberg extremely well, and he collected his early stories and prose pieces in *Historietter* (Stories), 1898, brilliant examples of a miniature art where the whole is completely mastered and the final points well calculated. The prose pieces span a register from rationalistic, religious criticism and stark depictions of the game of chance with human existence, to expressive and symbolic dream images. The dream plays an important role throughout Söderberg's authorship; in this respect also he was a child of the epoch that saw the birth of Freud's psychology of dreams.

In 1901, Söderberg published *Martin Bircks ungdom* (*Martin Birck's Youth*), a novel of personal development with certain autobiographical features, in particular the childhood memories. Martin Birck is a typically passive and listless Söderbergian anti-hero, who mechanically and without commitment pursues a modest bureaucratic career. However, below the anemic surface there is here a stronger element of feeling and protest, and the attack on the Church and on official hypocrisy is more vehement than earlier. There is an underlying rebellion against experiencing life as an unreal dream, and the disillusioned outlook on life, marked by resigned determinism, is illuminated by a positive understanding of love as life's only deep joy. Paradoxically enough, this melancholy developmental novel ends with a long, liberating kiss representing the whole of cosmic experience. However, Söderberg made his boldest contribution with the ideological novel *Doktor Glas (Doctor Glas)*, 1905, which has been called the best and most complete Swedish novel. It poses the problem of whether a private individual can take moral justice into his own hands by depriving an odious being of his life and, to a still higher degree, whether man through willpower can in some decisive way change life and the course of existence. Doctor Glas, who poisons the vulgar, narrow-minded clergyman Gregorius in order to help the clergyman's wife (whom he loves) gain happiness, does not succeed in this. The woman does not become happier, and life continues along other lines than those Doctor Glas intended. The tension between determinism and will appears more clearly than ever, and the vanity of human will becomes obvious. With a sharpness reminiscent of Dostoevsky, Söderberg replied to his own questions on existence, at a time when God no longer existed as an absolute ethical norm.

A tragic love experience deepened Söderberg's erotic portrayal in the drama *Gertrud*, 1906. The play between male and female psyche here shows that he also had a good grasp of dramatic effects. This was demonstrated all the more in the novel *Den allvarsamma leken (The Serious Game)*, 1912, which can challenge *Doctor Glas* as one of the foremost Swedish novels. This story about a reborn, but in the long run hopeless love affair is presented in the form of a historical chronicle, where contemporary events provide the frame for the sexual complications. The man's static commitment to a conventional, male way of life contrasts here with the woman's ability to stake everything on her happiness. The life of the main character, Arvid Stjärnblom, eventually collapses as a result of his meeting with Lydia Stille in this melancholy story that is conveyed with a low-key authenticity that indicates an attainment of maturity and insight in Söderberg's narrative art. This novel is also, like his earlier ones, an eminent depiction of the life and mores of the Stockholm of that time, but it is hardly an ideological novel. It is love's own dynamic game that stands at the center and that with implacable logic leads to its final downfall.

Otherwise, Söderberg's authorship moved increasingly toward philosophical and religion-critical observations. The intellectual work *Hjärtats oro* (The Heart's Unrest), 1909, is filled with strong yet humorous polemics against pragmatic philosophy of the will and an ever stronger stress on the importance of a rationalistic scepticism against everything that hinted of philosophical speculation and anti-intellectualism. After he moved to Copenhagen in 1917, where he remained until his death, he devoted a large part of his energy to theological research. An example of this is the story *Jesus Barabbas*, 1928, that launches the theologically somewhat questionable thesis that Jesus and Barabbas were one and the same person! Parallel with his inexhaustible struggle against religious dogma and belief in authority, against hypocrisy and superstition, ran an ever increasing political interest. In *Ödestimmen* (Hour of Destiny), 1922, a fictional drama about Germany's path into the First World War, there is an emphatic rejection of national ideologies of violence and totalitarian mass psychosis. This was strengthened during the 1930s, an otherwise unproductive period for Söderberg in terms of literature. He wrote furiously contemptuous articles about the growing Nazi barbarity with its anti-intellectual charlatanism and devotion to violence. It has been said that Hitler lengthened Söderberg's life by ten years. In the shadow of Nazism's racist dictatorship, his rationalistic scepticism grew into a fighting, compassionate humanism, marked by humanitarian pathos, a sense of justice and a passion for truth. His reactions against Mussolini's fascism and Stalin's communism were equally strong and directed against their inflated pretentions and equally mendacious and ruthless deception of the people. The threads of nineteenth-century radicalism proved to be equally tenacious in Söderberg when they were confronted with the ideologies of modern dictatorship—as was also the case with the poet Bo Bergman, who is closely identified with Söderberg in Swedish literature. The anemic intellectual and polished sensualist thus powerfully demonstrated a firm inner resistance to the destructive doctrines of violence and an uncompromising defense of truth, justice and reason. It can be seen as a symbolic irony of fate that at the age of 72 he died in Nazi-occupied Copenhagen.

Ellen Key and "The Century of the Child"

The struggle of the Swedish women's movement during the final phase of the nineteenth century, after the earlier pioneering period of Fredrika Bremer, has unjustly been eclipsed in the popular image by Strindberg's notorious hatred of women. As a matter of fact, a long series of good female authors appeared in the progressive spirit of the eighties, with feminist-oriented works which further developed the struggle for women's emancipation, and in general the women's movement grew stronger. One of those who most energetically contributed to this was Ellen Key (1849–1926). Her diverse contributions do not lie on the literary plane proper but on the plane of the creation of ideas and public opinion. In the perspective of the history of ideas they can without a doubt be labeled the most significant during the epoch in question. As the daughter of a landowner and politician, Ellen Key developed progressive, liberal political interests early on, and an educational trip to the Continent broadened her philosophical and aesthetic views. In the climate of ideas of the 1880s she was attracted by positivistic and evolutionary ideals, and she went from an idealistic Christianity to a belief in development and a "faith in life" with utopian characteristics. In many respects her world of ideas is a further development of those held by Geijer, Fredrika Bremer and Almqvist on the questions of the home and sex. She also contributed actively to the rediscovery of Almqvist's writings. In the question of women's rights she took—in works like *Missbrukad kvinnokraft*

(Misused Power of Women), 1896, and *Kvinnorörelsen* (The
Women's Movement), 1909—a controversial stand by stressing the mother's special social role, something that aroused
vehement reactions from more radical feminist quarters. In
works like *Tankebilder* (Mental Images), 1898, and *Livs-
linjer* (Lines of Life), 1903–6, she developed a view of life
with both monistic and pantheistic features. The idealistic
legacy is brought to mind in strong demands for an intense
morality. She urged a more consciously aesthetic upbringing, which she also considered to be ethically beneficial. Her
faith in life came from a warm and original world of the
senses, and she did more than anyone else for women's
emotional liberation. Her commitment gradually came to
embrace the causes of the working class too, and socialism
was an important source of inspiration. She worked for
peace and, outraged by the outbreak of the First World War,
she developed an active, radical pacifism that has not lost its
urgency during the course of the twentieth century.

Ellen Key's utopian vision—in its way typical for a certain Swedish, emotionally colored tradition of idealism bordering on mysticism—can be said to culminate in the work
Barnets århundrade (The Century of the Child) which with
spectacular timing came out in the very first year of the new
century. Her most remarkable work, it has been translated
into a number of languages, and it gave her a certain standing
outside Sweden. It contains several of her most central contributions on the subject of the home and women, but it was
above all her prophetic appeal for the new era to put the
child first which caught on then and later. "The Century of
the Child" became synonymous with Ellen Key's name and
deeds. In contrast to the child's peripheral position in earlier
conceptions of the family, hers called for a new, positive and
tolerant way of viewing the child's role and potential for
development and foreshadowed the revolution in the views
on child-rearing and the focus on children that would
characterize the twentieth century—even if these developments partly went along other lines than those Ellen Key
intended. Her ideas about a renaissance for the child also
typified the era in other respects. The new ideas about child-
rearing began to be reflected in the literary field in such a
way that increased attention was directed at literature for

children and young people, following Topelius and culminating during the years around the turn of the century. An abundance of newspapers and magazines for children saw the light of day. Many of the epoch's foremost authors wrote works directly for children and young people: Viktor Rydberg, Verner von Heidenstam, Selma Lagerlöf and later Hjalmar Bergman. Of great importance too was the founding of the Saga Children's Library, a long series of children's books that reached children from all backgrounds in relatively large numbers. These laid the foundation for a wider reading of literature and good reading habits which in time were to benefit adult literature.

In the strikingly strong children's book tradition that developed from the end of the nineteenth century on, from Topelius to Selma Lagerlöf's *The Wonderful Adventures of Nils*, several distinctive figures with a direct commitment to children's writing appeared. An important contribution to this rich tradition was made by Elsa Beskow (1874–1953), who wrote a long series of now classic children's books which she illustrated herself, often in the Jugendstil spirit. Among these are most notably *Puttes äventyr i blåbärsskogen (Peter in Blueberry Land)*, 1901, and *Tant Grön, tant Brun och tant Gredelin (Aunt Green, Aunt Brown and Aunt Lavender)*, 1918. These have been able to maintain their attraction for children even though they are permeated by an ethical strain typical of that earlier period. Another classic in the area of children's books is *Kattresan* (The Cat Journey), 1909, by the artist Ivar Arosenius. It gave children's book illustration an independent aesthetic value, just as did John Bauer's burlesquely fantastic fairy-tale drawings for the children's stories in the Christmas publication *Bland tomtar och troll* (Among Gnomes and Trolls) that appeared from 1907. A national Romantic picture of life on a farm was given in *Sörgården* (South Farm), 1913, by Anna Maria Roos, frequently used as a reader in schools. The children's song gained prominent and creative proponents in Alice Tegnér and Jeanna Oterdahl. Together, these authors gave the children's book a value of its own which has survived and strengthened in today's Swedish literature.

THE TWENTIETH CENTURY MODERNISM AND PROLETARIAN REALISM

At the beginning of the twentieth century Swedish society found itself in a state of change. Many of the social and political changes that the nineteenth century's authors and thinkers had fought for began to produce results in the field of social restructuring. The most shaking political event was that the union with Norway, that dated from 1814, was dissolved in 1905 under somewhat traumatic circumstances. This was a severe blow, not so much for the nation as a whole as for conservative opinion, which, under the influence of the turn-of-the-century's nationalistic and patriotic sentiments, saw in the Swedish-Norwegian union a tool for maintaining some of the lustre from the days of the Swedish Great Power Empire. In general, the bastions of the conservative King Oskar's class society began increasingly to disappear. The popular movements started to grow stronger, among them a civil rights' movement that worked for a more democratic system of government. During the period from 1907 to 1921 universal suffrage, first for men and then women, was introduced; Sweden became a modern democratic state in which democratic institutions and principles became important foundations for the social and cultural national consciousness. The lower middle-class and the working class quickly acquired a considerably greater political influence, and the confrontations with the Establishment and higher social strata became initially sharp, although not revolutionary. On the internal political plane, the most shaking event at the beginning of the century was certainly the Great Strike of 1909, when close to 300,000 workers stopped work on a directive from the trade unions of the labor movement. Initially, the outcome—when work had to be resumed because of lack of money—was seen as a defeat for the labor movement. In time however, the event proved to be the spur to political and trade-union progress. In 1917 the Social Democratic Party participated in the formation of a government for the first time, and in 1920 they formed their own government with Hjalmar Branting as prime minister. On the cultural plane, social confrontations are most clearly reflected in the so-called Strindberg feud around 1910 (see p. 139). With hindsight, this can be said to have been a victory for a cultural radicalism that would become the dominant line in Swedish cultural life for the entire twentieth century. The conservatives would never again play any effectively significant role there; the so-called 1914 ideas that pleaded for a Swedish entry into the First World War on Germany's side were on the whole insignificant, since Germany did not show the least interest in the matter.

The years around 1910 can thus be denoted as the port of entry to modern Swedish democracy. Society at this time, in keeping with international developments, came to be characterized by industrialization and the numerous technical innovations that followed. The new entrepreneurs and industrialists as well as the working class became the leading social groups, while the farmers, small businessmen and—at least initially—civil servants lost ground. Yet Sweden remained a sparsely populated, agrarian country far into the twentieth century; only at the beginning of the 1930s, for example, did the population of the towns surpass that of the rural areas. A strong division between different social groups arose at the beginning of the century, and it is reflected very clearly in the realistic novels that began to appear. This generation of realistic "writers of the 1910s" provided a many-faceted, sociological panorama of contemporary Swedish society, a broad social analysis ranging right across the political spectrum and from the still extant upper class to the rising lower class. The vanishing aristocracy with its increasingly outdated values is portrayed lovingly by Sven Lidman (1882–1960) in the so-called Silfverståhl-cycle, 1910–13, and in the novel *Huset med de gamla fröknarna* (The House with the Elderly Ladies), 1918. Sigfrid Siwertz (1882–1970) gives a sharply satirical picture of the nouveau-riche monied aristocracy and its mundane and emotionally cold existence in *Selambs (Downstream)*, 1920, an accomplished social analysis in which the egotism of the ultra-liberals is dissected with relish. The new strong northern entrepreneurs, the lumber barons, found an enthusiastic portrayer in Ludvig Nordström (1882–1942), e.g. in his collection of short stories *Herrar* (Gentlemen), 1910; he also depicted the poor fishing population in Norrland. Above all, though, he is remembered as an enthusiastic literary supporter of the new industrial expansion, which he portrayed as a centrifugal force in his visionary utopia of the new metropolis, Urbs. His own world view, bordering on mysticism, which he called "totalism" (the only independent Swedish "ism" in this internationally rich period of "isms"), was also centered on the force of the industrial expansion.

People from a broad and somewhat diffuse middle-class are portrayed by Gustaf Hellström (1882–1953), who in his extraordinary novel *Snörmakare Lekholm får en idé (Lacemaker Lekholm Has an Idea)*, 1927, gave a picture of typical Swedish class mobility, i.e. how a family generation after generation rises or falls on the social ladder. Women's position in various social strata was radically portrayed by Elin Wägner (1882–1949), e.g. in the novel *Norrtullsligan* (The Norrtull Gang), 1908. In many respects she continued Ellen Key's contributions and developed a personal vision of man and existence in which motherhood, pacifism and faith in the community are the main tenets. Martin Koch (1882–1940) emerged as the portrayer of the proletariat in novels like *Arbetare* (Workers), 1912, and *Guds vackra värld* (God's Beautiful World), 1916, the latter a thick, Dostoevsky-like chronicle of crime from the prison and underworld environments, and one of the period's most remarkable novels. The conditions of the female proletariat are central to Maria Sandel's (1870–1927) stories, which show class solidarity, as for example in *Familjen Vinge* (The Family Vinge), 1913. Lumberjacks and railroad construction workers are the subject of depictions by Gustav Hedenvind-Eriksson (1880–1967), an original, prose epic writer who integrated his social realism with the fantasy patterns of the legend. While the artistic quality can vary with all these authors, they have without doubt made an invaluable sociohistoric contribution with their large body of narrative art.

In spite of Swedish neutrality, the First World War was also for Swedish writers and intellectuals an experience that left its mark in literature. The early attempts at a typical Modernism emerge from this agony. The first part of the interwar era was on the other hand somewhat of a recovery period, marked by a harmonious, idyllic mood and by a cautious international orientation. In the 1930s, dark clouds again formed over Swedish society. The international depression was brought into sharp focus in Sweden by the collapse of the economic empire of the financier Ivar Krueger. This shook society to the foundations; social antagonism increased and unemployment became widespread. Proletarian realism reached a peak in Swedish literature during this decade, which also saw the emergence of a lively Modernism. However, beginning with the Nazis' assumption of power in Germany, the dominant line in cultural life was the "fighting humanism" that Pär Lagerkvist launched in 1934 and which he saw as a spiritual conscription against the destructive ideologies of dictatorship. The cultural struggle for freedom, reason and other western ideals continued in the "literature of preparedness" during the Second World War, when Swedish neutrality and the fear of German reprisals forced the writers under the rule of the censor. The postwar period, however, became one of unprecedented economic prosperity in Sweden. The country was favored, of course, by having been spared the destruction of the world war; a new stability had been achieved on the labor market through the so-called Saltsjöbaden Agreement of 1938, which regulated the terms of agreement between employers and employees. In this at least superficially harmonious "folkhem" (literally "people's home"— society viewed as a home for the people)—the expression coined by the Social Democratic prime minister, Per Albin Hansson—an unexpected social balance between classes and interests developed that would remain unbroken to the end of the 1960s. "The Swedish social model" became known worldwide, exports multiplied in volume, and prosperity quickly rose. In this harmoniously bubbling social pot, a vital Modernism thrived both in the area of prose and poetry, and the postwar period without a doubt became a new cultural heyday, which has already acquired something of the patina of the past.

Hjalmar Bergman
and the Fantasy of the Novel

Hjalmar Bergman (1883–1931) should also be mentioned among the many writers of the 1910s who depicted society. He was for the most part the well-informed portrayer of small-town central Sweden, with a wide register in his descriptions of different social strata, from the prosperous, family-conscious Establishment through an industriously striving, gossiping lower middle-class down to the dregs of society. But Hjalmar Bergman never got caught in Realism's illusory attempts to represent reality. His works invariably slip out of the realistic and into worlds of fantasy and dream, especially the nightmare. His reality is almost always transformed into a comic or tragic, high-spirited or ghostlike theatrical world, where the machinery inexorably controls people's fates and the sets assume the shape of the strange and unreal. As a novelist and as a dramatist Bergman took the step into twentieth-century Modernism, even if to an equally high degree he had his artistic roots in Romanticism. He can be said to start from where the late Strindberg—the Strindberg of the *Inferno* and the *Dream Play*—left off, and he played an important but still unexplored role for the Swedish novel writing of ensuing generations.

The son of a prosperous businessman, Hjalmar Bergman grew up in Örebro in central Sweden, the city that he later would depict with the authority of familiarity under the name Wadköping. He would also exploit his commercially oriented home environment as a background for his novels, in which financial complications play an unusually important role. However, his background did not lead him into a business career; on the contrary, from early on he was determined to become an author. His earliest work bears clear traces of a symbolistic literary climate: the legendary novel *Solivro*, 1906, and the moving and markedly cryptic psychological novel *Blå blommor* (Blue Flowers), 1907. Early on Bergman became a dedicated traveler and only ever put down roots for short periods. His strong love for Italy and Italian history is clearly expressed in the colorful Renaissance novel *Savonarola*, 1909, an accomplished historical chronicle, written in an intricate language filled with animated lyricism and a mannered rhetoric typical for the time.

However, around 1910 Bergman gave up his symbolistic sentiments, returned in his writings to his childhood town and its environs, and began to populate them with a crowd of fantastic and evocative figures from the past. In the works that followed there is an obvious strain of Balzac, and they can also remind us of the later William Faulkner and his Deep South, just as can his arabesque-like or accidentally disconnected manner of presentation. The first work with this new direction was *Hans nåds testamente* (His Grace's Last Testament), 1910, a burlesque comic novel that would later become better known and admired in a dramatized form. A wonderful depiction of a small town came in *Vi Bookar, Krokar och Rothar* (We Books, Kroks and Roths), 1912, which takes an almost sociological grasp of the material and action in its many-faceted portrait of the town's inhabitants. But reality's joints are creaky, and behind its facades there are constant hints of a marionette-like fantasy.

Hjalmar Bergman.

The tragic is mixed with the joyful, but underneath lies the ever-present sense of disillusion and fatalism which was already present in the early symbolist novels and which was to pervade Bergman's entire authorship. The darkly cynical is expressed still more strongly in *Loewenhistorier* (Loewen Stories), 1913, that tell of the tragic existence of a homecoming artist, his lack of willpower and unfortunate propensity for getting involved in criminal entanglements. The stories are written in an associative, compressed prose that looks ahead to the Swedish prose of the forties, when Kafka and Sartre were models. Emotions are absent, and the form of presentation is fragmentary in its subjective capriciousness, yet the stories are carried by an almost uncanny artistic perfection. The trilogy *Komedier i Bergslagen* (Comedies in Bergslagen), 1914–16, consists of a series of stories from Bergslagen's past, written with a stalwart narrative joy which took inspiration from Icelandic saga and from Selma Lagerlöf. But here too the dream and the grotesque play a large role and give a frighteningly unreal stamp to the events. Several of the stories in this historical fantasy belong among the peaks of Bergman's narrative art.

After all these preludes, Hjalmar Bergman then wrote in the course of some few years five novels that represent the culmination of his novel writing. The first of them, *Mor i Sutre* (Mother at Sutre), 1917, is written in an extremely compressed narrative prose that, with its repartee and short, evocative stage-directions, has an almost dramatic character. As in classical drama, the course of action is concentrated into a single day. At the center of this highly concentrated tragedy stands a strong-willed and domineering woman who thinks she can control what happens around her, but who finally becomes the cause of the murder of her favorite son. In Freudian spirit, the dream plays an important role in this drama of fate, where irrational forces play their ruthless game with people. The second of these novels, *En döds memoarer* (Memoirs of a Dead Man), 1918, treats the theme of death in life. It has been labeled a watershed, a work in which Bergman settled accounts with his past and made a move toward freedom and creativity. In form it is partly the chronicle of a family under a curse. When the main character, Jan Arnberg, flees to Hamburg from the pressure of a small-town scandal, he ends up in a symbolic kingdom of death where he gradually understands that one must kill ones own will and accept death in life—that the solution to life's problems lies in resignation. The third novel, *Markurells i Wadköping (God's Orchid)*, 1919, is on the surface of a lighter nature and also spans a single day's action. The protagonist is a grotesque, expansive tavern keeper who tries to bribe the examiners into passing his only son in the matriculation examination by holding a magnificent lunch. He pays the price for his audacity when he learns that this deeply loved son is not his own. The outcome of this tragicomedy, however, is that after a violent struggle with God he accepts life's merciless game and his own unhappy fate. Through its burlesque and splendid narrative joy it became Bergman's perhaps most popular novel.

The fourth novel, *Herr von Hancken* (Mr. von Hancken), 1920, is also a tragicomedy in which arrogance is punished and human dignity regained only after a total unmasking. At the center of the action, that takes place at the beginning of the nineteenth century in Bergslagen, is an unsuccessful nobleman who succeeds in making the guests at a spa believe that the king is about to pay a visit. When it is revealed that everything is a figment of his imagination, he is well and truly debunked during a cruelly humiliating ceremony. The story, written in a precise, pastiche-like style, takes on a deeply symbolic artistic meaning, and is highly symptomatic of Bergman's own artistic problems. The main character of the fifth novel, *Farmor och Vår Herre (Thy Rod and Thy Staff)*, 1921, is another domineering and strong-willed woman who is curbed by the fickle forces of existence. She lives in despotic symbiosis with Our Lord, but her authority is shattered when her beloved grandson, Nathan Borck, returns home as a rich and famous circus entertainer, no longer needing her goodwill and protection. This novel contains one of the most intense characterizations in Swedish literature and was successful not least in dramatized form.

After a prolific but more inconsistent period of novel writing during the 1920s, Hjalmar Bergman allowed Nathan Borck to return as the protagonist of his last work, the gripping novel *Clownen Jac* (Jac the Clown), 1930. It is one of his most personal works, originally written as a radio serial, for which he himself assisted at a reading a short time before his death. This is his own artistic catechism, in which he assembled the experiences of a busy lifetime as an author. The clown's tricks are a projection of his own fear. He appeals to the public's own feelings of terror and gets them to laugh at them. He despises the rules of the game on the American entertainment market, where he works, but at the same time he can feel humility and pride in his own art and a strong sympathy with the public. Nathan Borck, with his emotional vulnerability, reflects more than any other of Bergman's novel figures the writer's own neurotic, always tormented personality, the underlying anxiety of which was conjured up by figures of terror or comical pranks, sudden death or exuberant grotesquery.

All his life Hjalmar Bergman was a keen dramatist, and he is now counted as one of the twentieth century's great Swedish playwrights. In many ways he continued the striving for a theatrical revival that Strindberg began with his later drama, as for example in the so-called marionette plays from 1917, most notably *Dödens Arlekin* (Death's Harlequin) and *Herr Sleeman kommer (Mr. Sleeman Is Coming)*. Like many of the novels, they move in a mood-inducing landscape between reality and fantasy, between life and death, and are clearly close to an expressionistic aesthetic. The same holds for *Sagan* (The Fairy Tale) written in 1919, which integrates the fairy tale's structure with an original depiction of reality and where the actions are introduced and commented on in long, lyrical monologues of great beauty. In spite of its different, cynical view of the worlds of the fairy tale and the dream, this is one of Bergman's most poetic and at the same time theatrically effective works. Dramatically effective and innovative are also the three plays *Spelhuset* (The Gambling House), *Vävaren i Bagdad* (The Weaver in Bagdad) and *Porten* (The Gateway) that were published in one volume in 1923. In these are found reflections of Strindberg's dream-play technique and of the fiery Expressionism of the post-war years. Behind the hectic, theatrical, narrowly stylized casino atmosphere in the first-mentioned lies the memory of the decadence of inflation-ridden Berlin. The mildly parodical orientalism in the second reflects the fact that Bergman translated *The Thousand*

and One Nights. The Strindbergian resignation of the third play concludes with a message that is central for the late Bergman: "Life is consideration." The 1920s gave rise to some brilliant comedies, of which *Swedenhielms*, 1925, was the most successful. Its popularity has made it into something of a Swedish national comedy. With splendid comic bravura it depicts a charming, successful but extravagant engineer's family, whose expensive habits and vitality turn out to be paid for by the faithful housekeeper's forged signatures. It is perhaps something of a national blemish that is revealed when its idealistic conceptions of honor thus turn out to be hollow, yet this denouement takes place in an atmosphere of hilarity and exhilaration. Here—as earlier in the case of *Hans nåds testamente* (His Grace's Last Testament), *God's Orchid* and *Thy Rod and Thy Staff*—Hjalmar Bergman's paradoxical, literary clowning triumphs in highly colored character portraits that force the public to laugh in the midst of the tragic, pessimistic depiction of human life's capricious game.

Pär Lagerkvist
Modernist of Timelessness

With Pär Lagerkvist (1891–1974), awarded the Nobel Prize in Literature in 1951, Swedish literature got its first modernist, i.e. the first writer to link up more directly with the international movements. He was, however, only to a limited extent a pioneer and leading figure of the new artistic ideas. He went his own way, and the great existential questions always interested him more than contemporary literary life. When he formulated his modernistic program in 1913 in *Ordkonst och bildkonst* (Word Art and Pictorial Art) he tied in with modern art, in particular with Cubism and Expressionism. However, typically enough, he also cited as models the very oldest forms of literature: Homer, the Greek tragedies, the Old Testament, the Icelandic saga, the sources of primitive Indian and Persian religion and more. In the midst of his bold, artistic innovation is an obvious archaic element, a lingering fascination with timeless moods and attitudes, a strong link with metaphysical problems and the great religious questions. His writing can be seen as a powerful duel between the new scientific picture of the world, which he accepted early, and the Christian and Platonic-idealistic legacy from the nineteenth century. There is an immense tension between faith in life and disgust with life, between respect for man and a black, Swiftian misanthropy, between rebellion against world order and humility before a God whose being and existence he never stops seeking. Amid all the oscillations between Realism and Symbolism, simple old-fashioned style and literary experimentation, his rich and many-sided production, that comprises poetry as well as prose and drama, represents the enduring religious feeling for life in a secularized era. It contains an almost unique concentration on metaphysics in an era that has turned its back on metaphysical questions and is characterized by the decay, dissolution and fragmentation of ideas. Lagerkvist's work represents a classical reserve of timelessness in uneasily splintered twentieth-century literature, yet at the same time it has a profound affinity with modern man's rootlessness and innermost need of eternal values.

Lagerkvist grew up in a simple and strongly religious home in Växjö in southern Sweden. He has shaped his childhood memories in the autobiographical novel *Gäst hos verkligheten (Guest of Reality)*, 1925, whose depiction of milieu is powerfully realistic, yet where the stress lies on the young protagonist's inner liberation and departure from a stifling pietistic environment. From the socially simple circumstances of his childhood and adolescence, Lagerkvist inherited a natural feeling of affinity with the ordinary man, who as a rule stands at the center of his literary work. It was also natural for him, when he left home, to gravitate toward socialism's social ideals and to assimilate the modern scientific picture of the world. Yet it was toward aesthetics and existential problems that he directed his powers early on. A trip to Paris in 1913 brought him into contact with the latest art and its programmatic modernity, and he was able to acquaint himself with Gertrude Stein's art collection. Impressions from this revolution in artistic thought lie behind his polemical program in *Ordkonst och bildkonst* (Word Art and Pictorial Art) that was directed against what he interpreted as decadence in contemporary literature, and also came to affect his own writing. His debut work, the short novel *Människor* (People), 1912, already had a modern form in that it was written in a startling staccato style where most was left unsaid. His prose now developed toward boldly creative forms, as for example in the collection of prose poems *Motiv* (Motifs), 1914. However, his first significant work was *Ångest* (Anguish), 1916. It introduced a new darker and harsher style into Swedish poetry and stood out against the wartime's expressionistically desperate moods, as well as against a personal crisis. The imagery is directed against the brutal and the shocking, and it consciously defies traditional poetic values: "Anguish, anguish is my heritage,/ the wound of my throat,/ the cry of my heart in the world," "I spit at the dirty vault of space/ and the stars' pale snouts."

For some time ahead Lagerkvist concentrated his energies on drama. He aimed at a forceful settling of accounts with the illusory theatrical Realism of the Ibsen brand and advocated a stylized and theatrically effective drama. Like Hjalmar Bergman, he tied in with the late Strindberg dramas (yet not without polemical objections), but he had a considerably stronger affinity to the expressionist drama that was then emerging on the Continent. *Sista mänskan* (The Last Man), 1917, gives, as the name indicates, an eschatological picture of man's downfall, marked by the furious and high-strung nature of modern living. The masterpiece of Lagerkvist's early expressionist drama, though, is *Himlens hemlighet (The Secret of Heaven)* that was published in the volume *Kaos* (Chaos), 1919, and staged in 1921. The set is a hemisphere on which a number of people without any particular connection to each other happen to find themselves. They begin a discourse on conceptions of life in simple and natural language. A young man seeks the meaning of life, but he is surrounded by a ghostly futility, conveyed with biting ironic effect. In its fusion of cosmic universality and triviality, of simplicity and subtlety, this drama is both typical of the time and a masterpiece of its style. *Kaos* also contained prose and poetry. The story "Den fordringsfulle gästen" (The Demanding Guest) is a Kafka-like story about a man on a short stay in a hotel before he returns to the eternity from which he came. Irritated with the disorder and disarray, he is obsessed with the question of what kind of meaning there is in his life. In its tightly controlled style, this is a masterful piece of expressionist prose. On the other hand, the volume's poems, collected under the title "I stället för tro" (Instead of Faith), point toward more harmonious moods and contain among other things two of Lagerkvist's classic poems: "Nu löser solen sitt blonda hår" ("The Sun Is Loosening Her Light Blond Hair") and "Det är vackrast när det skymmer" (It is Prettiest When Dusk Comes), the timeless harmony of which takes on a psalm-like character:

> *Allt är ömhet, allt är smekt av händer.*
> *Herren själv utplånar fjärran stränder.*
> *Allt är nära, allt är långtifrån.*
> *Allt är givet*
> *människan som lån.*

> All is tenderness, all is caressed by hands.
> The Lord himself effaces distant shores.
> All is near, all is far away.
> All is given
> to man on loan.

Lagerkvist vacillated between sharp contrasts during the twenties. The gentle little story *Det eviga leendet (The Eternal Smile)*, 1920, takes place in a timeless and spaceless realm of death, in which a group of dead people sit and relate the stories of their life to each other "in order to make eternity pass." Upset by life's aimlessness and injustices, they decide to seek out God in order to take him to task for the meaninglessness of his Creation. However, God turns out to be an old wood-cutter who explains that the only intention behind the Creation was that no one should need to be satisfied with having nothing and that he experienced a great happiness in creating children. The dead resignedly take their leave of him, having gained an insight into the meaning of life.

The underlying mood of trust in this story differs sharply from the darkly pessimistic and harshly satirical prose pieces in *Onda sagor* (Evil Tales), 1924. They owe their blackness and roughness to Swift, to whom Lagerkvist acknowledged a certain debt. In particular the attack on the sensationalism, the platitudes and the insensitivity of modern existence has a grimly humorous absurdity and expressionistically frightening character, in which the proximity to Kafka is again striking. On the other hand, the poetry Lagerkvist wrote during this decade is mostly light and idyllic. The collection *Den lyckliges väg* (The Path of the Happy Man), 1921, contains many of his most beautiful love poems and is dominated by classical, timeless and confident moods. *Hjärtats sånger* (Songs of the Heart), 1926, Lagerkvist's perhaps foremost collection of poetry, is a religiously-conditioned homage to the eternal human spirit, contrasting with violent protests against the meaninglessness of life. The poems here often bear an unexpectedly archaic linguistic and poetic stamp. The drama during this period spans universal stylization—as in the verse drama *Den osynlige* (The Invisible), 1923, where man's spirit lives on eternally after the world's downfall—and paradoxical realism—in the tragedy *Han som fick leva om sitt liv (The Man Who Lived His Life Over)*, 1928, where a murderer gets a reprieve but whose new life becomes the cause of his son's suicide.

During the 1930s, Lagerkvist's literary production emerged against the growth of Nazism and the other dictatorships with their associated violence, and derived support from traditional western idealism of Platonic character. His motto became: "fighting humanism." A trip to Greece and Palestine resulted in the book of thoughts *Den knutna näven* (The Clenched Fist), 1934. Here he juxtaposed oriental irrationalism and misanthropy with western faith in reason and individualism in order to take a stand, strong in pathos, for western ideals. He saw the Acropolis in Athens as a symbol of western culture, a clenched fist directed against the subversive forces of the time. The poetry collection *Vid lägereld* (At the Campfire), 1932, had already given expression to desolate and apocalyptic sentiments: the human soul must arm itself for battle and resistance. The story *Bödeln (The Hangman)*, 1933, was Lagerkvist's first clear reaction against Nazism; it also enjoyed success in a dramatized version. It is divided into two sections: one medieval, where the hangman figure appears in a raw and primitive environment as an evil genius, and one a modern restaurant where the worship of violence, racism and cynicism is portrayed with dark, desperate satire. There too, the hangman appears both as mankind's constant fellow-traveler and as a tormented sacrificial figure in the service of evil.

Pär Lagerkvist.

There is a vehement tension in this work between the view of evil as an integral part of man's existence and the furious outbursts against the evil in the modern barbarian ideologies. The passionate fight for justice and humanity against evil's subversive forces was carried on in a number of poetry collections and plays during the 1930s and the war years. Lagerkvist's lyrical form of expression was now more and more tied to the great nineteenth-century tradition. With simple and easily understood conventions of expression and national and religious motifs it attempted to return to a vein of idealism in Swedish poetry reminiscent of Tegnér, Rydberg and Heidenstam. It was a low-key and slightly out-of-fashion "poetry of preparedness" in an evil and difficult time. Of more lasting significance, though, is the play *Midsommardröm i fattighuset (Midsummer Dream in the Workhouse)* from 1941, a light fantasy with dark shadows, in which the fairy tale mingles with realism. The dream about "love's great, eternal midsummer kingdom" is here a vision to counter a reality that is unbearable and all the evil forces that strive to destroy life and love.

During the war years, Lagerkvist gathered his strength for a major novel about the nature of evil: *Dvärgen (The Dwarf)* that came out in 1944. It was a considerable public success and also gained a certain international renown. On the surface, it is a historical novel set at a Renaissance court with a Macchiavelli-inspired prince and his dwarf as protagonists. The bloody course of action appears mainly to be steered by the dwarf's malevolent manipulations. He is the incarnation of evil and the denial of life, who can only feel joy at war and malicious sudden death and who abhors love, mercy and bird song. He is perplexed by and hostile to art, science and religious conviction and is beyond all sensual feeling for life. He thrives on destruction, and he allows its principles to guide his actions. To be sure, he is imprisoned for his evil deeds, but in his underground cell he awaits the hour when the prince will need him again. His destructivity can not be vanquished. Lagerkvist has brilliantly allowed the dwarf to narrate his own bloody story, thereby becoming shamelessly intimate with his readers. In spite of its clear and simple symbolism, the novel is a story with many unexpected layers, and without a doubt it stands out as one of the most important novels of twentieth-century Swedish literature.

After *The Dwarf* followed a long series of remarkable novels and short tales that represent the culmination of Lagerkvist's mature writing. These were interrupted only by the late poetry collection *Aftonland (Evening Land)*, 1953, where the moods are uncommonly peaceful and serene, yet also classical and full of melancholy. The first of these prose works, where the style throughout is simple and at the same time sublime, universal and concretely visual, was *Barabbas (Barabbas)*, 1950, which in significance is on a par with *The Dwarf*. The story of Barabbas, who was released instead of Christ, is an epic reflection upon misdirected religious feeling for life. Barabbas is mysteriously chained to the religious wonder without fully being able to believe and understand anything of Christ's doctrine of love. This simple, rough man can never liberate himself from the memory of his meeting with the pale Savior, and, largely by mistake, he too is condemned to crucifixion during the first wave of Christian persecution in Rome. *Sibyllan (The Sibyl)*, 1956, is also about man's permanent confinement to his conception of God and his brooding over an inexplicable God and a merciless world order. The setting is pagan, ancient Delphi, which is painted with astounding clarity. To Delphi comes Ahasuerus, the man who refused Christ's request to lean against his house and rest on His way to Golgotha and who is therefore doomed to wander eternally on the earth. He seeks out an old priestess who has been expelled from the temple because she partook of profane love. They communicate their unhappy fates to each other, both having met with cruel and incomprehensible gods. He is filled with suppressed hatred and contempt, she with a stronger and lucid insight into the paradoxes of existence. Ahasuerus' path toward a more positive experience of the divine is treated in *Ahasverus död (The Death of Ahasuerus)*, 1960, the first part of a trilogy of stories which also includes *Pilgrim på havet (Pilgrim at Sea)*, 1962, and *Det heliga landet (The Holy Land)*, 1964. Man's eternal quest stands at the center of this both naive and sublime pilgrim epic, where he is driven by a need for love and atonement from which he cannot liberate himself. *Mariamne (Herod and Mariamne)*, 1967, the novel about Herod's wife, whom he has killed but whose love lives on in his soul, also deals ultimately with the fact that divine love too is inseparably united with man's spirit. The thematic development in Lagerkvist's later work goes from eternal evil to equally eternal divine love. His work circles around this great contradiction in man, as if around two immutable poles. Not least in his late works he was able to formulate this eternal dualism, in universal pictures of transcendent beauty from a metaphysical landscape, in such a way as to make the great questions of life accessible for the reader.

Vilhelm Moberg and the Agrarian Epic

Among the socio-critical writers of the 1910s who were mentioned earlier, a significant portrayer of farming society is missing. Not until the interwar period did a flourishing literature emerge that depicted the people of the countryside and the way they lived with authentic insight. Lively depictions of the life of these people had certainly existed earlier, but the nineteenth-century stories had been written, as a rule, by authors of middle-class origins and urban perspectives, such as Almqvist, Strindberg and other writers of the eighties. Authors of humble extraction with real experience of life and work in the countryside now appeared, and through their well-informed descriptions they gave the Swedish realistic novel a new direction and a deepened social perspective.

The foremost portrayer of the farmer's life was Vilhelm Moberg (1898–1973). He grew up in a simple tenant-soldier's croft in the poor areas of southern Småland, where his father was eventually able to buy his own home and run a small farm. The agrarian society with which Moberg was familiar when young was, however, a society in decline—as mentioned earlier, during the interwar period the population of the towns surpassed that of the countryside—and at the same time a society undergoing a thorough structural change. The youth of the countryside moved to the towns in ever greater numbers, and this flight from the countryside became one of the period's most important social problems. At the same time, the age-old farming society with its small private farmers and its traditions began to dissolve and be replaced by modern industrialized agricultural practices. This whole process of transformation is reflected in Moberg's books. It is paradoxical, however, that when farming society finally got its own authentic portrayer, it had already become history. Moberg wrote social and cultural-historical chronicles about the changes that the farming society had undergone. He analyzed it, not without indignation, and cast nostalgic glances back to the life and values of the old agrarian society. There was a down-to-earth primitivist in Moberg who preserved an unbridled agrarian individualism and liberal values in the midst of modern mass society. There was also in him an apostle of justice, inspired by socialism, who attacked society's class differences and legal injustices with a vehement pathos. As a writer of prose epics he was something of a conservative, with a sort of classic realistic narrative art, vital and grand in scale, mixing the tragic and the comic, and with links to the chronicle style of both the Old Testament and the Icelandic saga.

After studies at a folk high school and many years as a journalist, Moberg made his real literary debut with the novel *Raskens. En soldatfamiljs historia* (Raskens, the Story of a Soldier's Family), 1927, behind which lies his own parents' story. The lives and privations of the simple small farmers are depicted with stalwart realism and cultural-historical accuracy, and the work is a kind of tribute to their will to survive and their courage in meeting adversity and tribulations. In the linked novels *Långt från landsvägen* (Far from the Highway), 1929, and *De knutna händerna* (Clenched Fists), 1930, the socio-historical perspective is expanded through the depiction of the development of farming society from the nineteenth to the twentieth century. The main character, who stands firm by the old and refuses to adjust to the new demands made by the modern era's agricultural rationalization, is a sympathetic figure, with a certain tragic greatness. *Mans kvinna* (Man's Woman), 1933, is a historical love story from eighteenth-century Småland, that shows clear traces of the D. H. Lawrence-inspired primitivism and sexual mysticism that swept through Swedish literature during the years around 1930. It is an intense and passionate story, drawn in strong, dark colors, and one of the foremost love stories in Swedish literature. But as in the previous books, the theme is to an equally high degree that of an individualist in conflict with external social pressure. This opposition would continue to characterize Moberg's writing in later works.

The literature of the 1930s gained a unique profile from the many autobiographical novels written by authors of proletarian origin. Moberg's contribution to this genre was a trilogy that appeared 1935–39, the first part of which, *Sänkt sedebetyg (Memory of Youth)*, became the best known. It is by and large a psychological depiction of the driving forces behind the flight from the countryside, the mechanisms of breakup and their consequences. The book's conclusion also contrasts peaceful working of the soil with the contemporary tendencies toward violence. During the war years, Moberg's political message was formulated still more clearly in the historical novel *Rid i natt! (Ride This Night!)*, 1941. This sketches the farmers' resistance to a strengthening aristocratic rule in seventeenth-century Småland in a way that conveyed the contemporary necessity of resistance to Nazi Germany's expansion; it was also an oblique criticism of neutral Sweden's government and its concessionary politics. The novel is largely based on studies of historical documents, and the story's strong pathos is borne by Moberg's powerful epic language, with its effective rhetoric, appropriate archaisms and lyric prose. A vehement settling of accounts with the Swedish policy of neutrality is also evident in *Soldat med brutet gevär (When I Was a Child)* from 1944. This is a novel with clear autobiographical features; but it is also an extensive chronicle of the history of the popular movements during the first half of the twentieth century. Here, again, Moberg links an individual destiny with broad and detailed social perspectives.

However, Moberg's foremost work was the colossal emigrant epic he worked on with inexhaustible energy during the postwar period. This comprises four parts: *Utvandrarna (The Emigrants)*, 1949, *Invandrarna (Unto a Good Land)*, 1952, *Nybyggarna (The Settlers)*, 1956, and *Sista brevet till Sverige (The Last Letter Home)*, 1959. It captures the history of Swedish emigration to America in the stories of some typical emigrants. These are poor smallholders in nineteenth-century Småland who, due to poverty, wretched working conditions, the harassment of the authorities and religious intolerance, emigrate to the promised land to start a new life. We follow them on their adventurous crossing of the Atlantic, during their first encounter with the new homeland and their hard life on a remote farm in Minnesota. The strength of the work's epic realism does not lie in Moberg's originality but rather in his representative, authentic and documentarily well-grounded treatment of the issues. It lies not least in an accomplished characterization. The main figures meet the reader with urgent clarity; they are commonplace yet surrounded by a grand epic aura. The simple individual destinies become the bearers of the great historical event. Here too, Moberg's epic art is well-grounded in the study of historical documents that gives the huge work a strong social and cultural-historical tangibility. Moberg was fascinated by the hidden history in people's lives, and toward the end of his own life he wrote a history of Sweden, in which he tried to promote a popular perspective of history as opposed to traditional academic conceptions.

A sequel to the emigrant epic came in the novel *Din stund på jorden (A Time on Earth)*, 1963, in which a Swedish-American emigrant looks back on his life with, for the author, unusually personal and intimate emotions. It was also very successful in dramatized form, as were several other of Moberg's novels. He was active as a dramatist throughout his life, with comedies, peasant dramas, satires and problem plays in his repertoire. His *Domaren* (The Judge), 1957, reflects an actual legal case and is significant for the intense struggle Moberg carried on against what he saw as judicial decay in Swedish society. As an indefatigable republican, debater and polemicist he found himself in constant opposition to the Swedish Establishment and its view of society; he felt himself constantly called upon to defend justice, freedom and truth and "to monitor the authorities." An almost symbolic dimension hovered over this powerfully individualistic Swedish agrarian figure with his need for freedom passed down from past traditions. It was with a mixture of fighting spirit and rage that he locked horns with the modern bureaucratic society which was beginning to grow during the postwar period and was rendering the new democracy increasingly closed and doctrinaire.

Ivar Lo-Johansson and the Depiction of the Proletariat

In Swedish literature, the interwar period meant a breakthrough on a broad front for self-educated authors of proletarian origin. The 1910s had already seen the appearance of a first generation of writers who described the life of the working classes: Koch, Hedenvind-Eriksson, Maria Sandel. With this new interwar generation, the depiction of the proletariat became a remarkable, indeed a dominant feature in Swedish literature. The new authors gave a voice and cultural consciousness to a stratum of the population that had earlier occupied only a more or less peripheral literary position and was always observed from outside and above in social terms. Now, working-class history, conditions of life and culture were put at the center of interest in a long series of realistic, or rather naturalistic novels. These reflected the life and work of the working class, its social and political struggle and its values and attitudes to life from a socio-historical and a sociological perspective, and with a focus on individual destinies. Just as the nineteenth century's middle-class novel portrayed middle-class life, the twentieth-century proletarian novel came to give a broad panorama of a social class that was emerging from centuries of obscurity to political power and importance. The social, political and literary advances are parallel for obvious reasons, and they were to give the proletarian author a respected place on the literary Parnassus. Unlike their middle-class fellow authors, the worker-writers had no academic background. Their educational process was different: that of the autodidact. Many of them have attested to their insatiable hunger for reading at an early age and their difficulties in satisfying it. Parish and workers' libraries were their access to literature, political and union clubs their "university." An important role was also played by the folk high schools that began to be built from the second half of the nineteenth century to give young people from the peasant and working classes the chance of some further education after the obligatory schooling. The folk high schools often became lively educational centers. The labor movement's own folk high school was Brunnsvik, founded in 1906, located in Dalecarlia and associated with many proletarian writers and leading popular educators.

By coincidence, several of the new proletarian authors came from farm laboring stock. Some of them came to be grouped together as "the Cotter School" *(statarskolan)*: the cotters were the poorest of the farm laborers. They got their wages mainly in kind, thus effectively placing them in a concealed form of degrading social slavery. That the cotter system, which had arisen during the eighteenth century, was finally abolished in the mid-1940s was surely to a certain extent a result of the cotter authors' literary and journalistic efforts. In particular this holds for Ivar Lo-Johansson (b. 1901), the clearly dominating personality of the Cotter School and the most monumental of the Swedish worker writers. Early dreams of becoming a writer drove him away from the socially restricted farm-worker environment in which he grew up, and he tried his hand at a long series of other working-class occupations. During the 1920s he moved around frequently and took work in Europe. Several depictions of society written during these journeys are refreshingly realistic and original in the sense that they give a proletarian perspective. They depict, for example, mining communities and big city slum quarters with powerful indignation. Lo-Johansson made his real novel debut with *Måna är död* (Måna is Dead), 1932, an impassioned, erotic narrative, where the conflict is between love and the proletarian writer's work and his ambition.

The big breakthrough, though, came with *Godnatt, jord* (Good Night, Earth), 1933, a broad collective panorama of cotter life with clear autobiographical background features. The novel is written in a powerful, realistic style, with roots in the narrative art of Zola, Tolstoy and Gorky, among others. Over the roaring flood of persons and episodes hover gently lyrical moods, and out of the course of events crystallizes above all a cotter boy's life and development and reactions to his environment that clearly go back to the author's own experiences. The book is both a kind of homage to a disadvantaged social class and a flaming appeal for social improvement. However it also attests to a sensual and concrete appetite for reality of great proportions. In retrospect it stands out indisputably as Lo-Johansson's foremost novel. Subsequently he sought to widen the theme of cotter depiction in short story form through the collections *Statarna I och II* (The Cotters I and II), 1936–37, as well as *Jordproletärerna* (The Agricultural Proletarians), 1941. These stress the socio-historical and sociological situation of the cotter population through a diversity of motifs and perspectives. Squalor and social deprivation are constantly exposed, yet are also illuminated by a radiant narrative mood and by a warm sympathy and sense of humor. Lo-Johansson's prolific short-story production is an impressive literary feat, stemming from a determined will to document a piece of unknown social life beyond the literary common ground. The successful novel *Bara en mor* (Only a Mother), 1939, also takes place in the cotter environment and is not without a certain monumental greatness. Here, the collective depiction yields to an intense and strongly moving portrait of an individualistic and bright cotter woman who dares to go her own way and has the strength to endure an existence of depressing melancholy. *Kungsgatan* (King's Street) from 1935 is, on the other hand, a novel about the flight from the countryside and about the problems that rural youth were confronted with in the anonymity, coldness and prostitution of the city. It caused a sensation at the time and offended many because of its brutal descriptions and sexual candor.

In his later writings, Lo-Johansson liked to return to his early experiences of the proletarian environment, and he wrote two autobiographical series. The first was begun in the 1950s—*Analfabeten* (The Illiterate), 1951, *Gårdfari-handlaren* (The Peddler), 1953, and others—and is characterized by an increased ironic distance from the material. In the first-mentioned work he gives a grand portrait of his illiterate father, effective and humanly very appealing. The second series, which has more directly the character of a memoir, was begun as late as the 1970s and comprises *Pubertet* (Puberty), 1978, *Asfalt* (Asphalt), 1979, *Tröskeln* (The Threshold), 1982, and *Frihet* (Freedom), 1985. Surprising here is the immediate sensualism in the memory images and the uninterrupted vital narrative joy. The main work in Lo-Johansson's copious production in later years is otherwise the huge short-story cycle *Passionerna* (The Passions), 1968–72, which comprises seven collections, each one centered around one of the deadly sins. This is an uninhibitedly dynamic fresco of short stories, with motifs from different eras and settings and with a richly varied gallery of portraits. With humor and exuberance he has thrown himself into a vicious literary cosmos, which he voluptuously populates with all sorts of grotesque, selfish and all-too-human figures, in a flow of imagination in which Lo-Johansson's ingenuity seems almost inexhaustible. The short narrative form suits him excellently here, as in the cotter short stories, and it is scarcely an exaggeration to call him the foremost Swedish short-story writer of all time. He has been faithful to Naturalism all through his writing career, and he has followed up the legacy from nineteenth-century Naturalism's heyday by putting problems under debate with journalistic fervor. Beside the cotter question he has turned his attention to the care of the elderly, where he has fought for an increased humanization and liberalization. He has also taken an interest in and defended a discriminated group, the gypsies. He has attacked modern sports and provocatively spotlighted the Swedish isolation of the individual and its catastrophic consequences on the emotional and sexual plane. His active and energetic synthesis of literary-creative and socially conscious debate has played a vital and constructive role in the Swedish "people's home."

Like Moberg, Lo-Johansson has reached a large public, not least through inexpensive popular editions that have spread to groups outside the main consumer categories of fictional literature. The same is true for the other so-called cotter authors. Moa Martinson (1890–1964) illuminated the woman's role in the world of the farm laborer in works such as *Kvinnor och äppelträd (Women and Apple Trees)*, 1933, and *Mor gifter sig (My Mother Gets Married)*, 1936. Her strength was in a cheerful and vehemently committed narrative art, marked by a talent for emotional insight and authenticity. She also wrote a prose epic with the aim of sketching the history of the cotters, and she was highly active as a polemicist who enjoyed debate. An unaffected boldheartedness characterized her narrative style and public appearances and made her a popular and controversial personality during her lifetime. Jan Fridegård (1897–1968) also achieved great successes with his books, in particular with his series of novels about *Lars Hård*, 1935–36, 1942, 1951, where with penetrating and warm understanding he depicts the life of a social outsider. His strong interest in history led to a trilogy with themes from the Viking era: *Trägudars land* (The Land of the Wooden Gods), 1940, *Gryningsfolket* (The People of Dawn), 1944, and *Offerrök* (Sacrificial Smoke), 1949, which for once depict the life, social situation and the rebellious attempts of the thralls consistently from a proletarian author's perspective. Fridegård's prose style is notable for its striking power—not least in his dialogues, his simplicity and his almost Gallic clarity.

Eyvind Johnson and the Modern Novel Tradition

In spite of the striving for literary innovation of a number of writers, the early twentieth century's narrative prose was dominated by a middle-class and proletarian realism. However, during the interwar period the modern novel tradition began increasingly to penetrate, and in the 1940s there was a preponderance of experimental prose over the conventionally realistic. Young authors in the 1920s readily went abroad and were inspired by current trends in prose. In Eyvind Johnson there are traces of Proust and Gide, Joyce and Thomas Mann; in Rudolf Värnlund there is Alfred Döblin and John Dos Passos. A wave of interest in American narrative art made headway during the 1930s, and Hemingway's characteristic prose won its first imitators in the young Walter Ljungquist and Thorsten Jonsson, thus becoming for a short time during the 1940s the dominant stylistic model. In the same way, traces of Faulkner are noticeable in a thirties' novel by Artur Lundkvist and in the works of Walter Ljungquist from the end of the 1940s on. The modern Swedish art of the novel was, thus, integrated with the international one, while also retaining a certain tradition-bound independence and, at least in some cases, developing a superb originality.

The obvious central figure in modernist prose is Eyvind Johnson (1900–76) who was awarded the Nobel Prize in Literature in 1974. He grew up under relatively simple circumstances in upper Norrland, and he is usually considered a proletarian author. In his early years he tried a number of manual jobs, and his path into literature went via socialist newspapers and left-wing organizations. However, he only gave himself up to proletarian realism to a very limited extent. He was more strongly stimulated by the changes of perspective that modern prose experiments allowed, and the autodidactic educational process to which he submitted himself with irrepressible energy led him more and more in the direction of traditional humanistic knowledge and concentration on man's timeless conditions of existence. During the 1920s he settled abroad for lengthy periods, in Paris and Berlin. His work from the 1920s, after his debut in 1924, is relatively modest. The novel *Stad i mörker* (Town in Darkness), 1927, is a stark depiction of a small town, while its companion-piece *Stad i ljus* (Town in Light), 1928, that was originally published in a French translation under the title *Lettre recommandée*, 1927, has a certain stamp of the twenties and attests to an interest in stylistic experiments. With *Minnas* (Remembering), 1928, and *Kommentarer till ett stjärnfall* (Commentary on a Falling Star), 1929, it became clearer that the ideal of the new novel was in Johnson's mind's eye. He introduced here the inner monologue into Swedish literature in the manner of Joyce and used it in depictions of more or less psychotic states of mind. *Bobinack* is a peculiar, allegorical novel from 1932, the height of the depression years, and depicts the excesses of the modern business world from a critical socialist perspective. *Regn i gryningen* (Rain at Dawn), 1933, is a contribution to the flood of primitivistic literature during these years.

Johnson wrote his first real important works some way into the 1930s with the four-part autobiographical *Romanen om Olof* (The Novel About Olof), 1934–37. Like all other autobiographical novels by proletarian authors, it is a depiction of a young writer's path from simple background and cultural hunger to self-insight, ambitions to write, and a newly-won commitment to education. But Johnson's contribution to the genre is a work with many artistic layers and a psychological shading of unusual sort. The perspective of the young Olof's turbulent path from one job to another steadily fluctuates between analytical seriousness and imaginative irony. The story's realistic framework is interspersed with tales that give different perspectives of the course of action with great artistic effectiveness.

Like other Swedish writers, Johnson reacted vehemently to the harsh political climate created by Nazism's advance during the 1930s, and his writing became a passionately committed "literature of preparedness" in defense of democratic values and against ideologies of violence and racism.

Eyvind Johnson.

His unusually active and militant cultural struggle against Hitler's Germany as well as Stalin's Soviet Union was a strong moral support for writers from the occupied neighboring Nordic countries during the war years. He made the heaviest contributions to this "literary conscription" with the gigantic trilogy about the real-estate broker Johannes Krilon: *Grupp Krilon* (The Krilon Group), 1941, *Krilons resa* (Krilon's Journey), 1942, and *Krilon själv* (Krilon Himself), 1943. The work has an allegorical structure that reflects events and sentiments in Sweden during the war years, but that above all illustrates the mighty ideological battle between western democratic life values and the contempt for man and worship of power of the dictatorial ideologies. In a masterly firework display of narrative-technical ideas and invention, comprising sections of argumentation, dream sequences and satirical jokes, he gives expression to a deeply grounded faith in man's basic common sense, his ability to master the destructive forces within himself, his desire for justice and freedom and his ordinary, simple, human decency. The novel is one long—lofty yet unrhetorical— defense of a free but humanly committed mankind, as seen from a liberal, socially conscious standpoint. It is in this quiet but intensive humanism that the novel frees itself from the temporal and becomes a timeless document about man's will to fight for his humanity.

Johnson would often later return to man's eternal predicament, reflected in the incessant flow of history. He moved to classical times in his next novel, *Strändernas svall (Return to Ithaca)*, 1946, a modern rewriting of Homer's *Odyssey*. The epic breadth and high-spirited anachronisms of this novel corresponded to the postwar period's submissive climate, with its kernel of individual inner confidence. Odysseus is no rhetorical hero here. Tired of violence and warring deeds, he returns to his Ithaca devoid of optimism for the future, only to find that he must resort to violence again to remove Penelope's suitors. History's mirror reflects our era's mass psychoses and brutal administration of the law in the novel *Drömmar om rosor och eld* (Dreams About Roses and Fire), 1949, that deals with the notorious witch trials in Loudun in 1634, when a sexually attractive priest was accused of witchcraft by the convent nuns. In a coolly observing manner, Johnson analyzes the social forces that control man's actions and the psychological tensions and explosions that burst the conventional patterns.

In a couple of autobiographical works from the early 1950s, Johnson worked in a sophisticated way with different time planes, a technique which returned in his next historical novel, *Molnen över Metapontion* (Clouds over Metapontion), 1957. Here, the classical action, which takes place in a Greek colony in southern Italy and which focuses on Xenophon's depiction of the March of the Ten Thousand, is contrasted with our own time. Man's bitter experiences from two epochs are juxtaposed, resulting in the conclusion that there are no good victors in history, but that individual man still has the power to survive and create a meaningful existence for himself. With his next work in the genre of the historical novel, *Hans nådes tid (The Days of His Grace)*, 1960, Johnson created one of his most sterling literary masterpieces. It takes place during the period of brutal revolutions that Europe went through under Charlemagne in the eighth century and paints with great historical accuracy a colorful and lively time fresco, where the concrete and timebound is always illustrated by the timeless and universal. As a novel, the book is surprisingly conventional in its prose epic structure. It oscillates between the dryly registering tone of the chronicle and a remarkably visionary narrative art with a rich language of symbols and dreams. The mood shifts between rebelliousness and melancholic resignation, between disillusionment and a paradoxical inner confidence. The story's characters ring out ever more clearly with individual life and a sort of greatness void of rhetoric, even if they are crushed under the ruthlessness of the era and the senseless events that obliterate their individuality.

Likewise in Eyvind Johnson's later works of importance, *Livsdagen lång* (Life's Long Day), 1964, *Favel ensam* (Favel Alone), 1968, and *Några steg mot tystnaden* (Some Steps Towards Silence), 1973, this quiet faith in the individual's potential and the values of life is shown amid the fluctuations of history's cruel and inexorable mechanism. The narrative perspective is regularly permeated by reflections and commentaries about the history writer's role as an intermediary between man's eternally similar conditions of life and his understanding of life behind history's flicker of political actions. Pervasive in Johnson's authorship is a tension between an observing analytical intellect on the one hand and a need for protest and revolt on the other. An anarchosyndicalism in the spirit of Kropotkin, to which he remained faithful from his youth, runs throughout. This is closely related to traditional western democratic liberalism, and it embraces at the same time a calm and secure commonsense philosophy, an emotional vulnerability to violence and social injustices and a need to hold under control the irrational forces that bring about confusion both in man and in the historical course of action. Johnson's complicated novel structures have often served the purpose of avoiding simplification, superficiality, the use of clichés and cheap solutions to problems in order to deepen artistic vision and democratic conviction. Over the years his youthful utopianism cooled to a considerable degree and was replaced by a resigned disillusionment, but even in the postwar era's bitter climate a kernel of warmth was preserved in the belief in man's inherent ability to endure history's harsh winters with inner freedom and dignity.

The narrative art of the interwar period was influenced in many ways by modernist impulses. The era's need for emotional and sexual liberation was clearly reflected in the novel series by Agnes von Krusenstjerna (1894–1940): the *Tony* series, 1922–26, *Fröknarna von Pahlen* (The Misses von Pahlen), 1930–35, and *Fattigadel* (Poor Nobility), 1935–38. These depicted customs and were psychologically penetrating. They also caused a literary debate typical of the day because of their erotic motifs, during a time, the 1930s, when human drives were being given Freudian labels. The narrative technique of the film together with modern American prose influenced Walter Ljungquist's (1900–74) novels, which developed increasingly intricate patterns. With ties to anthroposophic mysticism, he focused with tender fascination on the mystery that is man, as for example in *Resande med okänt bagage* (Traveler with Unknown Baggage), 1938, and the glorious depiction of childhood, *Källan* (The Spring), 1961. The anti-utopian depiction of the future as a reflection of a hardening contemporary climate gets an exponent in the novel *Kallocain (Kallocain)*, 1940, by Karin Boye (1900–41), who was most prominent as a lyric poet. Her evocative, frightening vision of a totalitarian and closed future society with a technocratically organized system of repression, is no less effective than Aldous Huxley's *Brave New World* or George Orwell's *1984*.

However, not until the 1940s did a quantitative breakthrough come for a modernist narrative art. A new generation of novelists followed after Eyvind Johnson. Foreign writers like Hemingway, Faulkner, Kafka and Sartre became for shorter or longer periods the leading prototypes, and their narrative methods came in one way or another to be put to serve an absurd and existential conception of life in a hardening intellectual climate. Among the many new individual profiles must be mentioned first and foremost Stig Dagerman (1923–54). His writing career was short, precocious and intensive; he is one of the decade's many who died young, and his life and work have come to be surrounded by an almost legendary aura. Like Eyvind Johnson, he came from a relatively simple background, and like him he committed himself when young to the anarchosyndicalist movement, which had an unusually firm and well-unified organization in Sweden. He became the cultural editor of its newspaper *Arbetaren* (The Worker), one of the epoch's foremost cultural organs, where among other things he became known for his quick and sensitive daily poetry. As early as age 22, he made his literary debut with the novel *Ormen* (The Serpent), 1945, the decade's most noticed debut work. On the surface it is a depiction of military service during the "preparedness years," beneath the surface it is the story of a young generation's desperation, anxiety and uncompromising intellectual seriousness. Through its nervously intense circling around feelings of terror, dread and fear, it gave a special stamp to the decade's literature: Angst. Its message was a defense of the right to be afraid and to have the "courage to look Angst in the eye."

Man's fear was also at the thematic center in Dagerman's second novel, *De dömdas ö* (Island of the Doomed), 1946, indisputably his most remarkable work. It is a description of how seven people are shipwrecked on an uninhabited island. In a desolate, Kafka-like expressionist landscape, filled with frightful lizards and a hostile nature, their civilized exterior breaks down and they are motivated by the mechanisms of fear and a primitive desire to survive. The book can be read both as a ruthless unmasking of western civilization and a penetrating psychological analysis. In its radical striving to tear loose all the veils from reality it seeks to demonstrate that awareness represents modern man's only chance to save himself and survive. Its penetrating analysis of the absurdity and the nightmares of modern consciousness is underlined by its fiery language and its visionary perceptiveness. The narrative language often borders on modernist lyric poetry, with a wealth of metaphors, free flow of associations and a musically swelling prose that vibrates with vulnerable sensitivity. Dagerman created some of his best pieces—*Nattens lekar (The Games of Night)*, 1947—in the short-story form. These demonstrate his mastery both of the symbolistic and the realistic narrative style. In the novel *Bränt barn (A Burnt Child)*, 1948, he abandoned Symbolism for a psychological Realism in the depiction of a young man's difficulties in adapting to a new family situation. It is an intense novel about alienated emotions, about man's need for purity and tenderness, and about his realization that the deceit all around him is also within him. In *Bröllopsbesvär* (Wedding Worries), 1949, Dagerman went one step further in his change of style and ended up in the realistic grotesque. The novel is a burlesque of the countryside that with disillusioned yet warm fascination portrays existence as a tragicomic chaos, filled with a myriad of activities and unforeseen, chance events. It makes a strongly dramatic impact that reveals that Dagerman was also an accomplished dramatist. In *Den dödsdömde (The Condemned)*, 1947, he shaped a tragedy of absurdity with traces of both Lagerkvist and Kafka. *Skuggan av Mart* (The Shadow of Mart) from the same year can be seen as a sort of tentative apotheosis of the anti-heroic human ideals of the postwar period. Dagerman's literary production was uncommonly concentrated in terms of time. His feverish productivity during the years 1945–49 soon abated, and during the last five years of his life he obviously had difficulty in writing. After he took his life (in 1954) he left only the fragment of a planned novel about Almqvist. In its concentration, his authorship stands out as important both universally and as symptomatic of his era. In more recent years it has aroused increasing attention abroad, particularly in France. There is a violent intensity in his prose that bursts the boundaries of time and space, and behind his theme of Angst and desperation there is a fascinating element of lucid sincerity and honesty. With a kind of benign resignation, he accepted that man's lot in the modern era was fear and icy consciousness, and that his only solution lay in being faithful to Angst.

Alongside of Dagerman, Lars Ahlin (b. 1915) appeared as

the giant of the 1940s in the field of the novel, but his reputation has been significantly greater at home than abroad. In spite of the fact that early on he protested against Modernism's pretentions of form he emerged as the revitalizer of the art of the novel who boldly broke away from Realism's well-plowed furrows and illusions. To a higher degree than any other modern Swedish novelist, he has developed his own aesthetic of the novel, which also has a significant degree of originality in an international perspective. Ahlin's basic view is—unexpectedly enough at a time when Swedish cultural life has largely been secularized—religious, and specifically Lutheran. It has been deepened by thorough studies in Lutheran theology. His world picture is somewhat visionary, but its immediate application is valid for contemporary human society. What he seems to see is democracy achieved by human value and human dignity, irrespective of social and moral hierarchies and levels. In this world of cooperation and interaction, the novelist's task is to be "mediator," to communicate, to speak and to answer when addressed. The novel becomes the instrument for a communication process with the reader; language becomes the world in which human community arises. The consequence is that Realism's illusory effect must be broken down and that instead language itself must become the novel's center: a conversational forum between the author and the reader touching major existential questions, an interplay and a ritual around a drama, where man first loses and then regains his fundamental values, his participation in and communion with the whole.

Through his radical gospel of equality, Ahlin—in spite of his theological point of departure—came to stand out as a proponent of modern Swedish democracy. He too came from a simple home, and he took milieus, characters and motifs from the experiences of his turbulent and socially unstable youth in his Norrland hometown of Sundsvall for the literary universe he created later, and which is mainly peopled by society's lower strata. His educational path went via the folk high school, and he was deeply affected by the years of unemployment of the 1930s. He depicted his experiences from this time in the debut novel *Tåbb med manifestet* (Tåbb with the Manifesto), 1943, a depiction of the unemployed which deals with the problem of social alienation. Essentially, though, it is a novel of ideas and argumentation that juxtaposes Marxism and Lutheran theology with visionary richness. Ahlin aimed at something of a synthesis, where Marxism's demands for social justice enter a paradoxical union with the Lutheran doctrine of righteousness and mercy. The collection *Inga ögon väntar mig* (No Eyes Await Me), 1944, showed the author as a masterly short-story writer, clear, simple and with an intuitive ability to reproduce the nuances of everyday human language. The breakthough, though, came with the lengthy novel *Min död är min* (My Death Is Mine), 1945, an exuberantly realistic grotesque that energetically tackles the theme of man's degradation and dignity. It is above all a story about life's losers, which tries to solve the problem of how a man should be able to live with his misfortune. At the same time it is a sort of social analysis and a play about the mystery of humiliation. It challenged the hierarchical thinking of social values and the "raising" of false moral pretentions to allegedly higher levels. In spite of its dark theme, it is a happy and constructive book, teeming with pregnantly drawn figures and scenes.

Ahlin carried out his boldest experiment with form in his next novel, *Om* (If) from 1946. Here he tried to illustrate his communicative novel aesthetic in the form itself. With effects that are reminiscent of Romantic irony, he broke up Realism's machinery of illusions and tried to give the narrative the character of a game of communication with the reader. The protagonist's inner identity with the narrator and reader is stressed: "Bengt who is you who is I who is anybody." The theme is that of a father/son relationship, in which the son is forced to take responsibility for his father, a social failure. This is one of Ahlin's favorite motifs, to which he returned in a couple of later novels. The book also attests to its author's predilection for wordy, cultural-synthetic discussion. It is an accomplished polemic against nineteenth-century liberalism's cult of freedom, which is contrasted with a Lutheran-inspired doctrine of community and dependence. The novel *Fromma mord* (Pious Murders), 1952, is also an advanced experiment with form. Its theological patterns are intricate, and the depiction of its Christ-like protagonist has a sharpness and a depth that is reminiscent of Dostoevsky. In a complex language charged with symbols, Ahlin here criticizes traditional Christian piety and pleads instead for a Christian humor or comedy that comprises a redeeming total experience of all aspects of human existence, hopeful as well as desperate. The work is both a mighty gathering of strength and an artistic turning point.

Later in the 1950s, Lars Ahlin created a long series of novels of uncommon artistic strength in which the theme of love is central. From a hard-won insight into life, they mediate a bright and conciliatory vision of the conditions of human existence. They are carried by a bright and freely flowing language, emanating from a high degree of inspiration throughout. *Kanelbiten* (The Cinnamon Stick), 1953, is a fine psychological study of a young girl's precocious development into a woman and her reactions to her mother's unreflecting acknowledgement of life. *Stora glömskan* (The Great Amnesia), 1954, is an analogous study of a precocious young boy's relationship with his father and of his almost superhuman insight into other people's emotional lives and what motivates them; the sensitive and sharp-eyed boy becomes in a Romantic sense the bearer of a truer and deeper relationship to life. *Kvinna, kvinna* (Woman, Woman), 1955, is an obsessive love story, a jubilant hymn to earthly love, to the union between man and woman that is important for Ahlin as a symbol of community. The masterpiece of this series of novels, though, is *Natt i marknadstältet* (Night in the Market Tent), 1957, where his perpetual theme of debasement and rehabilitation gets its artistically definitive expression. The dark tragedy in this everyday story about a marital crisis is illuminated by an all-forgiving insight into life that casts a conciliatory light over the sadness of a shattered existence and brings the rejected back to the community's mystical feeling of participation. In the lighter novel *Gilla gång* (Normal Course), 1958, Ahlin maps out the crisis in an incompatible marriage with the same perceptive, psychological caution. Here, the human conflicts are lightened by a mild harmony and a warm humor of unusual character.

In *Bark och löv* (Bark and Leaves), 1961, Ahlin returned to the problems of the artist, which just as in the 1940s had a strongly polemical character and where he tried again to show that the novel is a linguistic work of art that acquires its meaning in a social context. This work was followed by a period of silence lasting more than twenty years. The author himself explained this by saying that he had said what he wanted to say and that there was nothing to add. Not until 1982 did he make a comeback with a historical novel, *Hannibal segraren* (Hannibal the Conqueror), written together with his wife Gunnel Ahlin, who had earlier published a novel about the young Hannibal. As with Eyvind Johnson, a lively, detailed time chronicle is mixed here with reflections on the situation of the historian. In 1985 *Sjätte munnen* (Sixth Mouth) was published, a return to the father and son motif as well as to a more simple and realistic narrative art. In 1987 *Din livsfrukt* (Your Fruit of Life) appeared, a lengthy novel dealing with the problems of the Swedish "people's home" in an era of rising prosperity and welfare. Its main character is a tax lawyer and millionaire who is trying to preserve the social-democratic ideals of his youth in a period of changed social goals. His dilemma is solved by suicide, and he takes his mentally handicapped little daughter, his "fruit of life," with him in death—after first having bequeathed his private means to an aid program for developing countries. This novel is a tremendous literary achievement, a new peak in Ahlin's works. The hiatus in Ahlin's production has not reduced his topicality nor his influence on Swedish cultural life. During the "silent" period, he continued to inspire a younger generation of writers and critics, a constant source of spiritual and artistic stimulation. With his vision of human equality and spiritual democracy, he has to a high degree been a focal point for literary discussion in Swedish democracy—challenging, invigorating, always displaying new sides. His dynamic and original socio-literary aesthetics of communication and his rich and warm narrative art have made him one of the great figures in twentieth-century Swedish literature, and one who is still awaiting his international breakthrough.

In his will to break away from the aesthetics and form of the realistic novel of illusions, Ahlin has a comrade from his own generation in Lars Gyllensten (b. 1921), but there the similarities end. Gyllensten is a sceptical intellectual with an almost scientific attitude to his writing—by profession he is also a medical scientist, even if he gave up his career for that of the author. Gyllensten sees his works as tools with which to examine and continually test images of worlds and ideas, and as experiments in a ceaseless investigation of modern attitudes to life and systems of faith. He regards general visions and finite idea systems with distrust and subjects them to a relentless criticism. His ideal can be described by a term like "faithlessness," i.e. a view of life without faith, without superstructures above a simple natural life of love and work. The cool scepticism and distance which can be discerned in his intellectual attitude does not exclude a strong devotion to this ideal, indeed a positively fiery determination to fight against the simplified and falsified images of reality that surround modern man. This made Gyllensten a vital central point of the cultural debate in Sweden, particularly in the 1960s. Nor are religious questions and intellectual mysticism alien to him; Kierkegaard numbers among his companions, as well as Swedenborg. His now extensive œuvre can be seen as a continuous whole, a steady dialogue between positions and points of view, a dialectical process that steadily moves toward an elusive synthesis. It is a dialogue that goes on between and within the works, but also with other writers, for example Ahlin.

Gyllensten's real debut—after a somewhat notorious parody of 1940s modernistic poetry that attracted much attention—was *Moderna myter* (Modern Myths), 1949, a collection of stories of different types with the subtitle "dialectical fancy." Starting points in this successive unmasking of contemporary myths were Kierkegaard and Hieronymus Bosch. The fictional pieces are to be considered as literary experiments, as "artifacts," where the fiction itself is an intellectually conscious tool for the analysis of ideas, for discussion and argumentation and scientific testing. *Det blå skeppet* (The Blue Ship), 1950, was a "counter-message" to *Moderna myter*, a more unified, mythical narrative, which is played out in the Stockholm archipelago and where the intellectual analysis of "the bankruptcy of naive commitment" is replaced by a more naive picture of an intellectual commitment. Gyllensten has often carried out his dialectical experimentation in literary triptychs. One of these starts with

Barnabok (Children's Book), 1952, a ruthless analysis of the loss of naiveté and immaturity; followed by *Senilia*, 1956, a corresponding illustration of the attitudes of aging, passivity and resignation; and then by *Juvenilia*, 1965, where the desire for a direct and enthusiastic commitment is tested and rejected. It is striking that throughout all of these works the changes of position and the different viewpoints correspond to language and style variations which stress and often parody hollow and false attitudes, and that the intellectual experiment is at the same time a carefully devised experiment of form.

Senatorn (The Senator) from 1958 was a more convention-ally constructed novel about an Eastern bloc politician who lands in a human vacuum when he happens to break out of his social context. Gyllensten here, distinct and impartially testing, contrasts Communism's social discipline with Capi-talism's normless gospel of freedom. *Sokrates död* (The Death of Socrates), 1960, looks with farcical and anachron-istic effect at the legal action brought against the great philosopher and dialectician from the standpoint of the fam-ily and deglorifies his final choice by pleading for the simple, low life with its sensual palpability. *Kains memoarer (The Testament of Cain)*, 1963, is a pastiche-like chronicle about the sect of the Cainites that worshipped Cain and Satan and devoted themselves to useful and industrious work. Gyllen-sten here turns the religious concepts upside down and with clever irony plays with alternative views and faiths. Beyond his repudiation of all closed ideologies and doctrines, there is room for a "Nihilistic Credo"—the title of an essay collec-tion from 1964—and a sincere prayer to the mundane. He can also turn against western civilization's hedonistic exces-ses with strong moral indignation—as in *Lotus i Hades* (Lotus in Hades), 1966, where he depicts Europe as a glass veranda to the continent of Asia.

The intellectual and moral process continued unflaggingly in later works and moved toward individual liberation and maturity. In *Palatset i parken* (The Palace in the Park), 1970, he painted—in the manner of Giuseppe Arcimboldo—a portrait consisting of fragmentary sketches and memory images, a dream play in prose form about the problem of compassion. The dialectical triptych is accomplished in one and the same work in *Grottan i öknen* (The Cave in the

Desert), 1973, where among other things the choice of an ascetic, anonymous lifestyle is presented as a heroic alternative way of living, as well as in *Huvudskallebok* (Skull Book), 1981, a "novel in three turns" that oscillates between the lyrically meditative and burlesque Rabelaisian satire. The problem of human power relations is analyzed in *I skuggan av Don Juan* (In the Shadow of Don Juan), 1975, a book about both Don Juan's final impotence and his servant's vain lust for power. *Baklängesminnen* (Backward Memory), 1978, reverses the usual chronology of memoirs with the inherent comedy of a dream which places the novel in a European modernist Kafka-tradition. *Sju vise mästare om kärlek* (Seven Magi on Love), 1986, are delicious pastiches of Indian prose, displaying the wide range of Gyllensten's narrative art. As a whole, Gyllensten's works, with their variations of theme and their ever-shifting characteristics of style, constitute an incessantly changing intellectual fresco of life, in which the interplay of details and contrasts never ceases to fascinate. This continuous testing of views has been as valuable for intellectual life in the modern Swedish democracy as Ahlin's profound gospel of equality. Where the latter is a democratic visionary, Gyllensten is a sceptic and the conscience of democracy, who passionately guards the fundamental values and necessities of human life.

The desire to experiment found many forms of expression in the prose art of the 1940s, from Gösta Oswald's (1926–50) lyrical novels *En privatmans vedermödor* (A Private Person's Hardships), 1940, and *Rondo*, 1951, in which the epoch's attraction to esoteric, advanced stylistic forms reached its prose culmination, to Willy Kyrklund's (b. 1921) oriental stories, marked by a mischievous scepticism and a playful irony, e.g. *Solange*, 1951, and *Polyfem förvandlad* (Polyphemus Transformed), 1964. But the traditionally realistic Swedish rural narrative also underwent its metamorphoses in a modernist direction. Dagerman's *Bröllopsbesvär* (Wedding Worries) is not the only example of this. Tage Aurell (1895–1976) in novellas and especially in short stories gave new, compressed expression to small, everyday tragedies of the countryside, where the associatively evocative is given an almost classic dimension of objective clarity—*Skillingtryck* (Chapbook), 1943, *Smärre berättelser* (Lesser Stories), 1946. Sara Lidman (b. 1923), made her debut in this neoprovincial wave with its new advances in narrative technique, with novels like *Tjärdalen* (The Tar Still), 1953, *Hjortronlandet* (Cloudberry Land), 1955, and *Regnspiran* (*The Rain Bird*), 1958. These provoked a sensation by being written in a Västerbotten dialect that afforded southern Swedish readers certain difficulties. They also exploited new domains of narrative art with penetrating psychological portraiture and lyrical moods of a particularly introverted nature. With these works the character of Swedish folk-life depiction changed once again.

In contrast to the ever more complicated forms of prose writing, some authors strove for a more popular narrative without thereby losing literary quality. Among them was Frans G. Bengtsson (1894–1955), who made his foremost contribution as a British-inspired essayist, perhaps the foremost Swedish essayist of all time. He sought out colorful and grand historical subjects, that he fondly contrasted to our own time with its pale and psychologizing human ideals. However, his special talent was for essays of classical type, such as "Promenad till en myrstack" ("A Walk to an Ant Hill"). His historical prose epics culminated with a great work about Karl (Charles) XII, one of his historical favorites. His most popular book, though, was *Röde Orm (The Long Ships)*, 1941–45, which was his only novel. It is an eventful and lively story from the Viking era, where the heroic is united with the grotesque and the travesties of the Icelandic saga are sometimes exaggerated and farcical. The work became a great success and, through translations and a Hollywood film, probably helped to increase interest in the Vikings and their plundering expeditions. Frans G. Bengtsson's farcical temperament had an undergraduate-type character that he shared with another popular storyteller, Fritiof Nilsson Piraten (The Pirate) (1895–1972). The latter's narrative art has a strongly oral and homely nature that does not, however, exclude sophistication. There is a burlesque humor in practically all he wrote, but there is also a penetrating depiction of man and a dark pessimism in his insistence on the tragic aspects of existence. The Pirate—a nickname from his student years at Lund—won a large and appreciative public with his depictions of the young boy in *Bombi*

Bitt och jag (Bombi Bitt), 1932, and *Bombi Bitt och Nick Carter* (Bombi Bitt and Nick Carter), 1946, the novel *Bokhandlaren som slutade bada* (The Book Dealer Who Ceased Bathing), 1937, and the masterpiece of a short story, *Historier från Färs* (Tales from Färs), 1940.

Finland-Swedish Modernism
Edith Södergran and Others

A lyrical Modernism had gradually started to enter Swedish literature via Strindberg, Fröding, Ekelund and above all the young Pär Lagerkvist. The concept "Modernism" can most accurately be seen as a collective name for a literature that put the new and the modern at the center—and this in conscious and polemical opposition to older literary trends. The many different modernist movements and authors have certain common denominators, such as experimentation, the breaking of the norm and the deformation of earlier forms of expression, the challenge to established artistic taste and avant-gardism. The latter was a desire to appear as pioneers of literary development and answer the modern era's demands for an advanced form of writing, corresponding to modern world images and views, but sometimes also in intentional collision with technocratic civilization. In terms of ideas, though, it is difficult to give the concept "Modernism" a unified character. The term functions best perhaps as an umbrella term that includes the various modernist trends: Futurism, Expressionism, Imagism, Dadaism, Surrealism and more. In the area of lyric poetry, the modernist efforts were expressed above all in an abundant use of the free verse form without rhyme and meter, and in a freer and more advanced use of imagery. Images became the poet's most important material; they took an independent position in the text and could therefore be given free and varying interpretations. Other means exploited by the lyrical modernists were typographical effects and a structure that broke with logical and chronological principles. With the modernist poem a new triviality and objectivity also made its way into poetry.

For various reasons, lyrical Modernism made a stronger breakthrough and took on a more pronounced character of

movement and trend in Swedish-speaking Finland in the
1920s. Swedish-speaking Finland had over time become
more and more a minority culture that guarded its own
literary traditions and that felt an ethnic solidarity through
its own cultural manifestations. During the Russian Revolution, Finland broke free of the Russian empire and became
an independent republic in 1917, with a bloody and class-
based civil war as a consequence. The political, social and

Edith Södergran.

cultural relationships, however, were much too complicated for one simply to draw the conclusion that the modernist liberation was in keeping with a minority culture's situation or the new political independence. Equally, the leading modernists exhibited such great differences that general conclusions are difficult to draw. On the other hand, it is clear that the modernist breakthrough was to a high degree connected with one great and independent author with an uncommon personal radiance: Edith Södergran.

Edith Södergran (1892–1923) was born into a relatively affluent middle-class family in the Russian capital St. Petersburg, where she later went to German school. Her youthful poetry is written mainly in German, but also in Swedish, Russian and French. Her educational environment opened international windows, and proximity to contemporary German pre-expressionist poetry and to Russian Symbolism and Futurism was certainly one of the contributing factors to her later adoption of Modernism. In her teens she became gravely ill with tuberculosis and stayed for a while at a sanatorium in Davos. This environment to a certain extent further widened her international perspective, while her sickness and constant proximity to death—as well as a bitter disappointment in love—constituted the personal background from which her vital, life-acknowledging poetry sprang forth. After her sojourn in Davos, she settled down with her mother in the Karelian countryside, in a border area between Finland and Russia. It was from this geographically remote location that her boldly pioneering poetry emerged, a fact that further underscored the pathetic in this prophetically inspired and at the same time mortally ailing figure.

In her first collection, *Dikter* (Poems) from 1916, short poetry inspired by Runeberg folk ballads is interspersed by symbolistic legendary strains and Whitman-like catalogue style and repetitions. But unique is the new linguistic sensitivity with which she, with unfailing intuition, creates a broad register of erotic motifs, impressions of nature and fantasy. Throughout, the both cool and overheated intensity in her emotional aestheticism oversteps conventional poetic boundaries. Her desire for linguistic-artistic expansion becomes even clearer in the two following poetry collections *Septemberlyran* (September Lyre), 1918, and *Rosenaltaret*

(Altar of the Roses), 1919. In the midst of the civil war that broke out after the national liberation, she raised a heroic, Nietzschean lyrical protest against the bitter captivity of her life. With ecstatic, prophetic inspiration she foresaw here the new mankind who had liberated himself from the bonds and inhibitions of religion and who had the inner strength to let himself be intoxicated by the universal omnipotence. She places her ego at the center and lets it expand into an endless universe. She feels the "triumph of existing" and self-indulgently lets language create extraordinary impressions and experiences: "See in the sunset/ swimming fire islands proceed/ imperially over cream green oceans." In Dionysian intoxication she feels herself "with demented hands" holding on firmly to the wheel of the god's team: "the demented are capable of everything." In an introductory remark to the reader in the first-mentioned collection, she says that she has discovered her true dimensions and that "it is not fitting for me to make myself less than I am."

In *Framtidens skugga* (Shadows of the Future) from 1920, Edith Södergran's perhaps most remarkable collection of poetry, the cosmic mysticism culminates in a long series of blinding visionary poems, where the ecstatic moods of lofty spiritual intensity are replaced by a uniquely pure and clear beauty. Her path back down from Nietzsche's "sun-burned peaks" went via Rudolf Steiner's anthroposophy to a mild Christian mysticism. Attesting to this insight into life and reconciliation are the poems in the posthumous collection *Landet som icke är* (The Land That Is Not), 1925. Its title poem became Edith Södergran's best-known and most loved poem:

> *Jag längtar till landet som icke är,*
> *ty allting som är, är jag trött att begära.*
> *Månen berättar mig i silverne runor*
> *om landet som icke är.*
> *Landet, där alla våra kedjor falla,*
> *landet, där vi svalka vår sargade panna*
> *i månens dagg.*
> *Mitt liv var en het villa.*
> *Men ett har jag funnit och ett har jag verkligen vunnit—*
> *vägen till landet som icke är.*

I long for the land that is not,
for all that is, I am weary of requesting.
The moon speaks to me in silvern runes
about the land that is not.
The land where all our wishes become wondrously fulfilled,
the land where all our fetters fall,
the land where we cool our bleeding forehead
in the dew of the moon.
My life was a burning illusion.
But one thing I have found and one thing I have really won—
the road to the land that is not.

The feverish experience of life, the charismatic radiance and the enormous register of feelings and expressions in Edith Södergran's poetry render her the real portal figure of modern lyric poetry, and her influence on Swedish twentieth-century poetry has been enormous. For the Finland-Swedish generation of poets immediately following her, she was the great pioneer. A leader in the modernist succession was Elmer Diktonius (1896–1961), who also worked with expressionistic and American lyrical ideals in view. His poetry sprang from a political and social passion that was nurtured by communist sympathies during the Russian Revolution and the Finnish civil war, but there was also in him a musical artist with an unusually open and direct language of emotions. On the whole he was a poet of contrasts, where the strong, crushing and rapacious—as in the Nietzsche-inspired poem "Jaguaren" (The Jaguar)—unites with the weak, the tender and the warm, as in the many engaging poems about children. He supported the small and the weak and wanted to foreshadow with his poetry a new world free of starvation and misery. He gave a lyrical expression to the harsh beauty of Finnish nature that stands close to Sibelius' music. Through the realistic brutality with which, for example, he depicts life during the civil war, a clear poetry of the purest brand breaks forth. Diktonius was also a prose writer and a reflective aphorist, but it was for accessibility and for the unexpected meeting of the tender and the powerful in collections like *Hårda sånger* (Hard Songs), 1922, *Stenkol* (Hard Coal), 1927, and *Stark men mörk* (Strong But Dark), 1930, that he became perhaps the most admired of the lyrical modernists. The following imaginative impressions of nature are taken from the last-mentioned collection:

Ännu
är det blott
kammarmusikpizzicato
i vårens takdropp—
huschande framskymtande—
bortilande stämningar.
Men i snötyngd skog,
under fjärdens is
pågår ren orkesterrepetitionen
med alla instrument.
Snart står herr Sol i frack,
lackskor och bröstbriljanter,
och svänger pinnen,
kastar luggen över pannan
rytande:
intensivare!—mera glödande!—
for-tis-si-mo!

Still
it is only
a chamber music pizzicato
in spring's roof drip—
sprinkling intimating—
country sentiments.
But in snow covered forest,
under the bay's ice
there is already orchestra practice
with all instruments.
Soon Mr. Sun will stand in tails,
patent leather shoes and diamonds
and wave the baton,
throw the tuft of hair over his forehead
shouting:
more intensive!—more ardent!—
for-tis-si-mo!

The Finland-Swedish tradition of short poetry was always important for the modernist poets. The lyrical fragment reflects the diversity of existence and attests to the hidden totality. Such is the case in the poetry of both Gunnar Björling (1887–1960) and Rabbe Enckell (1903–1974). Björling was an eccentric who lived in a basement apartment in Helsinki that became famous in its own right over the years. He was philosophically schooled and passionately committed in his intention to create a unique emotional language for his complex and yet fundamentally simple experience of existence. In the 1920s he was receptive to Dadaist and other modernist stimuli from abroad. In order to be able to shape his mystical fundamental vision he developed a unique, distinct, lyrical syntax that makes his style easily recognizable and is found in some of the titles of his many poetry collections: *Men blåser violer på havet* (But Violets Blow on the Ocean) and *Att syndens blåa nagel* (That Sin's Blue Nail), both from 1936, and *Ord och att ej annat* (Word and that Nothing Else), 1945. The intimate, sensually obvious mysticism of life made Björling into a "poet of real life," and many of his poems, particularly in later collections, stand close to silence and the inexpressible:

> *Stryk ut, stryk*
> *dig, ditt ord*
> *stryk din*
> *kontur, den kan du ej*
> *förklara.*

> *Var vad du är*
> *var den musik*
> *var du, du själv*
> *som en ordkonsert*
> *var du, som en gömd*
> *i världs stumhet*
> *en drömd*
> *konsert.*

> Erase, erase
> yourself, your words
> erase your
> contour, you cannot
> explain it.

Be what you are
be the music
be you, you yourself
like a word concert
be you, like one hidden
in the world's silence
a dreamed
concert.

In Rabbe Enckell's swiftly illuminating "match poems" too, there is a sensually open life mysticism in impressions of nature which are as fresh and immediate as Björling's. However, the "flute player's happiness" of his youth—the title of a collection from 1925—came over the years to be characterized more and more by Greek myth and a classical view of life. He is the classicist among the modernists, who unites the modern fragmentary art of association with Greek clarity and purity. His poetry is a means of conquering painful life experiences and a tragic view of life, as in the magnificent collection *Andedräkt av koppar* (A Breath of Copper), 1946. Enckell also took the classical verse drama in a modern direction—*Orfeus och Eurydike* (Orpheus and Eurydice), 1938, *Agamemnon*, 1949—and made it reflect man's eternal conditions of existence. A high, cool and timeless atmosphere hovers over his neoclassical poetry, a brightness and a keenness that is unusual in modern lyric poetry.

In Finland-Swedish literature a large number of fine literary talents have also appeared more recently, both in the area of prose and of poetry, but only exceptionally have any of them been able to measure up to these "four greats." The vitality in the Swedish-speaking culture of Finland has, however, always been considerable—this is the case in the field of the theater too—and the number of people producing or committed to literature in other ways is remarkably high for such a small population. The contact with Finnish literature has diminished because of a widened language gulf—which to a certain degree is also a social gulf. At the same time, Finland-Swedish literature is sadly, indeed indefensibly, often neglected in Sweden.

Swedish Lyrical Modernism from Birger Sjöberg to Tranströmer

While a modernist movement prospered in Swedish-speaking Finland around 1920, literature in Sweden, after the young Lagerkvist's emergence, seemed to become immune to all influence from the latest continental trends. Even Lagerkvist tried to get back to more traditional forms of expression. The poetry of the era has a pronounced idyllic character, but from the idyll too something new emerged. Birger Sjöberg (1885–1929) first became extremely popular as a ballad writer of the small-town idyll in *Fridas bok* (Frida's Book), 1922. In 1926, however, when he published the poetry collection *Kriser och kransar* (Crises and Wreaths), the critics and the public were confounded by and cold to its fragmented content and cryptic forms of expression. The Frida-poetry's idyll had been shattered. In its place came "the acerbic ballad free of empty words," where the poet examined his own heart and his falsification of reality and strove for a new honesty in language and standpoint. Modern reality intrudes here in journalistic pictures which flicker by, and modernistically fiery metaphors of reckoning and world apocalypse convey neurotic moods:

Mudderverk med drypande skopor
vräkte syner jämt ur dyn.
Se, en köttblå råhet där!
Se, en vit och slagen hand!
Där på svarta mullen lyftes
fallna gudars brutna lemmar,
rivna proklamationsplakat.
Tidens gömda skräcknyheter
stego nakna upp på nytt,
hotande med vitnade händer,
stirrande med bristande ögon.
Flytt var allt—men dock ej flytt.

Futuristisk skola så
i ett hjärtas nattsalonger
vilda stycken exponerar:
Läppar, som av feghet tego,
händer, som av vinning dödat,
öga, grymhet givit sting...

Dredger with dripping buckets
regularly tossed visions out of the mud.
Look, a meat blue rawness there!
Look, a white and beaten hand!
There on black earth are lifted
fallen gods' broken limbs,
torn proclamation placards.
The era's hidden horrifying news
climbed up naked again,
menacing with withered hands,
staring with bursting eyes.
Shifted was everything—but yet not shifted.

Futuristic school so
in heart's night salons
wild pieces exposes:
Lips, silent from cowardice,
hands, having killed for profit,
eye, given sting by cruelty...

For the young modernists of the 1930s and 1940s, *Kriser och kransar* became as important as Edith Södergran's poetry. In certain respects, Sjöberg's linguistic innovation is a basic prerequisite for the changes that Swedish poetry was to go through in the immediate future.

The new Sjöberg achievements were firstly made use of by some "academic" poets in the 1930s, of whom Hjalmar Gullberg (1898–1961) soon became the leader. But Gullberg's poetry is more clearly rooted in the classical and Christian traditions and his form is simpler and clearer. With collections like *Andliga övningar* (Spiritual Exercises), 1932, and *Kärlek i tjugonde seklet* (Love in the Twentieth Century), 1933, he became the poet for a whole generation that was attracted by his lyrical technique of letting well-known patterns such as the verse of a hymn or a newspaper item convey metaphysical messages. It has been called "the lower string technique." His dominant motifs are love, classical myth and mystical experience. His mysticism was sometimes nourished by oriental sources and emanated from a strong disgust with the world:

Då skall ej vår jordiska lekamen
längre hindra och besvära oss.
Tyst i hallen står vid spegelramen
rockvaktmästarn som gör herrn och damen
från de tunga ytterplaggen loss.

Medan i fem fack han lägger undan
ögon, öron, tunga, näsa, hud,
står vår själ i andakt och begrundan.
Stjärnor brinner i den blå rotundan,
där vi äntligen skall möta Gud.

Then our earthly body will
no longer hinder and bother us.
Silent in the hall stands by the mirror frame
the cloak-room attendant who relieves men and women
of the heavy outer wear.

While in five compartments he puts away
eyes, ears, tongue, nose, skin,
our soul stands in devotion and reflection.
Stars are burning in the blue rotunda
where at last we shall be meeting God.

His later poetry *Dödsmask och lustgård* (Death Mask and Garden of Pleasure), 1952, is more exclusive and intricate, and attests to a reappraisal of the Christian-platonic world view that marked his 1930s poetry. His feeling for classical form still asserted itself in *Terziner i okonstens tid* (Terza Rima in Artless Times), 1958, with its often polemical attitude toward the present, but he won his greatest artistic victory with *Ögon, läppar* (Eyes, Lips), 1959, that emanated from a period of illness and had a new, greater authenticity. The obviously German-oriented Johannes Edfelt (b. 1904) belongs to the same generation. His dark, tragic-stoic themes are strictly controlled in form, and the collection *Högmässa* (High Mass), 1934, appeared as a "liturgy in an era of the wolf," where eroticism was cloaked in Christian ritual. In recent years he has become one of the century's foremost prose poets, trying to overcome a constantly intrusive consciousness of death with a broadening of his register of themes and a new mobility of form. Bertil Malmberg

(1889–1958) also appeared in the 1930s as a German-oriented, "academic" poet, with his literary roots in turn-of-the-century decadence. *Dikter vid gränsen* (Poems on the Boundary), 1935, is a masterly proclamation of downfall in the spirit of Spengler, clad in a splendid verse structure, which he was later to deconstruct, equally voluptuously, amid the reduction and revision of postwar Modernism. His lasting contribution, though, is the finely-tuned depiction of childhood, *Åke och hans värld (Åke and His World)*, 1924.

Partly in contrast to these traditional poets, the real breakthrough for lyrical Modernism in Sweden came with the group The Young Five. Largely autodidacts of proletarian origin and possessing enormous energy, they acknowledged the new era and the new opportunities it gave civilization and culture. The group appeared approximately contemporaneously with the functionalist exhibition held in Stockholm in 1930. Behind its literary ideal can be sensed Futurism, as well as Expressionism, and not least the sexual liberation program of D. H. Lawrence and others. They preached a new vitalism—a new joy of and appetite for life, which was quickly dampened, though, in the shadow of the dark political clouds that began to cast a shadow over the 1930s. The two leading figures of The Young Five were Artur Lundkvist and Harry Martinson—the former a leader and inexhaustible innovator, the latter a literary child prodigy who brought public attention to the group more directly. As a literary grouping, however, The Young Five was a temporary phenomenon, and their original, energetic program underwent powerful metamorphoses over the years.

Artur Lundkvist (b. 1906), who came from a Scanian farmer's home, saw early on in Modernism the right medium for his striving for change and renewal and his strong need of protest. The ecstatic, life-acknowledging poetry of his youth found prototypes in among others Whitman, Carl Sandburg, Nietzsche and Diktonius. In collections like *Glöd* (Glow), 1928, *Naket liv* (Naked Life), 1929, and *Vit Man* (White Man), 1932, a new ideal of civilization appeared, primitivistic yet also acknowledging technology—a new, liberated, life-accepting culture in sharp contrast to traditional academic culture. Lundkvist the poet stands close to the lives of the farmer and worker, and he embraces a sexual mysticism of the Lawrence brand. A trip to Africa at the beginning of the 1930s provided further nourishment for his Romantic primitivism. At the same time, Freud gained a footing in his world of ideas, and at the middle of the decade his poetry glided into a surrealistic world, where the image and the dream play a large role. The collection *Sirensång* (Song of the Sirens) from 1937 is marked by a visionary and mythical fantasy which was later to figure prominently in his authorship:

Dagarna flyger förbi som eld i torra buskar.
Månen manar till uppbrott; och kamelerna som gripits
av hemlängtan vägrar att ge sin mjölk.
Hemfärd; och nattens skuggor rör sig bredvid oss som
följeslagare utan ansikten, stumma, tålmodiga.
Och tanken går till hemkomsten: en tid i jorden,
men där bortom anar vi nya höjdkrön, det ena bortom
det andra i oändlighet.
Ty världen är som en ros med oräkneliga blad; och inte
är väl denna ros den enda i den eviga trädgården?

The days fly by like fire in dry bushes.
The moon calls for departure; and the camels gripped
by a longing for home refuse to give their milk.
Home journey; and the night's shadows move alongside us like
companions without faces, silent, patient.
And the mind goes to the arrival home: a time on earth,
but beyond we divine new high crests, the one
beyond the other in eternity.
For the world is like a rose with countless petals; and this rose
is not the only one in the eternal garden?

Lundkvist's next essay collection, *Ikarus flykt* (Icarus' Flight), 1939, which was important for Swedish Modernism, was an inventory of the entire international modernist tradition, and his later collections in the 1940s attested to how deeply he drank from its springs. Collections like *Korsväg* (Crossroads), 1942, and *Dikter mellan djur och gud* (Poems Between Animal and God), 1944, have a darker theme, with vehement oppositions and inner conflicts. Lundkvist's poetry from the postwar era again came to be marked by lighter and more constructive moods, as in the large collections *Fotspår i vattnet* (Footprints in the Water), 1949, *Liv som gräs* (To Live Like Grass), 1954, and *Vindrosor, moteld* (Wind-Roses, Counterfire), 1955, where the poet in long, image-filled poems celebrated life's endless diversity and the inner dynamics and changeability of existence. A strong element of social and political preaching again penetrated his authorship, and his visionary aerial panorama of the world was permeated with socialist-revolutionary sympathies, which were nourished not least through numerous trips to all parts of the world. At the same time he also increasingly began to use prose as a medium. He cultivated an imaginative, modernistically inspired narrative art, as, for example, in *Malinga*, 1952, which often borders on poetry in its flood of images. *Darunga eller varginnans mjölk* (Darunga or the Wolf's Milk), 1954, is a huge prose fresco depicting a social revolution, which was inspired by that in Egypt at the beginning of the 1950s and which in a remarkable way seems to anticipate Fidel Castro's revolution in Cuba a few years later. But Lundkvist is not a stranger to an exuberantly realistic narrative art. In *Vindingevals* (Vindinge Waltz), 1956, he returned to his Scanian home with an irresistibly fresh and vital depiction of man.

It is the inexhaustible flow of existence that always interests Lundkvist. His literary work is a steady stream of sensory impressions, images, visions and dreams, and of actions and reflections, where the dynamically variable and the static condition each other. His literary production, which has become ever more abundant over the years, is a constant variation on the theme of existence as an endless, constant process. Work after work is a building block of an imaginative, multifaceted poetic edifice of dimensions never previously seen in Sweden. But while the world of his youthful poetry was limited to utopian-visionary and revolutionary paths, his perspective has darkened considerably in the later poetry. His appraisal of civilization has now become pessimistic and desperate, yet this has not held back the literary productivity. With furious energy Lundkvist has continued to create "dreams at a time of storms"—the title of a prose work from 1963. It is true that poetry takes up a more modest position here than in the earlier writing, but a strong, moving highpoint is the poem sequence *Agadir*, 1961, written against the background of the Moroccan earthquake that Lundkvist himself witnessed and that was perhaps one of the main reasons for the appearance of desolation in his world of ideas. But poetry flourishes with undiminished force in the numerous prose works that continued to follow both a modernistic-experimental and a realistic line, often in a fruitful symbiosis. Lundkvist the narrator took on a fresh lease of life in a series of novels with historical motifs. *Himlens vilja* (The Will of Heaven), 1970, tells about the Mongol prince, Genghis Khan, *Tvivla korsfarare* (Doubt, Crusaders), 1972, about the first crusade against Jerusalem. *Krigarens dikt* (The Warrior's Poem), 1976, is "a true story" about Alexander the Great, *Slavar för Särkland* (Slaves For Särkland), 1978, an adventure story about Vikings going eastward. Broad geographical perspectives and historical depth characterize these novels. In his late work there is also an essay novel about Goya, *Livsälskare, svartmålare* (Lover of Life, Painter in Black), 1974, which also has autobiographical strains. *Färdas i drömmen och föreställningen* (Journey in Dream and Imagination), 1984, is a remarkable report that has attracted considerable attention, based on Lundkvist's visionary dream experiences from a state of coma during a long, serious illness.

Artur Lundkvist has also been in a class of his own as the most significant introducer of foreign literature, especially North American and Latin American, into twentieth-century Swedish culture. His literary criticism has been as broad as his own literary domains, and he has thereby actively contributed to internationalizing the Swedish cultural climate. Furthermore, he has revived the travel book as a genre and given it a more poetic, literary character. The revolutionary and protest maker, vitalist and dynamic innovator has made an extensive cultural contribution over the years, which led to his being elected to the Swedish Academy in 1968. He stands out as a veritable giant in twentieth-century Swedish literature, and the dimensions of his huge literary world remain for the future to explore.

Harry Martinson (1904–78) also emerged in interwar Swedish literature as something of a literary miracle. Behind him was the humiliation of a childhood as a fostered parish child and an unsettled and adventurous youth as a sailor. Everything he wrote is marked by a unique empirical originality. The world was his university: he stepped forth as a new graduate and seemed to transform Swedish literature by writing in an entirely new way. In his early poetry, in large part collected in *Nomad* (Nomad), 1931, and *Natur* (Nature), 1934, memories of childhood are mixed with impressions from his years as a sailor. A common denominator is the intensely experienced, cosmic feeling for nature in precisely etched miniatures as well as universal macroperspectives. Martinson continued and revitalized the nature tradition in Swedish literature that was initiated by Linné. His free and poetically imaginative diction was well suited to clever snapshots and unexpected lighting effects, always rendered with a natural, Romantic feeling for the wonders of nature, a devoted worship of life:

Vi låg i gräset
och våra ögon insög åt anden
*   allt det sammansatta som är liv och Gud.*
Vår undran för dagen tog vid
där alla somrars undran slutat.
Bisarra små hushåll var gömda i tuvorna.
Knappt till att fatta var insekternas liv
förrän tanken förirrat sig in med dem
i gåtfulla tunnlar där inga språk bodde.

Så blev vår förundran en tillbedjan
och vi sänkte våra pannor såsom genom djupt
*   vatten inför livets heliga välde.*
Sävsångarn brast i gråt i vassens skog,
av sorger mindre än av överfyllda år och
evig stämning av blommors ouppnådda renhets vår.
På gyttjan flöt en liljebård,
dagsländor dogo där invid
på junitysta vattenstenar.
Och allt var väsensfyllt av ögats egen undran.

We lay in the grass
and our eyes absorbed into the spirit
  everything put together that is life and God.
Our wonder for the day started
where the wonder of all summers ended.
Bizarre little households were hidden in grassy hillocks.
Hardly to be comprehended were the insects' lives
before the thought got lost with them
in enigmatic tunnels where no language lived.

Then our awe became a worship
and we lowered our foreheads as if through deep
  water before life's holy realm.
The sedge warbler broke into tears in the forest of reeds,
from sorrows less than from too many years and
eternal mood of the flowers' spring of unattained purity.
On the mud floated a lily border,
mayflies died close by
on June-silent water stones.
And everything was filled with the eye's own awe.

The two prose works *Resor utan mål* (Aimless Journeys),
1932, and *Kap Farväl (Cape Farewell)*, 1933, took their
material from the years at sea. Reportage and poetic
sketches, social and philosophical comment and dramatic
stories about the sailor's life are blended in an original,
sometimes lyrical sometimes narrative or essayistic form.
His language is full of bold metaphors, unchecked playful
associations, minute observations of reality and verbal innovations. In this creative language he delivered a message
critical of civilization that was constantly to be further
developed in his writing. As a utopian program he proposed
the idea of "the world nomad," the constant traveller who
avoids the stagnation of a permanent residence, and "the
Geosophism," the wise caretaking of the earth which is to
make better use of modern civilization so as to enrich man's
inner life. Martinson returned to the privations and hardships of his childhood years in the two autobiographical
novels, *Nässlorna blomma (Flowering Nettle)*, 1935, and
Vägen ut (The Way Out), 1936. These are free literary
depictions of his childhood experiences, classic in their

psychological analyses of the reactions of the vulnerable child to an insensitive environment and at the same time completely free of sentimentality in their struggle for a moral coming to terms with the lies, mechanisms of flight and ingratiation of the defenseless.

In some works about nature from the late 1930s, Martinson sharpened his criticism of civilization against the background of the darkening political climate. He contrasted the contemplative life of nature and the everyday with the era's brutal, violent tendencies and modern western civilization's superficiality and lack of soul. In the rich poetry collection *Passad* (Trade Winds), 1945, and in the great philosophical novel *Vägen till Klockrike (The Road)*, 1948, Martinson tried to build up a warm and generous cultural philosophy, a positive and constructive counter message to the era's stale ideals. What he tried to evoke was a universal humanism inspired by, among other things, Chinese philosophy. There is also a strong element of Indian mysticism and reincarnation in the novel, which deals with the lives of Swedish vagabonds at the end of the last century. The foundations of his growing humanist synthesis are now respect for life and everything living, sensual joy in all that is close to life and ordinary, mercy and respect, the principle of good will, reflection, insight and inward meditation, memory and dream, as well as knowledge and science. In the area of natural science especially, Martinson had amassed a considerable knowledge which began increasingly to stimulate his creative fantasy.

Martinson played on this alternative ideal of civilization in his late poetry collections: *Cikada* (Cicada), 1953, *Gräsen i Thule* (The Grasses in Thule), 1958, *Vagnen* (The Wagon), 1960, and *Dikter om ljus och mörker* (Poems About Light and Darkness), 1971. At the same time he reacted with desperation and impotence to the technocratic development that increasingly seemed to alienate modern civilization from his own cultural-philosophical beliefs. It is in the light of this violent opposition that the evolution of the space epic *Aniara (Aniara)*, 1956, whose first songs were already printed in *Cikada*, can be seen. In this, his most remarkable work, whose science-fiction theme revitalized the verse epic as a genre and created a synthesis of literature and modern

Harry Martinson.

natural science, he depicts in 103 songs how the space ship Aniara ferries emigrants from an earth damaged by radiation during a nuclear war to the planet Mars at some point in the future. However, the ship strays off course, is damaged and heads inexorably and blindly out into a cold and desolate space. For the passengers on board there remain only various forms of desperate escapism—particularly when they learn of the earth's final destruction—as they await the final annihilation, the nirvana ascent into an unknown universe. Symbolically, the epic narrative can be read as a coming to terms with the modern technocratic culture that has alienated man from the norms of life prescribed for him on the planet Earth. Through his destructiveness man has broken the laws of life and is thus instrumental in his own annihilation, while life itself has new universal potential, if chance so pleases.

Harry Martinson was also a dramatist, his greatest stage success being *Tre knivar från Wei (Three Knives from Wei)*, 1964, whose theme of destruction took its material from a Chinese story. But it is on *Aniara*, on poetry and on the lyrically lucid prose that his fame rests. Martinson received the Nobel Prize in Literature in 1974 and has stood out since his death as one of modern Swedish literature's great classics, leaving behind an abundantly rich body of works. Creative sensitivity is combined with a deeply ethical seriousness; the great questions of our era about civilization and culture are illuminated and enriched with a gentle and timeless wisdom.

The modernist tradition, with its background in Romanticism, is very much present in Gunnar Ekelöf's (1907–68) poetry. He could identify both with Swedish Romantics such as Stagnelius and Almqvist and with Baudelaire and Rimbaud. His poetry shows obvious similarities with Surrealism and with Eliot—although he obstinately denied all influence. Music and oriental mysticism left deep traces in his lyrical art. However, he succeeded in melting and catalyzing all stimuli and impressions into a deeply personal whole. Like Eliot's, his poetry is a huge temple echoing with cultures, widely separated in time and space. However, in contrast to Eliot's, it has an unmistakably intimate tone that gives it a genuine originality.

Ekelöf, who came from an upper middle-class Stockholm family, studied oriental languages in Uppsala and London. At the end of the 1920s in Paris he came in contact with the latest literary movements and modern music. This provided inspiration for the poems in the collection *Sent på jorden (Late Arrival on Earth)*, 1932, the most sensational debut work in the history of Swedish Modernism. The boundary-bursting imagery and shocking formulations might appear surrealistic—and created a good number of outbursts in the newspaper columns for their abstruseness—but the poems were consistently well crafted. They can be seen as a desperate personal document, a "suicide book," where the need for verbal protest sprang forth from helplessness in a personal crisis. The prophetic, poetic-revolutionary character was strengthened in the next collection *Dedikation* (Dedication), 1934, in the spirit of Rimbaud, while *Sorgen och stjärnan* (Sorrow and the Star), 1936, with its solitary nature moods and its striving for a cosmic universality, makes a strongly Romantic impression.

Behind the development of *Färjesång* (Ferry Song), 1941 —equally as important a cornerstone in Ekelöf's production as his first collection—lay the poet's need for a sweeping reappraisal of prophetic claims and Romantic affectation. The poetic style is now more direct and stark, and the collection is dominated by a rather abstract poetry of reflection close to Eliot's idiom. Ekelöf developed here an intellectual mysticism that seeks something beyond the endless conflicts of existence, something unexplained. There is also an individualistic existentialism that tries to embrace man's eternal conditions of existence, the naked and true circumstances of his life. In the "state of preparedness" of the war years, he wanted to protest with his collection against every form of "totalitarian narcosis" and he wanted to deliver his credo: "I believe in man the individual" against the modern mass psychoses. More programmatically, he later adopted a more existential stand and maintained that the poet's most important task was first and foremost to be a human being, to acknowledge the futility of existence and to put himself into the situation of every ordinary human being. In different ways, the large collections *Non Serviam*, 1945, and *Om hösten* (In Autumn), 1951, attest to this programmatic standpoint; they contain many of his most remarkable poetic creations, such as the magnificent, visionary "Samothrake," the musical-mystical "Absentia animi," the lyrical dream play "Röster under jorden" (Voices Under Ground), and bitter satires of the welfare state, such as in "Non serviam." The cycle *En Mölna-elegi (A Mölna Elegy)* can also be seen as a lyrical dream play, which the poet began during the 1940s but which was not published until 1960, and then in an apparently unfinished version. This poetry is a large, masterly work of quotation and allusion in the spirit of Eliot, where in particular eighteenth-century Swedish poetry is resurrected in what is intended as a cross section of fleeting experiences.

From the 1950s on, Ekelöf's poetry became ever more simple and occasional in form. An almost anti-poetic program lies behind poetry collections such as *Strountes* (Trifles), 1955, *Opus incertum*, 1959, and *En natt i Otocac* (A Night in Otocac), 1961. The poems are now playful, pastiche-like, ascetically reductive and refrain from poetic and musical effects. Antiquity plays an important role in these poems, but it is a different antiquity. Here he presents an everyday and popular antiquity, the antiquity that is represented in graffiti, a down-to-earth, intrusive and often obscene antiquity in sharp contrast to the traditional antiquity of humanism. It often corresponds with Ekelöf's intense experience of contemporary reality in the Mediterranean countries, in particular with the simplicity and the timelessness of the Greek countryside. Against the strong, sensual openness stands an ever starker negative mysticism, an ever stronger experience of nothingness that can have its origins in both serious and burlesque ideas.

The dimensions of great mysticism completely dominate Ekelöf's last lyrical phase of development. During a serious illness there arose under an unusually great inspirational pressure the orientally-influenced trilogy of collections that are usually called "the akrit cycle": *Diwan över fursten av Emgión* (Diwan on the Prince of Emgión), 1965, *Sagan om Fatumeh* (The Tale of Fatumeh), 1966, and *Vägvisare till underjorden (Guide to the Underworld)*, 1967. The poems are painstakingly composed, often in symmetrical patterns, and build on Byzantine legends and tales. They span a huge register of themes and are filled with obscure references to oriental and hermetic mysticism, myths and iconography. They are simple and appealing while also esoteric and closed. There is both a stormy intensity of experience and a cool intellectual control, both intimacy and distance. This poem cycle represents a summit in Ekelöf's authorship—and in Swedish poetry in general, where probably only Stagnelius can measure up to him in mystic-lyrical intensity. Internationally, the trilogy can have few, if any, counterparts from this period. Ekelöf's poetry is paradoxically enough both exclusive and popular. It is obscurely associative and esoteric and ranges over a widespread and often little known cultural territory. But at the same time it is private, human, intimate and it leans confidingly and lovingly toward the reader. This remarkable balancing act has made Ekelöf into a poet for all, and his position as one of the very greatest in Swedish poetry is solidly established. His poetry contains softly elegiac moods and desperate, volcanic outbursts of feeling, analytically intellectual reflections and intimate meditations, serenely elevated moods and grotesque and humorous ideas, and everything is held together by a striving for an ever elusive whole. While his poetry is highly Swedish in its feeling for nature and its belonging to tradition, he is a sharp critic of the modern Swedish welfare state with its "social brain" instead of a "social heart." He has a natural footing in a global culture—and ultimately in the no-man's-land of mysticism. The joy of life is as strong as the obsession with death in this poet, who with increased authenticity staked all his inner strength on uniting the antitheses of existence in a poetic synthesis:

Så bär på ikonerna Johannes Döparen huvudet
dels på helbrägda skuldror
dels och samtidigt framför sig på ett fat
Den offrade framställer sig som en offrande
Så bekänner jag mig
till det omöjligas konst
av livskänsla och av självutplåning
samtidigt.

Thus on the icons John the Baptist carries the head
partly on healthy shoulders
partly and at the same time in front of himself on a dish
The sacrificed presents himself as a sacrificer
Thus I profess
in the art of the impossible
a feeling for life and self annihilation
at the same time.

The 1940s signified a quantitative breakthrough for modernist poetry. After 1945 fewer and fewer poets used the traditional bound-verse forms. In its overall structure, Swedish poetry went into a new phase. The decade also came to be marked by intense debates about the inaccessibility and pessimism of poetry. On the whole, the postwar period was an intellectually and artistically lively period, in which poetry occupied a strong position. Its character was, to a high degree, molded by two prominent poetic figures: Erik Lindegren and Karl Vennberg.

Erik Lindegren (1910–68) wrote the most noted poetry collection of the 1940s. His *mannen utan väg (The Man Without a Way)*, 1942, has been described as something of a literary bible for its generation. Behind it lay many years of restless artistic seeking and studies of the symbolist and modernist traditions. However, what released the poet's own, long dammed-up artistic energy was evidently the outbreak of war in the fall of 1939, and perhaps in particular the war between Finland and Russia later in the fall of the same year. For it was then that the seven-strophe, "blown-up" sonnets began to appear that would later make up the forty similarly shaped poems in the work which gave him his breakthrough. The poet himself had to subsidize the publication of the first edition; the time was still not ripe for the established publishers to handle such boldly experimental poetry. Outside immediate literary circles it found little understanding to begin with, but by the middle of the decade it had acquired something of a legendary fame. By pushing language's potential for artistic expression to the maximum, Lindegren sought in these poems to present the complications and contradictions of the modern consciousness in a time of chaos, marked by destructive political events and a radical upheaval of the world picture. In a preface never published he maintained that it was the poem's task "to prepare for the future by refusing to distort the present, to give expression to perhaps unwelcome but strong feelings ... to experience and express the depths of the times, their dizzy differences of level with as physically intrusive a clarity as possible." No simple interpretation of these poems is possible. Later, the poet emphasized that they could be read on various levels and described his poetic method as a "realism of feelings" that aimed to give the poem the character of vision, where thought, feeling and sensual impression enter an inseparable union.

In the 1940s, Lindegren became the central figure of a grouping of younger authors called the "writers of the forties," who were united by the experiences of their generation and by a common front against a conservative literary establishment. A virulent literary debate broke out in 1946 on the occasion of the second edition of *The Man Without a Way*, and Lindegren's own defense of the case for lyrical Modernism contributed strongly to cementing its position in Swedish literature. His next poetry collection, *Sviter* (Suites), 1947, was also a remarkable success with the critics and the public. The poems, often more easily accessible, musically structured and evocative, came into existence over a lengthy period from the end of the 1930s. The collection consisted of poems with sometimes classically rhetorical features, and intensely ardent love poems, which quickly won a certain popularity, and are now considered among the great examples of Swedish erotic poetry, as for example "Arioso":

Någonstans inom oss är vi alltid tillsammans,
någonstans inom oss kan vår kärlek aldrig fly
Någonstans
    o någonstans
har alla tågen gått och alla klockor stannat:
någonstans inom oss är vi alltid här och nu,
är vi alltid du intill förväxling och förblandning,
är vi plötsligt undrans under och förvandling,
brytande havsvåg, roseneld och snö.

Somewhere within us we are always together,
somewhere within us our love can never flee
Somewhere
    oh somewhere
all the trains have gone and all the clocks have stopped:
somewhere within us we are always here and now,
always bound unto confusion and commixtion,
suddenly we are the miracle of wonder and transformation,
breaking ocean wave, fire of roses and snow.

The final, brightly ringing "Pastoralsvit" ("Pastoral Suite") is an artistic highpoint, where the maximal linguistic will of expression is combined into a harmonious whole with new musical structures.

Lindegren's third large poetry collection, *Vinteroffer* (Winter Rites), 1954, has a darker theme, against the background of the cold war and international tensions. Behind the symbols and motifs of cold that play a prominent role in the poems, strictly private sentiments can also be sensed. The mythically ritual pattern is striking, with its echoes of Stravinsky's Rite of Spring. It concentrates on the motifs of death and rebirth. As earlier, the artistic will of expression often struggles against enormous intensification, as in a grand poetic vision like the famous introductory poem "Ikaros" (Icarus). However, in several poems there are also new, simpler, more subdued accents, a new conciliatory resignation. With these three large poetry collections of highest artistic quality, Lindegren had completed his lyrical production. He made outstanding cultural contributions on other fronts, for example as a gifted translator and as an author of ballet synopses and opera libretti—such as the one for Karl-Birger Blomdahl's opera *Aniara*, based on Harry Martinson's space epic. He became a central figure in the lively cultural climate of the postwar era. With his boundary-breaking, volatile artistic authority, he is today recognized as a classic of Modernism. His poetry flowed from an unusual linguistic talent combined with a sharp intellect and a rich emotional life; it came from a concentrated and expansive feeling for life and the need for "high, spiritual temperature." He sought to overcome the era's disharmonies and contradictions in a strong lyrical synthesis that gives his poetry a lasting and luminous intensity.

Karl Vennberg (b. 1910) is in many respects Lindegren's polar opposite. In the already legendary collections from the 1940s, *Halmfackla* (Straw Torch), 1944, and *Tideräkning* (Chronology), 1945, his sceptical and critical probing created an effective and stylistic lyrical instrument for a first-person existential analysis and a shattering revision of ideas. The distrust of ideological and religious superstructures that generally characterized the poets of the 1940s has its ironically dialectic power center in Vennberg. With his roots in

an evangelistic small farming milieu in the province of Småland, he is at the same time strongly linked to a religious
problematic and his stark and pessimistic world view is
never far from mysticism. The poems in the two collections
span a wide register, from exquisitely beautiful mystic visions to penetrating analyses of conscience, seemingly rhetor-
ically ironic invocations and touches of grim humor. They
represented a liberation from an inner powerlessness in
which the existential choice stood between "the indifferent
and the impossible." However, the poet never abandoned
his role as intellectual moral conscience; in fact he rather
maintained it with an almost ascetically clear vision.

Vennberg went on to expand his register with reflective
and didactic poetry. In large collections like *Fiskefärd* (Fishing Trip), 1949, *Synfält* (Field of View), 1954, and *Vid det
röda trädet* (At the Red Tree), 1955, the tone is clearer and
purer and the moods often more relaxed and conciliatory.
He wrote classically didactic poems about Greek philosophers and late Roman poets, into which an elevated tone
of the Horatian stoic ode would occasionally creep: "Do not
kindle a hope of victory,/ no fear in your defeat./ Maintain
your surprise." A limitless visionary picture of the world is
paradoxically united, with an almost voluptuous joy of
beauty, with the spartan poetic ideal, in a poetry where the
inner tensions dissolve spasmodically and with harsh self-
irony, resulting in liberation and reconciliation. At the same
time, Vennberg participated with strong commitment in the
great debates of the time. He advocated the so-called "third
standpoint" that attracted many writers and intellectuals like
Artur Lundkvist and Werner Aspenström during the years
around 1950, and that pursued a balanced stand between and
beyond the two political Great Power blocs of the postwar
era. Vennberg, with his scepticism and his instinctive aversion to being enrolled into any kind of closed and finite
philosophy, also played an important role in the debate
about faith and knowledge that was initiated by the moral
philosopher Ingemar Hedenius.

From the 1970s on, Vennberg's poetry went into a new,
strongly productive period with a long series of poetry
collections, of which *Sju ord på tunnelbanan* (Seven Words
in the Subway), 1971, and *Visa solen ditt ansikte* (Show the

Sun Your Face), 1978, should be mentioned here. In their political, philosophical and mystical register of themes they show a remarkable continuity even as the sexual motif is expanded. Many of the poems deal with the emotions of aging love, and there is both a sensual freshness and a stark melancholy of uncommon poetic strength. As a whole, Vennberg's rich lyrical work stands out as a remarkably personal and uniform symbiosis of poetic and anti-poetic, of intellectual and mystical, of sensual and ascetic, of bitter pessimism and bright, glorious visions. Behind this frenetically dialectic game there is an unusually intense inner warmth and a constantly vigilant openness to man's ability to survive the spiritual and moral corruption of our era with his self-esteem intact, and his ability to seek moments of breathing space, consciousness, trust and hope.

Werner Aspenström (b. 1918) also has his origins in the antitheses and new ideas of the 1940s. In collections like *Snölegend* (Snow Legend), 1949, and *Hundarna* (The Dogs), 1954, there are both huge, symbolic image structures and small, precise nature miniatures in the style of Martinson. In the shadow of the cold war, he developed a disquieting and evocative theme of destruction, while at the same time he could assert, with a deeply felt confidence in man, that "there is a faith more powerful than rock." The aesthetically sophisticated in Aspenström merges naturally with a subtle, popular scepticism that distrusts the modern rationalistic world picture and prefers to express itself through folkloristic conventions and archaic myths. In the pastoral collection *Dikter under träden* (Poems Under the Trees), 1956, the simple and the natural dominate, and the perspective of eternity is more clearly underlined than before. In a thought-provoking and often amusing way, Aspenström succeeds in playing out the chaotic absurdity of modern existence against experiences of timelessness and mysticism. His world is that of chance and paradox, and it is filled with genuine poetic revelations and ever fresh impressions of nature. His later poetry comprises not only new collections—such as *Inre* (Inner), 1969—but also much drama. Here too he illuminates our era's prejudices, utopias, faith in science and meddlesome rationalism from a playfully satirical or folkloristically naive but sound philosophical perspective. There is something charmingly captivating in these plays. They are simple in their structure, but uncomplicated only in appearance. The legacy from the scepticism and dialectics of the 1940s plays its subtle role also in their simple, everyday settings, their symbolic scenic structures and fairy-tale worlds. Around 1950, the base of Swedish poetry had widened substantially, and a number of fine poets appeared. Against the pessimism and distrust of the 1940s, many of the young poets wanted to defend a more Romantic ideal and make poetry more easily accessible. Lars Forssell (b. 1928) maintained that the poet ought to express himself on various levels. He introduced Ezra Pound in Swedish translation, struck a blow for the ballad and gained acceptance for French-style political ballads in Swedish. Poetry collections like *Narren* (The Jester), 1952, *Telegram* (Telegram), 1957, and *Röster* (Voices), 1964, attest to his broad poetic spectrum, in which genres, styles and poetic levels are mixed freely and easily, and where everything is permeated by the same genuine lyrical vein. *En kärleksdikt* (A Love Poem), 1960, revived erotic poetry through a broader sexual openness and directness. The political element in his work was strengthened in the late 1960s and early 1970s in collections such as *Ändå* (Nevertheless), 1968, *Oktoberdikter* (October Poems), 1971 (a long poem cycle about Lenin), and *Det möjliga* (The Possible), 1974, while *Sånger* (Songs), 1986, shapes personal and classical motifs in an accomplished sonnet form. Forssell has also been successful as a versatile dramatist with a preference for working innovatively within established genres, preferably simple ones. A more cerebrally introverted world marks the poetry of Östen Sjöstrand (b. 1925), which revolves mainly around religious problems that emanate from a Catholic world of ideas, and which makes great use of symbols from the realm of natural science. Sjöstrand owes most to modern French poetry, and his own poems, presented in a long series of fine collections, such as *Främmande mörker, främmande ljus* (Strange Darkness, Strange Light), 1955, *Hemlöshet och hem* (Homelessness and Home), 1958, and others, have a more international than Nordic character, even if he has also written powerful and deeply-felt poetry on the theme of Nordic nature.

Tomas Tranströmer's (b. 1931) poetry also has a markedly international scope. His favorite theme is that of Swedish nature, but this provincialism has not hindered him from appearing on the world poetry market with poems that are both universal and exotically Nordic. His poetry is extremely compressed, with an accomplished use of the metaphor, often expressing intensely concentrated emotional and mystical experiences. The image is as strongly developed as the genuine musicality. His first collection, *17 dikter* (17 Poems), 1954, immediately aroused great attention for its unusual maturity. Since then he has regularly published exquisite collections, such as *Hemligheter på vägen* (Secrets on the Way), 1958 (a title which could stand for his entire authorship), *Den halvfärdiga himlen* (The Half-Finished Heaven), 1962, and *Klanger och spår* (Bells and Tracks), 1966, where international and political themes are broader. In *Östersjöar* (Baltics), 1974, there is a clear tendency toward a greater looseness of form. Throughout Tranströmer's poetry there is a boundary-breaking dimension, a striving to broaden and make concrete the inner perspective. His point of view is that of the individual, and in his world of ideas there is a certain tension between the individual and the mass, between subjective and collective. In many ways his unique talent for imagery represents a culmination, a perfection in the Swedish tradition of lyrical Modernism. Within a relatively narrow range of themes, the images of the individual poem (here "Kyrie") flourish with a fantastic luster:

> *Ibland slog mitt liv upp ögonen i mörker.*
> *En känsla som om folkmassor drog genom gatorna*
> *i blindhet och oro på väg till ett mirakel,*
> *medan jag osynligt förblir stående.*
>
> *Som barnet somnar in med skräck*
> *lyssnande till hjärtats tunga steg.*
> *Långt, långt tills morgonen sätter strålarna i låsen*
> *och mörkrets dörrar öppnar sig.*

> Sometimes my life opened its eyes in the dark.
> A feeling as if crowds drew through the streets
> in blindness and anxiety on the way towards a miracle,
> while I invisibly remain standing.

As the child falls asleep in terror
listening to the heart's heavy tread.
Slowly, slowly until morning puts its rays in the locks
and the doors of darkness open.

Ballads and Other Well-Loved Poetry

During the twentieth century, poetry has, virtually without
interruption, occupied a very strong position on the Swedish
book market. The number of poetry collections published
annually is remarkably high—even if the demand only
exceptionally corresponds to the supply. This was especially
true for modernist poetry, which was met by a relatively
weak public response and in general sold only in small
editions. Poets such as Gullberg, who maintained traditional
forms, enjoyed the public's attention in an entirely different
way. It is only in the most recent decades that the lyrical
modernists have begun to penetrate into the general consciousness of the literary public to a greater extent.

Some poets, namely those who wrote songs and other
popular types of poetry, have met with a particularly strong
response from a broader public. At the beginning of the
twentieth century, many followed in the footsteps of the
writers of the 1890s, in particular Fröding and Karlfeldt.
One of these was Dan Andersson (1888–1920), whose roots
were in Bergslagen and who had worked as a charcoal
burner. In *Kolvaktarens visor* (*Charcoal-Burner's Ballad*,
partly tr.) 1915, he gave expression to working life in the
forest in poems filled with a strong empathy with nature,
mysticism and superstition. The ballads were splendidly
rhythmic and mellow and permeated by sentimental strains.
Many of them belong to Swedish poetry's most popular
numbers: "Helgdagskväll i timmerkojan" ("Saturday Night
in the Log Cabin"), "En spelmans jordafärd" ("A Fiddler's
Last Journey") from *Svarta ballader* (Black Ballads), 1917,
"Jungman Jansson" ("Sailor Jansson") and others—all
became well-known set to music.

With Birger Sjöberg (see p. 223), ballad writing and modernist, avant-garde poetry stand side by side. His *Fridas bok*
(Frida's Book), 1922, consists of the poetically ethereal and
clever pastiche-like songs purportedly penned by a naively

idealistic shop clerk in an idyllic small town. The Frida songs can be said to be a twentieth-century counterpart to Bellman's poetry, and through the years they have retained a popularity which can be closely compared with that of the eighteenth-century poet. The charm of the Frida songs lies above all in the contrasts between the poetic shop clerk's comical seriousness, the mundaneness in his environment and the down-to-earth objectivity of his muse, Frida. But the depiction is tenderly understanding and sympathetic, and the comedy in the songs lies to a high degree in the parodic language. The songs and post-Romantic poetry of the nineteenth century can be discerned behind these subtle and yet moving pastiches, while there are echoes of Fredman's epistles in the following small-town vignette:

Allvarsam
blickar där fram
vår kommunala Fattiggård med ankor på sin damm.
Rosigt ljus
på Sparbankens hus;
markiser fladdra vilt och skönt vid blåstars ryck och sus.
Så lugn, förutan rök och tjut,
Fabriken sova får.
Vårt Föreläsningsinstitut
bak gröna buskar står.
Lilla Paris,
Lilla Paris,
du ligger trygg och tindrande i sommarns friska bris.

Seriously
peeps out there
our communal Workhouse with ducks on its pond.
Rosy light
at the Savings Bank building;
sun blinds flutter wildly and beautifully at the pull and sigh
of the wind.
So calm, without smoke and howling,
The factory may sleep.
Our Lecture Institute
behind green bushes stands.
Little Paris,
Little Paris,
you lie secure and sparkling in the summer's fresh breeze.

Sjöberg set his poems to music himself and performed them on long tours around the country that made him inordinately popular. When he later tried more difficult poetic forms, his reaction to the curse of popularity played a central role. Otherwise, the most typical troubadour among the twentieth-century Swedish poets is Evert Taube (1890–1976). His ballad art was consciously tied to traditional ballad prototypes: folk songs from various parts of the world, sea shanties, and more. Equally conscious was his opposition to modern poetry's overly contemplative and pessimistic character. Taube's songs aimed to be timeless in their homage to life, nature and love. There is a fresh affirmation of life in his ballads, whether they employ motifs from Latin America (where he spent some years during his youth), from the seven seas, from Italy or from the areas of Sweden he especially celebrated: Bohuslän and Roslagen. Taube performed his ballads himself with great bravura and became an immensely beloved figure. It was more difficult for him to gain recognition in literary life, but this happened, nevertheless, around 1950 when he was honored by the Swedish Academy and respectfully embraced by younger writers. He came to occupy a supreme position as a poet, popular yet also learned, commanding an extensive knowledge of the Provençal and Elizabethan ballad.

But a writer who struck a darker tone also attained a much greater popularity than is usual for a poet. This was Nils Ferlin (1898–1961). His poetry collections, among which can be mentioned *En döddansares visor* (The Ballads of a Death-Dancer), 1930, *Barfotabarn* (Barefoot Children), 1933, and *Goggles*, 1938, sold in remarkably large numbers. Many of his poems gained popularity when set to music. Ferlin was an artistic individualist who tied in to the rhythmical ballad-writing tradition of Fröding and Dan Andersson. His themes, usually dark and obsessed with death, form a bridge back to the occasional poets of the Baroque era, such as Lasse Lucidor. The hymn and the spiritual ballad often provided models and ideas for his poems. Ferlin's alienation is combined with a sharp and jesting criticism of contemporary society; his bitter satire hits at well-to-do and socially inflated egos, modern society's pursuit of efficiency and the dehumanized, striving mentality. But above all Ferlin is a resigned and melancholic lyric poet, always confessing his own loneliness and sense of alienation:

> *Med sitt rödaste bläck, under dagarnas lopp,*
> *har Vår Herre på lek ritat stjärnorna opp,*
> *det är bilder för barn.*
> *Det är bilder för stora och bilder för små*
> *dessa gåtor som Salomon grubblade på.*
> *Det är dikter i eld.*
> *Tusen dikter i eld tar min andedräkt ner,*
> *jag stapplar och stammar och vet ej mer,*
> *—En gycklare är jag—ett torkat trä,*
> *en kvidande hund, och ett barn på knä.*

With his reddest ink, during the course of the days,
Our Lord for fun drew the stars in the sky,
they are pictures for children.
They are pictures for large and pictures for small
these riddles that Solomon brooded on.
They are poems in fire.
A thousand poems in fire take my breath away,
I stumble and stutter and don't know any more,
—A jester I am—a dried tree,
a whining dog, and a child on its knee.

Ferlin also wrote for the revue theater, but it was Karl Gerhard (1891–1964) who first elevated the biting revue to the level of literature. French-style spirit and elegance often characterized his texts with their cutting satires of the celebrated personalities and vices of the times. Karl Gerhard's political song writing culminated with the passionate anti-Nazi revue song "Den ökända hästen från Troja" (The notorious horse of Troy), 1940, which played on fifth column activities during the Second World War and aroused Nazi Germany's displeasure and suspicion. After the war, the revue satire, as represented by Povel Ramel (b. 1922), became both milder and crazier. The song texts in Ramel's *Knäppupp* revues (Loosen Up Revues) from the 1950s are characterized by a wild and clever play on words and a subtle pastiche art—an art that was successful in among other things travesties of the masters of pastiche like Bellman and Birger Sjöberg. Ramel's joy with words can be seen as a more popularly attractive variant of the desire for verbal play that characterized the era's modernist poetry. With Hans Alfredsson and Tage Danielsson, the revue song again became more socially and politically conscious, with a clear socialist accent. In a long series of revues, these two versatile men created a number of already classic song texts of ironic keenness; Tage Danielsson, especially, was recognized as a supreme master of light verse of our times.

The 1950s brought a renaissance of the ballad. Credit for having discovered Evert Taube's literary worth can be given not least to Lars Forssell, who in an essay from 1950 praised the poetic qualities of the latter's poetry. Forssell, as mentioned, became a ballad writer of rank. His texts are rooted in the politically stark and pathetically pessimistic tradition of the French postwar song. Together with the novelist Pär Rådström he created a cabaret on the French pattern. He collected his songs, of which several were reworkings of French originals, in the volume *Snurra min jord* (Spin My Earth), 1958. In the 1960s, his songs took on a more acerbic political character, as in *Jack Uppskäraren* (Jack the Ripper), 1966. Several other young poets, such as Beppe Wolgers and Olle Adolphson, attached themselves to the ballad tradition of the 1950s, and this renaissance continued into the 1960s and 1970s, nurtured in the political and popular culture of the time. Among a swarm of troubadours associated with the era, a couple of sharper personalities can be mentioned: Cornelis Vreeswijk with his bitter and sentimentally ironic ballads and Alf Hambe with his finely-tuned, folk ballad pastiches.

Ingmar Bergman—Theater and Film

While the novel and poetry underwent a major rejuvenation toward the middle of the twentieth century, drama was trapped in a certain stagnation, and the Swedish plays written after Strindberg, Hjalmar Bergman and Pär Lagerkvist were seldom significant, even less revolutionary. Several of the epoch's most productive dramatists—Vilhelm Moberg, Rudolf Värnlund and Stig Dagerman—were more successful as novelists. However, in the 1940s a dynamically

inspired figure emerged who quickly vitalized Swedish theater life and who, above all in the area of film, was to become
our era's foremost and internationally best-known Swedish
cultural personality: Ingmar Bergman (b. 1918). Ingmar
Bergman's contributions to contemporary Swedish theater
life are primarily linked with his activity as director, artistic
adviser and head of the Royal Dramatic Theater in Stockholm during the years 1963–66. Practically all his produc-
tions have attracted exceptional attention and had a stimulating effect on the general theatrical climate.

The works that Ingmar Bergman himself wrote directly
for the theater, though, have won little recognition, which
perhaps can be seen as an injustice and an omission. He
appeared as a dramatist as early as 1942 with *Kaspers död*
(Kasper's Death), followed in 1946 by *Jack hos skåde-
spelarna* (Jack with the Actors). These plays reveal a good
deal of the passion and the vulnerable artistic sensitivity that
would later become an almost constant theme in his work.
However, the central point in his youthful drama lies in the
three plays that were published in 1948 under the common
title *Moraliteter: Rakel och biografvaktmästaren, Dagen
slutar tidigt* and *Mig till skräck* (Moralities: Rachel and the
Movie Guard, Early Ends the Day and To My Terror). They
are very clear indications of the anxiety-ridden and existen-
tially oriented moods of the 1940s, but at the same time they
are distinguished by a distinct, intense mood. *Dagen slutar
tidigt* (Early Ends the Day) particularly, in its disgust for
life, fear of death, anxiety and impotence, is typical of Bergman. In *Mig till skräck* (To My Terror), rebellion is juxtaposed with numbness, desperation with bitterness and resignation. It is a world of unrelieved and locked positions we
meet here, an existence filled with metaphysical needs, without mercy or escape. Technically, however, Bergman is not
especially creative in the theater. He attaches himself quite
clearly to a Swedish drama tradition. He has read his Strindberg closely, and the latter's later drama especially, with its
Symbolism and repartee, without a doubt exerted a fundamental influence on his overall dramatic conception. He can
also, in his way, be said to have succeeded Strindberg as
cultural giant in an international perspective within the
framework of an intimate native tradition. The nightmarish

elements, the shadow-play of anxiety and the stagnation of these plays remind us of Hjalmar Bergman, while when some of the main characters at the end of *Dagen slutar tidigt* (Early Ends the Day) leave "life's outermost headland" and go out into darkness, the stylized view of eternity of Pär Lagerkvist's expressionist drama is very close. But at the center of this Swedish legacy is a new, nervous vulnerability that points ahead to the particular force that constitutes the kernel of Bergman's mature film art.

It is as a film maker that Ingmar Bergman has made his greatest contribution, an activity that has both a literary and cinematic side. He writes his own film manuscripts, and these take on a strongly literary character. He is thus markedly different from most other film makers, for example from his two great predecessors in Swedish film, Mauritz Stiller and Victor Sjöström, who often based their films on literary works. Bergman, on the other hand, has always been cinematically and dramatically creative, from the first germ of an idea for a film manuscript to the actual filming. As early as 1943 he had written a manuscript to Alf Sjöberg's highly regarded film *Hets (Torment/Frenzy)*, with its unforgettable portrait of a sadistic, emotionally stunted high school teacher. In 1945 he made his debut directing his own film with *Kris* (Crisis). It was, however, not until the films of the 1950s that he made his great international breakthrough: *Gycklarnas afton (The Naked Night/Sawdust and Tinsel)*, 1953, an existential tragedy of fate in a simple, artist's environment; the cynically elegant comedy *Sommarnattens leende (Smiles of a Summer Night)*, 1955; the darkly visionary medieval legend *Det sjunde inseglet (The Seventh Seal)*, 1957; the dream-play like *Smultronstället (Wild Strawberries)*, 1957, and the evocatively stylized medieval ballad *Jungfrukällan (The Virgin Spring)*, 1960. These classical Bergman films also stimulated an international interest in his film scripts, which began to be widely studied and discussed. This side of his art was neglected in his homeland in a deplorable, indeed almost scandalous way; only from the 1960s on did Bergman's film scripts—the film trilogy *Såsom i en spegel, Nattvardsgästerna* and *Tystnaden (Through a Glass Darkly, Winter Light* and *Silence*) from 1960–62, with their bold chamber cinematic simplicity, *Persona (Persona)*,

1966, and other of his more recent great films—start to be published in their original language.

It is not wrong to assert that Bergman with these works created a new literary genre—the film script, with independent literary quality and structure. These texts take on their own specific genre character by being both epically narrative—in the present tense—and dramatic in dialogue form. At the same time they have their own, peculiar genre problems. As a rule, they assume their really great artistic value when they are made concrete in cinematic form, yet much of what is artistically meaningful in the great films already lies hidden in the manuscript's literary shape. It is difficult to imagine these manuscripts without Bergman's own filmatizations—and who would really dare to use these manuscripts as scripts for new films? On the other hand, though, they often give rise to free, independent interpretations, and the finished film frequently deviates noticeably from the manuscript. The film manuscripts also vary clearly from each other in character and appearance. *Höstsonaten (Autumn Sonata)*, 1978, the psychologically masterly portrayal of a mother-daughter relationship, is almost wholly dialogue in printed form, like a play, while *Fanny och Alexander (Fanny and Alexander)*, 1982, has the character of an epic family chronicle with interspersed elements of dialogue, in which turn-of-the-century, small-town environment gives rise to a many-sided and often witty narrative art. The evocative and cautionary depiction of Berlin in the 1920s, *Ormens ägg (The Serpent's Egg)*, 1977, also has a supreme narrative stamp in manuscript form that makes it a harrowing read and gives it an independent position vis à vis the film version. As the important film writer that he is, Ingmar Bergman undeniably belongs to literary as well as to cinematic history.

As a film writer he has been able to use the puritanical legacy of his strict Protestant upbringing in a clerical family, described in his captivating memoirs *Laterna Magica (The Magic Lantern)*, 1987, to express modern western man's disgust with life, fear of death and metaphysical rootlessness. His existential world, where the great metaphysical questions are posed again and again, and where God's silence is just as great as man's frantic searching, derives its peculiar bitter flavor from a modern neurotic obsession with a destructive life process of erotic desperation, elements of violence and furious death passion. As with Hjalmar Bergman, deep fear can only be controlled by the magic of the theater, by symbolic-magic visions. However, many of his later cinema and TV films, such as *Scener ur ett äktenskap (Scenes From a Marriage)*, 1973, *Ansikte mot ansikte (Face To Face)*, 1976, and *Ur marionetternas liv (From the Life of the Marionettes)*, 1980, deal with the human conflicts of cohabitation and the difficulties in breaking away and achieving self-fulfillment. There is a milder climate in these upper middle-class, everyday dramas, just as the opportunities for contact and reconciliation and the simple affirmation of life in Bergman's later production grows ever stronger. *Fanny and Alexander*, that lively panorama of Bergman's central themes, is a vehement settling of accounts with ascetic-sadistic religiosity and ends in a jubilant hymn to life. In this magnificent work the threads come together into a conciliatory summing-up of Bergman's inexhaustibly rich film-writing talent.

Astrid Lindgren and the Children's Book

The Swedish children's book had made substantial advances at the turn of the century, and a number of excellent writers for children and young people emerged and became classics of their genre (see p. 173). However, it was not until the 1940s that a new wave of revival appeared. Several eminent authors now emerged who embraced a freer view of the nature and function of the children's book, as well as inspiration from modern pedagogy and child psychology. Astrid Lindgren (b. 1907) was responsible for the most obvious and most successful rejuvenation; her global breakthrough gradually made her internationally the most widely-read Swedish author of our time. She has come to occupy a supreme, unique position in the world of children's books. Her works have literary qualities far beyond what had hitherto been common in the genre. She has thereby effectively contributed to raising the quality and status of the children's book.

Her story about *Pippi Långstrump (Pippi Longstocking)*

from 1945 has attracted more attention and has been more widely-discussed than any other children's book this century. The self-reliant, fiercely independent Pippi, who answers the child's secret dreams of inordinate strength, unbound freedom and power over adults, has been called "the child of the century." New Pippi books soon followed, and Pippi is still Astrid Lindgren's most internationally popular creation. In these works there are elements of both the fantastic fairy tale and the realistic story about the mischievous child, both of which were further developed in her subsequent works for children. The latter feature flourished in the books about the children in "Bullerby" (1947–52) and to a certain degree in those about *Mästerdetektiven Blomkvist (Bill Bergson Master Detective)*, 1946–53, which display her splendid ability to create tension and mystery. A highly individual, poetic fairy-tale style characterized *Nils Karlsson-Pyssling* (Nils Karlsson Pyssling or Simon Small), 1949, and became great literary art in books like *Mio min Mio (Mio, my Son)*, 1954, and *Sunnanäng (Summer Meadow* in *Mio, my Son)*, 1959, where both dream and social reality play an important role. It is often in the synthesis of fantasy and realism that Astrid Lindgren achieved her best results, for example in *Rasmus på luffen (Rasmus and the Vagabond)*, 1956, the story of an orphan boy, and above all in the good-natured burlesques about *Emil i Lönneberga (Emil in the Soup Tureen)*, 1963, the naughty prankster with a heart of gold.

Astrid Lindgren's ability to achieve a sort of inner communication with her young readers is an important key to her great success, but her books also greatly attract adult readers. While previous children's literature often consisted of adult literature adapted for young people, Astrid Lindgren can be said to a certain extent to have made the children's book into something for adults too. This is very much the case with her later books, the publications of which have to a great extent become literary events. With *Bröderna Lejonhjärta (The Brothers Lionheart)*, 1973, she achieved one of her greatest successes, remarkable not least by the fact that the book tackled something as dark as the subject of death for young people. With *Ronja Rövardotter (Ronia the Robber's Daughter)*, 1981, she created a lively, historical adventure story, which like many other of her books proved well-suited to imaginative cinematography. Astrid Lindgren's position today corresponds to a certain degree with that of Zacharias Topelius at the end of the nineteenth century. However, via translations, films and TV she has achieved a popularity to which no other Swedish author could lay claim. Within her own lifetime she has become an unusually vital classic in her field.

Among other prominent writers of books for children and adolescents can be mentioned the Finland-Swede Tove Jansson (b. 1914), who with her many books about the Moomin troll and his family made an original contribution to the fairy-tale and nonsense genre. The Moomin world is a mirror image of the adult world, and like Astrid Lindgren, Tove Jansson has exerted a strong attraction on adult readers in books like *Vem ska trösta knyttet? (Who Will Comfort Toffle?)*, 1960, *Det osynliga barnet (Tales from Moomin Valley)*, 1962, and above all the remarkable *Pappan och havet (Moominpappa at Sea)*, 1965. Her imagination has also created myths that have been absorbed into the general cultural consciousness. In children's literature, the nonsense tradition has undergone a remarkable revival in the poet Lennart Hellsing's (b. 1919) original and masterly verbal enchantments in books like *Krakel Spektakel*, 1952, *Sjörövarboken (The Pirate Book)*, 1965, and *Boken om bagar Bengtsson* (The Book About Baker Bengtsson), 1966. A deepening of the psychological depiction and themes of the children's book was achieved by Maria Gripe (b. 1923) with books like *Josefin (Josephine)*, 1961, *Hugo och Josefin (Hugo and Josephine)*, 1962, and *Hugo (Hugo)*, 1966. In Maria Gripe, the modern children's book—with its aim of treating the reading child as a serious reader, prepared also to accept more difficult material—has an extremely sensitive and tender representative. Among her other works can be mentioned *Pappa Pellerins dotter (Pappa Pellerin's Daughter)*, 1963, and the dark tale *Glasblåsarens barn* (The Glassblower's Children), 1964.

Books for children and adolescents presently occupy a relatively strong position on the Swedish book market, and the number of good authors is considerable. Other stories which can be mentioned here are Gösta Knutsson's books about the tailless cat Pelle, in which the animal is represented as a human adult; Edith Unnerstad's *Kastrullresan (The Saucepan Journey)*, 1949, *Nu seglar Pip-Larssons (The Pip-Larssons Go Sailing)*, 1950, that mix realism and fairy tale, moral and narrative joy; Åke Holmberg's cheerful parodies of the detective novel (the Ture Sventon series) and his fine books about the girl called Gritt, which do not flinch at difficult themes; Anna Lisa Wärnlöf's books about the girl called Pella, and Hans Peterson's long series of children's books which are characterized by a penetrating understanding of the child's psyche. For teenagers, Harry Kullman and Sven Wernström in particular have written much-loved books—the former, novels that focus on the problems of adolescence, the latter, political novels with strong left-wing sympathies. New recruitment in the area has been very good, and in more recent times several writers for children and adolescents have appeared with books that, as in many earlier cases, have been successful on the international book market.

LITERATURE AFTER 1960

Twentieth-century Swedish literature had to a significant extent developed in harmony with Swedish democracy and the Swedish welfare state. A large new group had been recruited to the Parnassus from among autodidacts of proletarian origin. The labor movement had been able to count on strong support for its policies of social change from these authors, indeed from large portions of the literary establishment in general. The tendency dating from the nineteenth century of many Swedish authors having radical, left-wing sympathies has been kept alive to a high degree during the twentieth century. As a professional, with roots in a Romantic-humanistic view of the writer's lofty, pioneering task, the author aligns himself with the small, weak and exposed groups in society. If democracy seems threatened, he comes to the defense of its basic values—as during the 1930s and 1940s. During the postwar period there is still—in spite of the fact that the climate is largely oriented toward the problems of aesthetics and Weltanschauung—a certain secure literary foothold in the Swedish welfare state's fundamental principles and a certain general sympathy for the values that lay behind its powerful economic growth.

During the years around 1960, however, the conditions for such an understanding between politics and cultural life changed considerably. A global perspective became more common. Asia, Africa and Latin America came under the spotlight to a greater extent than previously. Economic injustices and the chasms between the developing and the industrialized countries, starvation, poverty, overpopulation, lingering colonialism and racial policies came increasingly to penetrate cultural discussions, thereby putting the Swedish welfare state and its expansion in a somewhat different light. At about the same time, there emerged an awareness and criticism of the negative side of western industrial society—its chemical dumping, its air and water pollution, acidification and all the other threats it poses to man's health and life and to the continuation of civilization.

Toward the end of the 1960s, cultural life was to a high degree impregnated with the new ecological ideas. The most fundamental change, however, came on the political and ideological plane, through heavy involvement in the Vietnam war issue. In 1965, the young poet Göran Sonnevi published a poem where he expressly spoke about "the USA's repugnant war in Vietnam." This was the signal that led to a stormy, revolutionary period of anti-Americanism and Marxist conviction for at least a decade to come. During this tumultuous time, with its greatly heightened political dualism, Swedish cultural life's left-wing sympathies were very much strengthened, thus placing the well-established Swedish social democracy in an ambiguous light. People persistently questioned its policy of compromise with its free economy, thereby stimulating the sharpened social class antagonisms that caused the image of the ideal "Swedish model" to peel somewhat around the edges. A radical attack on the values of the welfare state was launched on many fronts. People reappraised its established forms and sought new, more global paths for the future.

Crisis became the watchword for the new cultural consciousness: crisis in the welfare state and democracy, western industrial society, economic world order and energy supply, global distribution. After the end of the Vietnam war, many of these central crisis areas still remained: the ecological crisis, the peaceful use of nuclear energy, the Great Powers' nuclear arms race, etc. As far as literature was concerned, this committed, outward-oriented cultural stand led, especially during the 1960s, to many authors preferring factual books and the essay as media of expression; journalistic reportage flowered for a time before declining in popularity again over the last decade. The theater is perhaps the traditional literary medium that most successfully lent itself to the new climate of crisis and commitment; it seemed best suited to communicating messages and stimulating debate and provocation quickly and effectively. Casual debate plays were often created by the actors themselves, by free theater groups, etc. This led to a highly active, but with time ephemeral theater activity that in more recent years has dwindled in a cooler cultural climate, tired of revolution. In the field of poetry, a new variant emerged, in which the new political force found expression. The political song, as mentioned earlier, also flourished, yet, the past ten years have been mainly characterized by a return to the poetic ideals of Modernism. The most energetic genre throughout, though, is the novel. Over the years a long line of good novelists have continued to appear, who with greater or lesser political ties have created a renaissance of good narrative art.

The revolutionary fervor that dominated the climate up to around the mid-1970s has recently been replaced by a more literary atmosphere, in which the radical poses have become calmer, not to say more conservative. The fighting spirit has been channeled into an intensive promotion of literature, which also receives good support under relatively favorable economic conditions. An active cultural policy has improved the social standing of authors considerably. Through state contributions, the Swedish Authors' Fund can give a very large number of established writers a guaranteed author's salary that provides them with a basic income. This salary is intended to complement the payments authors receive for library use of their books, which are calculated according to special guidelines. Furthermore, authors can receive special author grants for five years, as well as other types of work and travel grants. The improved standing of authors has to a high degree been made possible through active efforts by the Swedish Writers' Union. One of these efforts, in 1969, took the form of a demonstration, where the authors literally emptied the libraries in order to obtain higher remuneration for library loans. The new literary policy has to a certain degree turned the author into an official public servant, who can often be said to make "a literary career" for himself and who can have representative tasks in international cultural exchanges. The role of the writer has thereby radically changed when compared with the nineteenth century's Romantic-bohemian writer ideal. It is still too early to say what consequences this will have for literature and for cultural life in general.

The New Political and Global Consciousness

In the Sweden of the 1950s, there was a tendency toward a narrow provincialism, with a very strong stress on aesthetic problems, a sheltered welfare-state culture which lacked close contact with society but which, on the other hand, was not in conflict with society either. That the gates of this closed and somewhat self-satisfied Garden of Eden opened up to a global and more contentious perspective was certainly connected with an improved economy and better air communications, as well as with general international trends and a need for stronger commitment. It was Africa, the young Africa on the verge of overthrowing the yoke of colonialism, that first opened Swedish eyes to global problems. In a manner typical of the era, it was two young authors of the 1950s, Per Wästberg and Sara Lidman, who via Africa took the first steps out into a broader international consciousness.

As a precocious young writer, Per Wästberg (b. 1933) had established himself as a sensitive portrayer of Stockholm, for example with the novel *Halva kungariket* (Half the Kingdom), 1955, a well-written and fresh narrative about the big city youth of the 1950s. With *Arvtagaren* (The Heir), 1958, he took an educational journey on the Continent. A scholarship sojourn in Africa, though, turned him into a passionate Africa reporter, and his two books of African reportage, *Förbjudet område* (Forbidden Area) and *På svarta listan* (On the Black List), both from 1960, introduced the strong contemporary wave of international political commitment. In sober and effective documentary prose, he illustrated the devastation caused by colonialism in Africa and the birth pangs and enthusiasm of the new African nationalism; he also violently attacked, in particular, South African apartheid policies. These travel depictions were free from the traditional subjective-exotic tourist attributes and charged with a new political and social consciousness. Africa was no longer a remote part of the world, surrounded by a mythical-primitive aura, but rather a human and political concern for contemporary Swedes. Wästberg went on to establish himself as a well-informed and committed Africa expert, and introduced African literature into Sweden. At the end of the 1960s, when he made his return as a novelist, it was with a successful trilogy: *Vattenslottet* (The Water Castle), 1968, *Luftburen (The Air Cage)*, 1969, and *Jordmånen (Love's Gravity)*, 1972. Here, the main characters inhabit a new consciousness, marked by a global web of tensions and the symptoms of the new social crisis. They are modern professional people in an upper middle-class environment: an air-traffic controller at Stockholm's Arlanda airport, workers in aid programs for developing countries and nature conservationists. At the same time it is a bright and constructive love story, about the possibility of love in the new existence, about the chances for self-realization, about sensualism as a condition of existence. In Wästberg's novels there is an extraordinarily fine balance between the potentials of modern existence and its threatening future perspective; they are some of the few significant novels about contemporary people and conditions of life in recent Swedish literature.

In the early 1950s, Sara Lidman (b. 1923) had been successful as a portrayer of Norrland life with novels in which she depicted, in dialect, Norrland village life and took up the cause of the socially handicapped, "the unloved" (see p. 214). There is a fine moral thread connecting this commitment and the commitment for the oppressed and destitute of Africa that was awakened in her during a visit to South Africa in 1960–61. The novel *Jag och min son* (I and My Son), 1961, deals with racial persecution and apartheid policies and depicts with great moral indignation the contrasts between the situation of the black Africans and naive Swedish attitudes towards them. In *Med fem diamanter* (With Five Diamonds), 1964, Sara Lidman put the Africans themselves at the center of the action and depicted the destructive collision between African society and new western civilization. Her Africa commitment led to a more and more intense political passion, in which the inner strength of moral conviction became her foremost weapon. For a time she left the literary form and wrote, in *Samtal i Hanoi* (Talks in Hanoi), 1966, vehemently charged political reportage about the Vietnam war, marked by passionate anti-American, left-wing sympathies. On the home front too she found reason to deliver strong polemical attacks from a radical left-wing position. In *Gruva* (Mine), 1968, she reported with indignation on the working conditions of the Norrland mine workers and the exploitation of human labor. The book showed a different picture of the Swedish welfare state; its emotional power provoked debate, and it clearly played a direct role in the crippling mine strike that broke out in the Norrland ore fields at the end of 1969. Sara Lidman had shown that a book can serve as effective political action, and she stood out more than others as the moral conscience of the Swedish left-wing movement. Like Per Wästberg, though, Sara Lidman later returned to the novel with a long series of stories: *Din tjänare hör* (Thy Obedient Servant), 1977, *Vredens barn* (The Children of Wrath), 1979, *Nabots sten* (Naboth's Stone), 1981, and other works. It is a remarkable prose epic from late nineteenth-century Norrland, revolving around the building of the railway. She returned here to the geographically conditioned themes that she had depicted in her first novels—*Tjärdalen* (The Tar Valley), 1953, *Hjortronlandet* (Cloudberry Land), 1955, *Regnspiran (The Rain Bird)*, 1958—but now gave a historical perspective of life in these poor parts of Sweden, where the people had always felt themselves inferior to the country's southern and central regions. Her depiction of their struggle for justice and better living conditions reflects an unusual sensitivity and sharp ear. In her dialectal and strongly lyrical prose she clings fast to the moral stance in her authorship and stands out as one of the very best novelists of contemporary Swedish literature.

Jan Myrdal (b. 1927) was also a novelist—in the 1950s, when he wrote a little noticed series of satirical novels about the welfare state—before he tackled travel accounts of his journeys in Asia and works of political debate. Asia became his literary territory, and in several travel depictions he gave well-informed pictures of countries like Afghanistan and China, concentrating on social, historical and political issues. His major breakthrough came with *Rapport från en kinesisk by (Report from a Chinese Village)*, 1963, which gives a documentary presentation of life in a village in revolutionary China, chiefly using the interview method. The book, with its literary-sociological mode of presentation, also became an international success, and it contributed greatly to the strong interest in revolutionary China that permeated the Swedish left-wing movement in the 1960s. Myrdal also developed a personal, journalistic, essayistic art in the highly regarded book *Samtida bekännelser av en europeisk intellektuell (Confessions of a Disloyal European)*,

1964, that analyzes the reasons why he took political stands during these years. His sharp, individualistic prose—behind which one can clearly sense his admiration for Strindberg—also appears in his effective, polemical journalism from the heyday of the left-wing movement. This was collected in several volumes, *Skriftställning* (Writings), from 1968 on. Myrdal's versatility appears further in his manuscript for the film *Myglaren* (The Fixer), 1967, a satirical illustration of the manipulative bureaucracy in today's society. It aroused a good deal of debate about the basic values of welfare-Sweden. Myrdal has continued to debunk bureaucracy and careerism and made literary analyses of the way in which power functions. His autobiographical novels about his childhood in a well-known family of political academics, *Barndom* (Childhood), 1982, and *En annan värld* (Another World), 1984, created a sensation.

If Jan Myrdal has in many ways been the leading figure of left-wing commitment, with an inexhaustible vitality and ability to provoke, Sven Lindqvist (b. 1932) has rather been its intellectual, philosophically schooled strategist, ingenious and analytical, but lacking the personal image that has made the former into a well-known, in fact almost popular figure in all camps. However, as a politically conscious journalist with the whole world as his field of work, Lindqvist has made an essential contribution by inspiring and informing and placing problems under debate. During the 1950s he established himself as a writer in personal, essayistic books about ways of looking at life—*Handbok* (Handbook), 1957, *Hemmaresan* (Journey at Home), 1959—until a longer sojourn in China gave him a well-informed familiarity with China's internal social life. In 1963, the same year as Myrdal's report from a Chinese village came out, Lindqvist recorded his experiences in *Kina inifrån* (Inside China), a book where his essayistic schooling is fertilized by new political consciousness. It was followed the next year by *Asiatisk erfarenhet* (Asiatic Experience), also a work where facts and discussion are combined with high literary quality. He has continued untiringly to write political travel reportage of high class from many places, including India and Latin America. One of his best works is the collection of essays *Myten om Wu Tao-tzu* (The Myth of Wu Tao-tzu),

1967, where he juxtaposes art and political consciousness. Moral vigilance, which has always characterized Lindqvist's writing, has taken a good deal of inspiration from Vilhelm Ekelund, whose soul-searching, traditional line he in many ways pursues in his political works. In the more individualistic climate of recent years with its "new privatism," he has published intimate books about his love life: *En älskares dagbok* (A Lover's Diary), 1981, and *En gift mans dagbok* (A Married Man's Diary), 1982, without thereby relinquishing a political perspective.

Göran Palm (b. 1931) emerged during the 1950s as a poet and literary critic in the modernist tradition. However, at the beginning of the 1960s he rebelled against "aristocratic Modernism" and sought new aesthetics and other artistic forms of expression. The poetry collection *Världen ser dig* (The World Sees You), 1964—whose title is significant for the new climate that had set in—gives expression to the feelings of breaking up and points to the potential for a more direct, everyday and political poetry. With the book of essays *En orättvis betraktelse (As Others See Us)* from 1966, which was characterized by intellectual perspicacity and moral keenness, Palm published one of the most important works of the 1960s, an intelligent and rough settling of accounts with western ethnocentrism and its economic, political and cultural oppression. *Indoktrineringen i Sverige* (Indoctrination in Sweden), 1968, sought to show the extent to which Swedish welfare society was permeated by capitalist and American values. Palm pursued for many years a very active left-wing journalism that culminated with his reportage accounts about the large corporation LM Ericsson, *Ett år på LM* (One Year at LM), 1972, and *Bokslut från LM* (Balance Sheet from LM), 1974. He had obtained material for the books by working at the factory without betraying the fact that he was an author—somewhat in the spirit of Günter Wallraff. Palm has also criticized the traditional concept of culture in a debate book from 1978. In his latest writing he has tried to reintroduce blank verse into Swedish poetry, namely in the brilliant verse narrative *Sverige en vintersaga* (Sweden, A Winter Tale), 1984. Here, contemporary, crisis-ridden Sweden is portrayed with enormous vitality from a historical and satirical perspective, against the background of the waning political Left. It is an epic of left-wing disappointment, written with a good helping of infectious humor. The historical images in particular, with their unexpected and unfamiliar material, have a force and a freshness that make this narrative into one of the best literary works of recent years. And in the bitter indignation over present day moral corruption lies the seed of a strong revival of left-wing criticism.

The Novel

Poetry had undeniably occupied a dominant position in the postwar era's modernist literary climate. Toward 1960, though, it was apparent that the most exciting events were occurring in narrative prose. 1957 was an unusually good year for high-quality prose debuts, and in general it can be said that an exceptionally vital generation of narrators emerged in the years around 1960, with an astonishing number of excellent novelists. The desire for renewal was clearly connected with foreign stimuli (the new novel in France, Gruppe 47 in West Germany), but there was also a strong effort to tie in to traditional narrative patterns and Swedish models. Side by side can be discerned links with experimental narrative techniques as well as more popular and established narrative patterns. Generally, the development has gone from a temporary intellectualization of the novel during the 1960s to a more powerful and emotional narrative joy in more recent years. Yet during the first half of the 1980s, it was the novelist generation from around 1957 that ruled on the Parnassus.

One of these 1957 debutants was Per-Olof Sundman (b. 1922). His short story collection *Jägarna* (The Hunters) contained highly concentrated depictions of Norrland; the behavioristic narrative technique is reminiscent of the Icelandic saga and of Hemingway's "iceberg prose." The difficulty in getting at the truth, along with our uncertainty about people's motives and their inner character, are also the dominating themes in his subsequent novels *Undersökningen* (The Investigation), 1958, and *Skytten* (The Marksman), 1960, both set out as real, objective investigations that end in uncertainty and circumspection. With *Expeditionen*

(The Expedition), 1962, Sundman—like Sara Lidman—left his Norrland theme for Africa. The tightly stylized story is based on Stanley's expedition to relieve Emir Pascha, but is a free interpretation of the theme. It has a certain kinship with the new French novel's experimental methods, and it allows a political reading with typical criticism of European expansionism and colonialism. Sundman's best work, though, is the novel *Ingenjör Andrées luftfärd (The Flight of the Eagle)*, 1967, that depicts an ill-fated Swedish balloon trip to the North Pole at the end of the nineteenth century. The story is based on authentic diary material and can be read as a settling of accounts with the nineteenth century's superman ideal and blind faith in progress. In the 1970s, Sundman returned with *Berättelsen om Såm* (The Story About Såm), 1977, a retelling in a modern setting of an Icelandic saga. It is a violent depiction of power and justice that attests to the author's deep roots in a Nordic narrative tradition. Sundman has—especially in his earlier works—succeeded in giving this terse, evocative stylistic tradition a new function, namely that of expressing ambiguity and uncertainty amid the knowledge-theoretical relativism of our age. He is one of the most translated Swedish authors of recent years.

The tightly stylized narrative has also been Birgitta Trotzig's (b. 1929) trademark. She made her debut in the early 1950s, but her breakthrough as a novelist came with the historical novel *De utsatta* (The Exposed), 1957—a darkly intense, legendary depiction of the life of a country clergyman in seventeenth-century Scania. Appalling suffering and extreme degradation are the main themes in her world of ideas, dominated by religious (Catholic) and existential questions. This is also true for her later historical novels—*En berättelse från kusten* (A Story from the Coast), 1961, set in medieval Scania, and *Sveket* (The Deceit), 1966, where the events are played out on different time planes—both darkly visionary and existential psychological dramas of intense force. In the somewhat longer novel *Sjukdomen* (The Illness) from 1972, that takes place during the interwar period, the fate of a mentally ill boy is woven together with destructive contemporary events. Birgitta Trotzig has also had success with shorter prose forms, such as the prose poem, which suits her extraordinary visual sharpness. In her writing there is also a thoroughly reflected synthesis of aesthetic expression and ethical and metaphysical problems that makes her more or less unique in Swedish literature today. With a passionate consistency, she peels away from human existence everything inessential and reduces it to a central kernel of guilt, suffering, hate and humiliation. She poses the most fundamental questions about the meaning of human life. In order to gain the right perspective on her nakedly brutal stories about mental suffering and human alienation, one should remember that they were written during a period of singular material expansion and welfare. Her latest novel *Dykungens dotter* (The Marsh King's Daughter), 1985, attests to her inexhaustible desire to restore human existence to its basic metaphysical conditions. The universal validity of her harrowing stories has brought her international attention, particularly in France.

Unlike Birgitta Trotzig, Lars Gustafsson (b. 1936) is more philosophically than religiously oriented. In a series of novels from 1957 onwards, that are characterized by neo-picaresque action and Romantic dream-play structures, he has shaped a personal view of the world strongly influenced by contemporary philosophy, e.g. Ludwig Wittgenstein. Among these works can be mentioned *Poeten Brumbergs sista dagar och död* (The Poet Brumberg's Last Days and Death), 1959, *Bröderna* (The Brothers), 1960, and *Den egentliga berättelsen om herr Arenander* (The Actual Story About Mr. Arenander), 1966. The brightly poetic character of these novels is striking—Gustafsson is also one of the present era's foremost Swedish poets (see p. 278). In the 1970s, though, his narrative art changed character considerably. The series of novels he then wrote within the frame of a novel project he calls *Sprickorna i muren* (The Cracks in the Wall) have a darker, more fragmentary and chaotic stamp. Each novel has in itself an independent status, but taken together the cycle aims to reflect the present era's inner tensions and problems from different angles. *Herr Gustafsson själv* (Mr. Gustafsson Himself), 1971, is a variation on the theme of "a contemporary intellectual's confessions" and questions the ability of the individual to maintain a coherent personal world view in the tumultuous chaos of the present. Other parts give critical insights into how school and bureaucracy function in today's Sweden, while *Sigismund (Sigismund)*, 1976, is a splendidly imaginative depiction of contemporary Europe on different time planes and with playful, science fiction-like elements. It is a novel that demonstrates the freedoms and scope of prose. It has been called by the author himself a novel "about the era's collective subconscious, about its dreams and nightmares." *En biodlares död (The Death of a Bee Keeper)*, 1978, which concludes the series, is a story about how a man gravely ill with cancer withdraws from the world of his own free will to live resignedly at one with life. In the acclaimed *Bernard Foys tredje rockad (Bernard Foy's Third Castling)*, 1986, the author exploits the narrative structure of the spy novel to deliver a clever story with many political and philosophical layers. The strength in Gustafsson's narrative art is his ability to cast thought-provoking intellectual perspectives over our present situation, something which has given him a certain international reputation, above all in Germany. In recent years he has been active as a professor of philosophy at the University of Texas at Austin in the USA. From his foreign "exile," he has taken up the position of Swedish "dissident" and vehemently attacks what he sees as totalitarian tendencies in Swedish democracy.

A more exuberantly inventive narrative talent is Sven Delblanc (b. 1931), who in recent years has stood out as perhaps the most obviously illustrious central figure of contemporary Swedish novel writing. An Uppsala academic, he relies heavily on scholarly allusions and pastiche, even while choosing popular, epic forms for his stories. More recently, however, an epic realism has become more pronounced. In his first novel *Eremitkräftan* (The Hermit Crab), 1962, the main character is torn between democratic emancipation and disciplinarian dictatorship. In rejecting both he ends up in a position of extreme vulnerability. Delblanc's breakthrough came with *Prästkappan* (The Cassock), 1963, an imaginative and racy historical novel from eighteenth-century Prussia that alternates the heroic themes of the Hercules legend with irony and comedy. During the latter half of the 1960s, Delblanc's works took on a radically sharpened ideological character, clearly following popular narrative trends.

However, it was with a broadly realistic epic about life in

the Swedish countryside during the 1930s and early 1940s that Delblanc won a distinguished place among Swedish novelists of today. *Hedebyborna* (The Inhabitants of Hedeby) comprises four parts: *Åminne* (Memories), 1970, *Stenfågel* (Stone Bird), 1973, *Vinteride* (Winter Lair), 1974, and *Stadsporten* (The City's Gate), 1976. With a masterly firework display of narrative-technical ideas, he depicts the revolutionary structural changes in the Swedish countryside during these years: the decline and fall of the aristocratic property owners and the traditional affluent, patriarchal farmers, the growth of large scale agriculture and unions, etc. In the midst of this socio-historical collective, individual human destinies are sketched with fine psychological sensitivity; particularly memorable are the portraits of women. Artistic arrangement and symbolic perspectives deepen the depiction of reality throughout. *Speranza (Speranza)*, 1980, is a historical novel set in the late eighteenth century which, in the harrowing depiction of the slave trade, contrasts idealism and faith in freedom against a brutal reality. In the 1980s, Delblanc has otherwise mainly devoted his energies to a new, realistic narrative sequence that, taken together, makes up a tragic family chronicle rooted in the story of his own family. The series consists of the following works: *Samuels bok* (Samuel's Book), 1981, *Samuels döttrar* (Samuel's Daughters), 1982, *Kanaans land* (Land of Canaan), 1984, and *Maria ensam* (Maria Alone), 1985. In these, particularly the first, Delblanc's sketches of tragic human destinies, harrowingly powerful within the frame of a broad epic flow, become an unbridled protest against the destructive forces of existence. In the later parts, the novel cycle becomes a story about emigration. The closeness to Moberg's emigrant epic is sometimes noticeable in the actual character of the narrative, but the individuality of the heroic, pessimistic human depiction, in particular in the portraits of women, is significant.

The strongly politicized post-1965 literary climate clearly influenced the works of many of the period's novelists. Sara Lidman ceased writing novels for many years because of her passionate political commitment, before once again taking up her broad Norrland epic with its socio-geographical perspective. Delblanc sought to make his writing popular and realistic with the Hedeby cycle. Another author who increasingly oriented himself to the left during these years was Per Olov Enquist (b. 1934), an Uppsala graduate like Lars Gustafsson and Sven Delblanc. Initially, he seemed mainly to be attracted to intellectually analytical narrative forms with obvious affinity to the new French novel and the German Gruppe 47. In 1964 he made his breakthrough with the historical novel *Magnetisörens femte vinter* (The Fifth Winter of the Mesmerizer), which in its depiction of the eighteenth century is really a typical novel of ideas about faith and scepticism, about the needs of the masses and the responsibilities of the individual. *Hess*, 1966, puts the notorious Nazi leader in a sort of symbolic focus and is a technically complex novel which placed Enquist in the vanguard of avant-garde novel writing. He combined the documentary and the fictional in the novel *Legionärerna (The Legionnaires)*, 1968, which dealt with a much-discussed event in Swedish postwar politics: the extradition of some refugees from the Baltic states to the Soviet Union. The novelist here transformed himself into an investigative historian who sought to give a new picture of a politically and emotionally loaded event, but who throughout accepted his own subjectivity. The novel has a clever structure that provoked discussion and strong feelings. *Sekonden* (The Second), 1971, is a story from the world of sport—also anchored in reality—that is shaped as a socio-political allegory with strongly critical barbs directed against social democratic revisionist policies. The short-story collection, *Berättelser från de inställda upprorens tid* (Stories from the Time of the Canceled Revolts), 1974, reports on the post-revolutionary sentiments of the mid-1970s with analytical sharpness and global themes. With *Musikanternas uttåg (The March of the Musicians)*, 1978, Enquist returned to his native Norrland in order to narrate in a broad and rich prose epic the early struggles of the labor movement out in these wilds. But even in this burlesque and cruel story about isolation and distrust, passivity and desperation, there is still an obvious element of documentation and the desire for analysis. The frenetically charged episodes are executed with a dramatic verve which reminds one that Enquist has recently also had great success as a dramatist (see p. 280).

In this generation of novelists there is a stronger technical awareness than earlier and a highly developed professional attitude to novel writing. An excellent example of this is P. C. Jersild (b. 1935), who after his debut in 1960 tried various novel forms with the same cunning skill and who illustrated contemporary social problems from various angles with polemical effectiveness. Throughout his writing there is a sharp attraction to the fantastic and the absurd. In his early novels he could let fantasy break through the dreariness of modern suburban life by, for example, having people on the way home from a company party get lost in the subway for several days without being discovered. *Calvinols resa genom världen* (Calvinol's Journey through the World), 1965, an exuberant Rabelaisian fantasy, is played out on various time planes and swings the scourge of satire over age-old human folly. Most persistently, Jersild has used his satire against modern bureaucracy. In *Grisjakten* (The Pig Hunt), 1968, he depicts how a bureaucratically organized decimation of the pig stock on the island of Gotland takes on absurd proportions, along lines which have great similarities to Nazism. *Vi ses i Song My* (See You in Song My), 1970, is a satire on military bureaucracy, which shows how modern democracy can outgrow its ideology and assume totalitarian forms. *Djurdoktorn (The Animal Doctor)*, 1973, is a futuristic novel that combines social satire with a scientific stand, directed above all against animal experiments in medical research. In *Babels Hus (House of Babel)*, 1978, one of Jersild's most widely read novels, he depicts a large modern hospital as a chaos of specialization and overorganization, where linguistic confusion threatens to become total and the solitary individual is left to wander. In *En levande själ (A Living Soul)*, 1980, a story with strong overtones of science fiction and a great artistic success, a human brain kept alive in a nutritional solution in a laboratory tank stands at the center of a symbolic horror story of evocative force, both tragic and comic. But Jersild has also developed an accurate and nuanced contemporary realism; *Barnens ö (Children's Island)*, 1976, is a psychologically finely-tuned novel about a young boy's encounter with adult life during a few days spent on his own in Stockholm. With *Efter floden (After the Flood)*, 1982, he has created an intensely harrowing, futuristic novel, an anti-utopian story about a desolate world after a devastating nuclear war, where the scattered remains of humanity struggle for survival. Jersild has constantly striven to illuminate and comment on a conflict-filled contemporary world, where threats and catastrophes lurk all around.

In the women's movement climate of the 1970s, a long series of female authors emerged and placed sex role questions and women's lives and working conditions under the spotlight. Foremost among them stands Kerstin Ekman (b. 1933), who began her career as a successful detective story writer. At the beginning of the 1970s, she left that genre and made her real literary debut. Her most important work hitherto is the trilogy *Häxringarna* (The Witches' Circles), 1974, *Springkällan* (The Spring), 1976, and *Änglahuset* (The House of Angels), 1979, a socio-historical prose epic about the destinies of several generations of women during the twentieth century. Geographically, and partly even historically, these lie quite close to Sven Delblanc's books about the inhabitants of Hedeby, but Kerstin Ekman's novel cycle focuses on female life and work, with a unique clarity and an inner effectiveness. It can genuinely be called a women's epic and is written with a classical realism that focuses both on a milieu depiction of great familiarity, warmth and dignity, and on a psychologically intimate understanding, conveyed in human portraits. It avoids exaggeration and bombast and allows an unobtrusive humanism to permeate the depiction of anonymous women's lives and their struggle to survive everyday hardships and humiliations. At the same time, the depiction gives a sociological illustration of a small Swedish community and its development during our century. *En stad av ljus* (A City of Light), 1983, is a free-standing continuation of the earlier novels and has a more subjective and lyrical stamp. Dream and fantasy play a larger role here, and the possibility of love at a time of incessant change is the central motif around which the action revolves. It is a tremendously rich book, in which Kerstin Ekman is able to strike up an even more polyphonic register than earlier.

In contrast to the political climate's predilection for collective and neoproletarian novels and works of socio-critical debate in literary form, the literary development of the most

recent years is characterized by an increased interest in man
the individual, his psyche, dreams and fantasies. At a time of
leveling, bureaucratization and anonymity, it is more interesting to turn inward to man's fount of creativity and to see
in literature an artistic, psychological and linguistic tool to
counter the rationalism of social life. An author who is
endlessly fascinated by man's mystery is Göran Tunström
(b. 1937). He has his roots in the Värmland cultural and
inventive tradition and is one of the finest poets of recent
years. He made his real breakthrough as a novelist with *De
heliga geograferna* (The Holy Geographers), 1973, and
Guddöttrarna (The Goddaughters), 1975, works which with
richly nuanced humor depict a geographical society in
Värmland in the shadow of the Second World War and
Nazism. He returned to the Värmland milieu in *Juloratoriet*
(The Christmas Oratorio), 1983, which was received with
unusual enthusiasm and is his foremost work to date. With a
warm, intimate understanding, he depicts dreamers who are
hurled out of their usual everyday circles by inner impulses
and the power of sorrow. The spirit of Selma Lagerlöf is
obviously present, and she personally figures in one of the
novel's episodes. But there is also a strong strain of Swedenborg's mysticism and a deep feeling for music. Tunström
says that he has chosen to give "a picture of the Word, the
Sound that emerges, disappears like water between the
stones, that appears again in a second or two." The Värmland motifs returned in *Tjuven* (The Thief), 1986, a new and
magnificent display of the art of blending realism and fantasy, everyday triviality and mysticism, the present and the
past. To a certain degree Tunström's works constitute a
Swedish, indeed specifically Värmland, variant of the magical realism of the Latin American novel.

Per Gunnar Evander (b. 1933) too is obsessed by man's
inner psychological processes. His novels are similarly
characterized by fantasy and unrealness and mystify the
reader with accomplished professionalism. Evander mixed
an apparently documentary approach with Kafkaism in his
breakthrough novel, *Uppkomlingarna* (The Upstarts), 1969,
an evocative narrative about the destruction of a night
watchman by some boys who profess to be his sons. The
main characters in novels such as *Det sista äventyret* (The

Last Adventure), 1973, and *Måndagarna med Fanny* (Mon-
days With Fanny), 1974, are also cast out of everyday,
familiar routines by mysterious, inner forces, while *Härlig
är jorden* (Glorious is the Earth) from 1975 has a lighter,
more positive theme. In 1978, Evander unexpectedly published a novel about Judas Iscariot, *Judas Iskariots knutna
händer* (Judas Iscariot's Clenched Fists)—the same year that
Göran Tunström surprised everyone with a novel about the
young Jesus: *Ökenbrevet* (Letter from the Wilderness). In
the works of both authors, despite their highly individual
characteristics, man appears as an impenetrable mystery and
a creative source of power. With Evander, this mystical
dimension stands in stark contrast to the misleading factual-
ness and rationalism of the documentary presentation.

The novel of the most recent years is also characterized by
other narrative-technical ideas than the broad, realistic prose
epic that thrived in the 1970s. One of the new novelists is
Torgny Lindgren (b. 1938). He already had several books
behind him when he made a remarkable breakthrough in
1982 with the novel *Ormens väg på hälleberget (The Way of
a Serpent Upon a Rock)*. Lindgren appeared there as a
narrator in the Sara Lidman vein, with a dark and fateful
dialectal story from Västerbotten. The novel takes place in
the nineteenth century and deals with economic power relations in a remote village. It was above all Lindgren's pregnant and humorous narrative style, free of illusion, that
consolidated his success. The dialectal feature is somewhat
strengthened in the slim collection of stories, *Merabs
skönhet (Merab's Beauty)*, 1983, which deals with harsh
everyday existence in Norrland: a man who works himself
to death breaking up an unusually obstinate tree stump, a
well-digger who digs down forty-five feet in the dry forest
only to die in an avalanche of sand. But Lindgren has also in
recent years tackled very different environments and motifs,
namely the biblical story, which has had a certain renaissance in the neo-conservative cultural climate that came in
around 1980. In 1984 he published his *Bat Seba (Bathsheba)*,
a rewriting of the Old Testament story about how King
David fell in love with the beautiful Bathsheba. There is an
artistic breadth and an intoxicating luxuriousness in this
personal reinterpretation of the Bible story. In *Ljuset* (The

Torgny Lindgren.

Light), 1987, Lindgren returned to the arctic regions of his narrative art in a story full of human hardship and priceless humor. Torgny Lindgren has gained a certain international attention, particularly in France, where *Bathsheba* won the Prix Fémina.

Another storyteller who has aroused considerable interest in France is Carl-Henning Wijkmark (b. 1932). His debut novel *Jägarna på Karinhall* (The Hunters at Karinhall), 1972, takes its motif from Nazi Germany and depicts with strong, quite sensational effect the harsh barbarity behind its grand facades. *Dressinen* (The Hand-Car), 1985, integrates realism and fantasy in an evocative and thought-provoking way. Wijkmark has not shied away from difficult, indeed taboo subjects. Among other things, he has reacted to the cynicism with which death is treated in modern society, something that is reflected in his most recent book, *Sista dagar* (Last Days), 1986. Peter Nilsson (b. 1937) is also close to the fantastic in his works. He is an astronomy professor by profession, and his best work up to now, *Arken* (The Ark), 1982, with the subtitle "the story about a trip to the end of time," is colored by wide, cosmogonic perspectives. It is a mythic-poetic saga of great beauty and evocativeness, full of reflections on modern natural science. *Guldspiken*

(The Golden Nail), 1985, on the other hand, is a partly realistic story with strong visionary elements set in the revivalist and emigration Småland of the nineteenth century.

Poetry

The postwar period was characterized by a very strong interest in poetry that resulted in the publication of large numbers of collections. This tendency continued in the early 1960s when concretist poetry that used the word as a pure medium, and a so-called new-simple everyday poetry were among the new movements. Toward the end of the decade, though, interest weakened considerably. To a certain extent, poetry had to make way for the political song, modern troubadour poetry, rock poetry, and more. During the course of the 1970s, however, poetry made a quantitative comeback with the publication of the works of large numbers of poets. Most of these have developed a sort of neomodernistic poetry, tied sometimes to an intimate, concrete and occasionally satirical tradition, sometimes to a symbolic and visionary one. This new poetic wave stimulated a certain response from the public, which was manifested in such events as poetry readings and "poetry days." Modernist poetry that was earlier considered "difficult" began to attract the public more, and even if certain poetry collections are still hard to market, it has become easier to sell modern poetry in larger editions.

Among the great lyrical profiles of recent years is Lars Norén (b. 1944). He began with a reductive Modernism in his first collections from the early 1960s, but then went over to a more concretist-related style where "picture poems" play a significant role. *Stupor* (Stupor), 1968, consists of a raging avalanche of visions that present a chaotic world springing forth from a schizophrenic consciousness and a violent need for expression. In Norén's subsequent production these rushing, uncontrolled masses of words are more restrained, and he ties in again more strongly to a modernist tradition in the manner of Hölderlin, Rilke and Paul Celan. Norén was able to revive this tradition with his explosive, visionary talent in collections like *Order* (Order), 1978, *Murlod* (Wall Plumb), 1979, and *Hjärta i hjärta* (Heart to

Heart), 1980. These have a severely reduced and existential character that sometimes borders on the ascetic. Norén's ability to break through barriers of feeling with desperate shock effects has been further developed in his drama (see p. 280), but in his poetry he is also able to give expression to feelings of an abstract, clarified beauty with intense, unique effect.

Göran Sonnevi (b. 1939) also occupies a distinguished place in the new poetry. His first poetic appearances in the early 1960s demonstrated his roots in a lyrical, modernist short poem tradition. But from the middle of the decade on, he stood out against others in contemporary Swedish poetry as the politically conscious and committed poet, with his unambiguous stand against the USA's Vietnam war and his anti-capitalist criticism, such as in the collection *Ingrepp—modeller* (Intervention—Models), 1965. Despite Sonnevi's fragmentary poem sequences (which are like random notes joined together into a larger whole), an intellectual mysticism in harmony with an important strain in the modernist tradition (e.g. Gunnar Ekelöf) is increasingly apparent, and his poems are filled with a great awareness of language, as in *Det oavslutade språket* (The Unfinished Language), 1972. Over the years, his register expanded to more large-scale collections of poetry, such as the 430-page *Det omöjliga* (The Impossible), 1975, which contains small fragmentary and occasional items, but which to an ever higher degree aims at a synthesis beyond the multiplicity. He made something of a public breakthrough with this collection. *Språk; Verktyg; Eld* (Language; Tools; Fire), 1979, and *Dikter utan ordning* (Poems Without Order), 1983, also have this paradoxically split character, where unexpected discoveries can be made in a myriad of passing fancies, ideas and notes, but where each element also has a definite function within a greater whole. *Små klanger; en röst* (Faint Notes; a Voice), 1981, was, on the other hand, a more unified collection of individually shaped, refined sonnets where Sonnevi's skills of concentration and intensity came well into their own. In contrast to Sonnevi, Tobias Berggren (b. 1940) works with longer, more connected sequences and larger, essay-like poetic compositions. They have political commitment as well as modernist roots in common, and Berggren works expressly in a tradition in which Eliot and Ekelöf are the most clearly discernible forerunners. His magnificent poem sequence "Resa i den integritetslösa världen" (Journey through the World Without Integrity)—in the collection *Resor i din tystnad* (Journeys in Your Silence), 1976—that depicts an existence in which man's individuality, worth and dignity have been eliminated, can be seen as a modern variant of Eliot's *The Waste Land*. Berggren's sense of the grand and pathetic also finds expression in collections like *Bergsmusik* (Mountain Music), 1978, which includes the long travel letter "Europa, en exil" (Europe, an Exile); *Threnos*, 1981, that spans vast cultural domains; and the magnificent *24 romantiska etyder* (24 Romantic Etudes), 1987, where each individual poem, or etude, corresponds to a different key, from C major to D minor.

Among the leading poets of recent years is also, as mentioned earlier, Lars Gustafsson. His poetry has a lucid, philosophical tone, in which wide-ranging cultural material and considerable erudition are illuminated by a lyrical spotlight that renders it clear, soft and gleaming. There is a sort of curious intellectual construction to his poems that makes them attractive and exciting, from the early collections *Ballongfararna* (The Balloon Travelers), 1962, and *En förmiddag i Sverige* (A Morning in Sweden), 1963, to later ones like *Artesiska brunnar, cartesianska drömmar* (Artesian Wells, Cartesian Dreams), 1980, and *Världens tystnad före Bach* (The World's Silence Before Bach), 1982—titles that say a good deal about Gustafsson's emotional and intellectual temperament. Philosophical speculations are mixed here with curiosities from the natural sciences and cultural history. Kjell Espmark's (b. 1930) poetry has a clear profile too. In the trilogy *Sent i Sverige* (Late in Sweden), 1968–75, he has made a long series of contemporary human portraits reflect a society in which personality and individuality are increasingly stifled. A new trilogy of collections—most notably *Tecken till Europa* (Signs to Europe), 1982—gives expression to a solemn, moral wrath over the indifference and disregard for man which threatens the individual in a de-individualized social machinery and amid the relentless progression of history.

Sweden is a highly productive country in terms of poetry. The number of poetry collections published every year is often large, around 60–65. It can often be difficult to distinguish the individuals in this large scale production of poetry. In most recent decades, though, many distinguished female poets have appeared, most of whom tend to deal with everyday experiences and women's lives. Sonja Åkesson (1926–77), who gave sad sketches from women's lives with a bitter and teasing self-irony, e.g. in the long poem "Självbiografi" (Autobiography) from the collection *Husfrid* (Domestic Peace), 1963, has exerted a strong influence on a younger generation of female poets. These in turn have given a sometimes satirical, sometimes desperate picture of marriage, life as a housewife and professional careers from a feminist point of view. This is the case, for example, with Kristina Lugn (b. 1948), who has also tried her hand at pop music lyrics. Another poetic field has been that of nature, but a different form of nature poetry now, more marked by the new environmental and ecological consciousness. Finally, language itself has also to a higher degree become poetry's own theme. Reflections about language are now common property in the field of poetry.

Drama

The 1960s brought a revitalization of the theatrical climate. The stage was extraordinarily well-suited as a medium for the new political consciousness, and a number of more or less impromptu critical and satirical dramas saw the light of day, often produced by non-institutional or free groups and shaped by the actors themselves. A strong stimulus also came from Peter Weiss (1916–82), through his connections with Swedish cultural life. Weiss had come to Sweden in 1940 as a refugee from Germany, and during the postwar period he wrote a number of prose works in Swedish, as well as a couple of plays. Although he went over to writing in his German mother tongue in the 1960s, the international success of these plays also became to a high degree a Swedish cultural affair. This is the case in particular with *Mordet på Marat (Marat/Sade)*, 1965, a revolutionary idea play of indisputable force, and the intense, harrowing *Rannsak-*

ningen (The Investigation), 1966, based on documents from the legal proceedings against the crimes at Auschwitz. Other newly written Weiss plays were premiered in Stockholm, such as *Sången om Skråpuken (The Song of the Lusitanian Bogey)*, 1966, with its anti-colonial message. Parallel with the vitalizing effect of Weiss' drama was a newly awakened interest in Brecht's theater and theater aesthetics; an interest that influenced the era's many political plays both for better and worse.

Recent years have offered Swedish authors fairly good opportunities to write for the theater. This is especially the case with radio and TV dramas, a field for which numerous plays of various sorts have been written. Many novelists have become involved in the field of drama, with greater or lesser success. Per Olov Enquist has won a certain international acclaim with the playwriting that has come to occupy an ever larger place in his literary production. One of these successes was *Tribadernas natt (The Night of the Tribades)*, 1975, a drama about Strindberg that with indisputable dramatic effect gives an unconventional and unflattering picture of the misogynistic writer. *Till Fedra (To Phaedra)*, 1980, focuses on inter-generational antagonisms in this classical theatrical theme. *Från regnormarnas liv (The Dance of the Rainsnakes)*, 1981, is a play on themes from the life of the Danish fairy-tale writer Hans Christian Andersen, also with a cleverly arranged overall dramatic effect.

Lars Norén's international theater successes have been still more striking. He began by writing for television theater, where his ability to conjure up an evocative and provocative visuality appeared to advantage. Around 1980 he finally made a breakthrough as a dramatist, with plays such as *Modet att döda (The Courage to Kill)*, 1980, and *En fruktansvärd lycka (A Terrible Happiness)*, 1981. The two plays which have consolidated his reputation more than any others, namely *Natten är dagens mor (Night Is the Mother of Day)* and *Kaos är granne med Gud* (Chaos Is God's Neighbor) are chiefly characterized by his technique of escalating an intense atmosphere, where desperation, revulsion and panic are always lurking, and of highly effectively playing on the viewers' nerves. Both of these are from 1983, with titles taken from a distich by Stagnelius (see p. 80).

Lars Norén.

These works tie in clearly with the theater tradition in which Ibsen, Strindberg and O'Neill are the foremost names, a dramatic technique that is characterized by dealings and revelations within a small group of people. At the center of these two plays stands a lower middle-class family. The father is an alcoholic and the youngest son is slowly sliding into mental illness. If the technique is not new, Norén's way of using it is highly individual. The dramas are to be seen as a desperate conjuring up of the incurable impotence and corruption of existence, in which people's methods of tormenting and humiliating each other often exceed the limits of the endurable. But there are also mild and conciliatory elements in these dramas, a Romantic longing to escape the inferno. Norén without a doubt gives—in spite of the shocking elements—a well-balanced overall scenic effect to his dramas, a widened dramatic dimension of brutal authenticity and emotional passions.

The culturally spartan Middle Ages, when Swedish literature took its first steps, is a long way from our own age, which rather resembles a cultural avalanche in which a torrent of imaginative literature has to vie for attention with an even greater flood of messages in the mass media. Swedish literature today makes an exuberantly vital impression, the total silence at the beginning of history has been replaced by an almost unmeasurable and unstructured verbal din that makes it difficult for the reader to orient himself. In the last 100–150 years, Swedish literature has also to a greater extent been able to hold its own internationally, and in most recent times a considerable number of Swedish authors have been translated into many foreign languages, thus participating in a broader cultural exchange. An internationalization of Swedish literature has also taken place over the past twenty years or so within the country's own borders, partially through the growing immigration of different nationalities. Immigrant authors have had some success in their new language on the Swedish book market. One example is the Greek-born Theodor Kallifatides (b. 1938), who has enriched Swedish literature with a novel cycle about Greece in the 1930s and 1940s—*Bönder och herrar (Masters and Peasants)*, 1973, and others. He has also depicted the situation of the immigrant in Sweden, as has Rita Tornborg (b. 1926) who is of Polish-Jewish descent and who has depicted the immigrant communities within Swedish society with great accuracy and a good deal of critical bile. But immigration in Sweden has also given rise to a considerable amount of literature in a number of foreign languages: Finnish, Turkish, Spanish, etc. Seen as a socio-cultural phenomenon, literature in Sweden today is a highly differentiated linguistic activity where watertight bulkheads exist between the different language areas in the literary field, and contacts between Swedish and foreign cultural life are virtually non-existent. At the same time, Swedish literature tends to take on a more international profile, where only the choice of geographical setting gives it a special national character. Poetry in particular today tends to assume a more and more uniform stamp throughout the world.

How will distinctive national characteristics fare in these circumstances? Will Swedish writers continue to hold their own on the international literature market as a result of their international adaptability, or perhaps because of a lingering Nordic exoticism? For the cultural life of so-called smaller language areas, these are vital questions for the national consciousness that is manifested through literature's development over the centuries. Answers to these questions, however, cannot be given here. In today's situation we can restrict ourselves to the assertion that Swedish literature is presently going through a dynamic and exciting developmental period and that many younger authors, for whom there has been no room for discussion here, stand ready to write new pages in the book of Swedish literary history.

INDEX

BIBLIOGRAPHIES

Gustafson, A.: *A History of Swedish Literature*. Minneapolis, 1961.

Rossel, S. H.: *A History of Scandinavian Literature, 1870–1980.* Minneapolis, 1982.

Aspects of Modern Swedish Literature, edited by Irene Scobbie, Norwich, 1988.

About Sweden 1900–1963, a bibliographical outline by Bure Holmbäck, the Swedish Institute, Stockholm, 1968.

Suecana Extranea. Books on Sweden and Swedish Literature in Foreign Languages. The Royal Library, Stockholm, 1963–1988. (Annual.)

Translations of poems by Frederic Fleisher pp. 219, 239; Robin Fulton pp. 244, 245; C. D. Locock p. 146; Michael Meyer p. 128; Robert T. Rovinsky p. 81; C. W. Stork p. 84.

Photos by Albert Bonniers förlag pp. 91, 179, 188, 201, 216, 233; Lennart Edling/Norstedts förlag p. 275; Bengt A. Lundberg/the Central Board of National Antiquities, Stockholm, p. 16; the Royal Library, Stockholm, p. 57; the Swedish Portrait Archives, Stockholm, pp. 44, 49, 79, 101, 130, 163; Lutfi Özkök p. 281.